VOICES FROM BEARS EARS

VOICES FROM BEARS EARS
SEEKING COMMON GROUND ON SACRED LAND

REBECCA M. ROBINSON

PHOTOGRAPHS BY **STEPHEN E. STROM**
FOREWORD BY **PATRICIA NELSON LIMERICK**

**THE UNIVERSITY OF
ARIZONA PRESS**
TUCSON

In association with George F. Thompson Publishing

The University of Arizona Press
www.uapress.arizona.edu

ISBN-13: 978-0-8165-3805-8 (paper)

Cover design by Leigh McDonald
Cover photograph by Stephen Strom
Interior design by Sara Thaxton

Frontispiece: Canyon, Goosenecks of the San Juan River

The epigraph on p. v is from *Secrets from the Center of the World* by Joy Harjo and Stephen
Strom. © 1989 by The Arizona Board of Regents. Reprinted by permission of the University
of Arizona Press.

Additional content and updates on the Bears Ears site can be found at https://www.bearsears
country.com.

Library of Congress Cataloging-in-Publication Data
Names: Robinson, Rebecca, 1984– author. | Strom, Stephen, photographer. | Nelson, Patricia,
    writer of foreword.
Title: Voices from Bears Ears : seeking common ground on sacred land / Rebecca M. Robin-
    son ; photographs by Stephen E. Strom ; foreword by Patricia Nelson Limerick.
Description: Tucson : The University of Arizona Press, 2018. | Includes bibliographical refer-
    ences and index.
Identifiers: LCCN 2018009197 | ISBN 9780816538058 (pbk. : alk. paper)
Subjects: LCSH: Bears Ears National Monument (Utah) | Bears Ears National Monument
    (Utah)—Pictorial works.
Classification: LCC F832.S4 R63 2018 | DDC 979.2/59—dc23 LC record available at https://
    lccn.loc.gov/2018009197

Printed in the United States of America
♾ This paper meets the requirements of ANSI/NISO Z39.48-1992 (Permanence of Paper).

All landscapes have a history, much the same as people exist within cultures, even tribes. There are distinct voices, languages that belong to particular areas. There are voices inside rocks, shallow washes, shifting skies; they are not silent. And there is movement, not always the violent motion of earthquakes associated with the earth's motion or the steady unseen swirl through the heavens, but other motion, subtle, unseen, like breathing. A motion, a sound, that if you allow your inner workings to stop long enough, moves into the place inside you that mirrors a similar landscape; you too can see it, feel it, hear it, know it.

—JOY HARJO, *Secrets from the Center of the World*

Badlands, near Red Canyon (aerial photo)

CONTENTS

Protecting Ancestral Lands: Exercising Tribal Sovereignty

A Path Forward: Establishing Trust, Healing Wounds

Seven Sisters Buttes

FOREWORD
Bears Ears and the Redemption of the Confounded

You and I ought not to die, before We have explained ourselves to each other. —John Adams to Thomas Jefferson, July 15, 1813

I have thus stated my opinion on a point on which we differ, not with a view to controversy, for we are both too old to change opinions which are the result of a long life of inquiry and reflection, but on the suggestion of a former letter of yours, that we ought not to die before we have explained ourselves to each other.

—Thomas Jefferson to John Adams, October 28, 1813, from Lester J. Cappon, ed., *The Adams-Jefferson Letters*

Blessed are the peacemakers, for they shall be called the children of God. —Matthew 5:9

In the mid-2010s San Juan County in southern Utah has become the setting for a collision of individuals and groups who claim a strong sense of place and who are thereby locked in intractable opposition.

In the early 1990s, in a phase of hopeful cheer that seems regrettably distant, many earnest people who love the American West got swept up in a wave of enthusiasm for the benefits of an ever-growing adoption of a sense of place. People who held this sense of connection were to gain a grounded sense of mission: recognizing the West as our chosen home, we would thereby be called to serve as the grateful stewards and guardians of the land where we had found our bearings. The most audible and articulate advocates of a sense of place wisely chose not to raise a confounding question: What should we expect when dissimilar and conflicting senses of place are directed, with force and conviction, *at the same place*?

The controversy over the proposed Bears Ears National Monument in southern Utah seems to offer a clear and direct answer to that question:

> Expect groups holding differing senses of place to collide with each other. Expect antagonism and hostility to rise in intensity. Expect memories of past injuries to surge back with new force.

In the early twenty-first century bitter conflicts over the lands and resources of the American West have rattled communities in many locales, providing an abundance of evidence to validate that answer. Those who would prefer an alternative to antagonism and polarization have reason to feel constantly confounded—or, to enlist a few of the word's colorful synonyms, to feel dumbfounded, staggered, bewildered, baffled, mystified, perplexed, puzzled, flummoxed, and confused.

This sets the stage for a theory I now present for its first test.

If we are going to be confounded by the proliferation of conflicts over the West's public lands, there would surely be wisdom in taking possession of this process, calling a halt to the unrewarding custom of letting it take possession of us.

In a state of affairs that even very alert observers might miss, the story of the conflict over the proposed Bears Ears National Monument presents an improbably promising situation: because Utah has a distinctive history that confounds the conventional wisdom on western land conflicts; and because two good souls have chosen to position themselves squarely in the middle of this conflict.

The example, set by the two purposeful and very skilled confounders who collaborated to bring *Voices from Bears Ears* into being, presents an opportunity we should not let slip from our reach.

Moved by a deep and intense sense of place, photographer Stephen Strom and his granddaughter, writer Rebecca Robinson, ventured into a setting where people have devoted years to the successful project of casting each other as antagonists. Strom and Robinson resolved to forswear predetermined conclusions and to refuse to hold their own perspectives and points of view with complacency. Moving with grace, in all senses, among this divided population, these exemplary confounders set out to capture the words of "residents of San Juan County," as well as "tribal members and environmentalists across the Colorado Plateau," so that those voices could "be heard with openness, compassion, and understanding for what they hold sacred."

Strom's and Robinson's commitment to congenial listening evoked a matching congeniality in the people they met. The interviews they conducted repeatedly demonstrated a confounding quality of human nature: it is perfectly possible for the same people to be at once genuinely very congenial and genuinely very contentious. That paradox seems to have found one of its most hospitable habitats in southern Utah. For all the goodwill they carry, the interviews in this book carry a discouraging message that cannot be veiled: congeniality makes frequent appearances, but consensus is keeping a very low profile.

By conventional wisdom, a fundamental rule of keeping conversation harmonic and tranquil is to avoid going near religion or politics. It would take an astoundingly clever engineer of conversation to figure out how to fit that rule to the Bears Ears conflict. A presidential designation of a national monument, over the objections of a significant number of citizens living in its proximity, permits no conversational exemption from politics. And in many western locales, but particularly in Utah, the border separating religious belief from environmental policy defies even the most earnest efforts to locate and chart it. Every aspect of the dispute over the proposed Bears Ears National Monument connects directly to the reality that both Indian people and Mormon people guide their conduct toward nature by religious belief. Rather than following the conventional wisdom and trying to avoid the subject of religion, a better move would be to put it front and center, especially since there is really no other option!

No one can pretend to understand the past, present, or future of Utah without paying close attention to the role of religion. Historical perspective has a proven capacity to offer an alternative to fruitless recitations of opposition and antagonism. In other words, Utah's distinctive history could provide the terms for a much refreshed and much more realistic debate than the one that has rattled southern Utah in recent years. The discussion of the proposed monument has been constrained by assumptions that are in urgent need of a lively round of purposeful confounding, and there is no better way to confound conventional wisdom than to depart from the too-familiar present and enter into the unexpected twists and turns of the past.

And so, following in the footsteps of Stephen Strom and Rebecca Robinson, I will step aside from the choice between supporting and opposing the designation of the Bears Ears locale as a national monument. Instead, mobilizing the distinctive power of Utah's history, I aim at a different, more complicated form of reflection than "support or oppose" would permit. This line of thought has the particular advantage of opening a route of escape from the trap of fatalism and inevitability: the way things are now is not the way they have always been and will always have to be.

The members of the Church of Jesus Christ of Latter-day Saints arrived in Utah with distinctive beliefs in the stewardship of nature and in the cultivation of good relations with Indians. Both of those beliefs set them apart from the majority of white settlers in the American West. And yet in a pattern shared with every other group of believers, the practices and conduct of the Mormons did not end up matching their ideals; moreover, with the passage of more than a century and a half, valuable dimensions of these ideals have faded in memories. And here is a point of great promise: as believers in a Restored Christianity, Mormons have a particularly compelling reason to examine their own conduct in relationship to their history and to revive and mobilize ideas that guided the first European American settlers in Utah.

The history of the Mormons' early start in environmental stewardship is rightly the basis of considerable cultural pride, constituting an inheritance to steer by in the disorienting times of the early twenty-first century. Retired Brigham Young University historian Thomas Alexander summed up the Latter-day Saints' tradition of stewardship: "Only after the Saints had learned to live in harmony as stewards with one another and with the earth, Brigham Young said, could they expect to inherit, presumably as exalted beings, from the Lord who owned it. . . . He told them that the earth belonged to the Lord and that human beings could hold no title to the land and its resources. Landholders might manage God's estates only as stewards."[1]

With their unshakeable support of the principle of stewardship, Joseph Smith and Brigham Young gave church members an awareness of the consequences of their conduct toward nature, an awareness that was far from common among European Americans in the mid-nineteenth century and is still far from universal in the early twenty-first century. Thomas Alexander has put forward an invitation, both generous and demanding, to mobilize the past on behalf of the present: "When faced with extraordinarily difficult problems, insightful and creative people with a cultural tradition may return to their roots to re-appropriate or reinterpret concepts and practices—religious or secular—forgotten in contemporary society, [but] which seem to apply to current problems."[2]

---

1. Alexander, "Stewardship and Enterprise," 345.
2. Alexander, "Stewardship and Enterprise," 364.

Alexander's invitation presents us with a feature of fortune that humanity, across a wide range of beliefs, has always treasured: a second chance.

Might there be a surprisingly close match between the tribal understanding of human beings as stewards of an earth that is both material and spiritual and the early Mormon conviction that God, not humans, was the owner of the earth?

Could there be more compatibility between Mormonism's founding ideals and the proposal of a national monument than we will realize if we keep our vision locked on the present?

Can we attend to the ideals that many residents of Utah held sacred in the mid-nineteenth century and unleash those ideals in the West of the twenty-first century?

These questions seem well suited for discussions at the Homestead Steakhouse, and Yak's Center Street Café in Blanding, and Duke's Bistro in Bluff, restaurants where Stephen Strom and Rebecca Robinson sat down and, fielding a redemptive force of good nature, talked with the people engaged in the current controversy.

Stephen Strom and Rebecca Robinson have endowed every photograph and every word in this book with the belief that everyone in their company joins them in the loyalties and responsibilities that a sense of place delivers to its holders, even as it confounds simple configurations of opposition and antagonism.

Will we rise to their example?

Patty Limerick
Center of the American West
University of Colorado, Boulder
December 2016

Canyon Walls, Goosenecks of the San Juan, Monument Valley in the distance
(near the southern boundary of Bears Ears National Monument)

PREFACE

The best way to comprehend Bears Ears country is to take wing. With the benefit of a bird's-eye view, the scale and rhythm of a landscape spanning three thousand square miles comes into full relief: endless spires, buttes, mesas, and canyons sculpted and painted by water and wind, glowing red at sunset and gleaming white at midday; streams and rivers through whose veins and arteries the desert's lifeblood and scarcest resource flows. The vast terrain bears scars as well: of explosive emergence and tectonic shifts that sculpted the earth into otherworldly formations of stark cinder cones, petrified sand dunes, and impossibly steep ridges, all painted with a wild palette of colors. It is country that both tests the body and stirs the soul.

During my decades of travel across southeastern Utah, I have come to know this country in all seasons. Muted midwinter light rests gently on the mesas, the red rock landscape subdued with a dusting of snow. The brilliant sunlight of midsummer intensifies the harshness of the landscape, its ruggedness revealed in jagged shadow. The cracked earth and parched plants of a scorching July day are transformed in minutes by monsoon rains, releasing long-dormant scents imprinted in my memory.

In a landscape that often looks and feels empty, one is constantly reminded that humans made a life and a living here long before our time. Enter any of the canyons in this nearly three-thousand-square-mile region—each one, like a sandstone fingerprint, completely unique—and you will find evidence of ancient civilizations that thrived in a harsh climate, building stone structures and crafting pottery, tools, and weapons, remnants of which have survived for centuries, even millennia. The canyons bear silent witness to the earliest settlers of this land, the ancestors of today's Pueblo people, who migrated southward to Arizona and New Mexico over seven hundred years ago but whose spirits remain. Faded tepee rings and half-collapsed octagonal mud-and-wood structures known as hogans speak to the presence of early Ute, Paiute, and Navajo peoples. Their descendants are still here, continuing to draw spiritual and material sustenance from the land.

Weathered wooden fence posts and old cattle corrals dot the many miles of open range in San Juan County, evidence of the area's first Anglo settlers, Mormon pioneers who in the 1840s traveled from upstate New York to the edge of the Great Salt Lake and thirty years later sent an expedition four hundred miles to the southeast to settle along the banks of the San Juan River.

San Juan County's modern-day inhabitants follow different faiths and have varying traditions of living on the land. What binds them together is that, in their own ways, they each view the land as sacred and feel that they are called to steward it so that it sustains their people today and into the future. Their competing visions for how best to do so animate one of the central struggles for the future of the American West. The voices on the following pages bring the debate to life with passion, authenticity, and, above all, a deep respect for and love of their homeland.

In January 2015 we began work on what would become this book, exploring southeastern Utah through conversations with people who have their own personal connections to the land. We interviewed tribal leaders and local citizens, archaeologists and environmental activists, a range of county, state, and national political leaders, and other stakeholders currently engaged in efforts to shape the future of Utah's largest county. After the first few of more than seventy interviews, we learned of the efforts of five tribes and their supporters to protect nearly two million acres of public land surrounding the iconic Bears Ears buttes as a national monument—and of the fierce opposition by many locals to any new land designation that they believed might threaten their livelihood. The focus of our book expanded in scope to capture a rich narrative: a juxtaposition of Native and Mormon cultures; a clash between local, state, and federal interests; a study of the complex forces at work in rural America today.

We decided that the most powerful and respectful way to relate what we have learned would be to share the stories of people's connections to San Juan County's public lands, connections that for some span five generations and for others, millennia, and to share their hopes for the future.

This book is arranged to give personal histories a central role in the telling so that voices can be heard. It is written with the belief that through getting to know and respect each individual and his or her connection to place, we can all move closer to the fundamental human understanding and respect that are essential to discovering common ground.

A NOTE ON THE STRUCTURE
OF THIS BOOK

We made the conscious choice to place individual voices and personal histories at the center of our narrative. As a result, the story unfolds conver-
sationally, with critical information embedded in the personal stories of
those involved in the debate over the future of Bears Ears. Recurring themes
emerge as each perspective adds richness and detail to the whole. With our
commitment to giving voice directly to individuals, explanatory sections
providing background information that might traditionally appear earlier
in the manuscript are placed as interludes between personal histories or
in the appendices. To provide context, we have included detailed maps, an
extensive historical time line, and a list of people interviewed along with a
brief summary of their role in this story.

The fate of Bears Ears country remains unresolved. This book provides
historical context leading up to current conflicts and captures a snapshot
in time, primarily between the summer of 2015 and the fall of 2016, when
the debate over the designation of Bears Ears as a national monument was
at its peak. At the time, two approaches for determining how public lands
in southeastern Utah would be managed were being considered: legislative
passage of the Utah Public Lands Initiative (PLI) proposed by Utah representative Rob Bishop and unilateral designation of a national monument by
then president Barack Obama.

We have added updates through February 2018 as critical decisions were
made and challenged. Former president Barack Obama established Bears
Ears National Monument in December 2016, and President Donald Trump
reduced the size of the monument by 85 percent and established two much
smaller monuments on the remaining 15 percent of the land a year later.
In response, Native American tribes, environmental and archaeological

organizations, and outdoor retailers challenged President Trump's right to alter the boundaries of national monuments declared by his predecessors. The resulting litigation is likely to continue for years. (Follow the blog on www.bearsearscountry.com for continuing updates on the status of the monument.)

With no clear resolution to the seemingly intractable problems surrounding public lands in Utah, the voices and ideas shared in these pages remain deeply relevant today in the search for a way forward.

VOICES FROM BEARS EARS

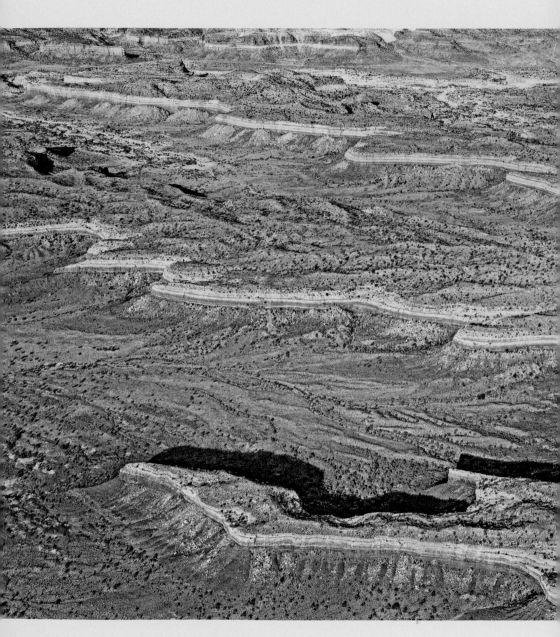

White Canyon looking south from Jacob's Chair (aerial photo)

INTRODUCTION

Land and People

To travel across the Colorado Plateau is to learn the meaning of deep time. A seemingly infinite array of stone spires and buttes stands sentinel over a vast expanse of land, creating a world that feels primeval and timeless. A jagged, thousand-foot-high sandstone spine snakes its way through the landscape, while towering mesas, water-carved canyons, and petrified sand dunes provide dramatic testimony to the region's multimillion-year history.

The land encompassing Bears Ears, the Colorado Plateau, first emerged above the oceans 2.2 billion years ago near the equator. As the land inched north on its 2,500-mile tectonic journey toward the Four Corners region, the earth's climate warmed and cooled, causing sea levels to rise and fall with the melting and freezing of polar ice. By seventy million years ago the land had reached its current location when powerful geologic forces lifted it upward by more than a mile above the ocean, finally creating the plateau.

During this uplift, rivers that once flowed gently atop the sea-level plain rushed downward, cutting into the rising land, creating deep, multilayered, multicolored canyons that reveal a complex natural history. Elsewhere, layers of sandstone, crossing at different angles, were exposed as the plateau rose, providing a fossil record of the ebb and flow of water and of shifting winds in ancient times.

At the heart of the Colorado Plateau and the center of our story lies San Juan County, Utah, an eight-thousand-square-mile expanse in the southeastern corner of the state. The poorest and one of the most sparsely populated counties in Utah, it is bordered on the east by Colorado's San Juan and La Plata mountain ranges; on the west by the sinuous paths of the Colorado and Green Rivers; on the north by the city of Moab and the eastern half of

Canyonlands National Park; and on the south by the Arizona state line and that state's portion of the Navajo Nation.

Within its boundaries lie wild, exquisite canyons and high mesas; the meanderings of the Green, Colorado, and San Juan Rivers passing under towering cliffs surrounded by rich riparian areas; and the watershed and forests of the majestic Abajo Mountains. In the midst of it all, there is the dramatic Comb Ridge, a jagged thousand-foot-high monocline known to Native peoples as the backbone of the earth, snaking sixty miles northward from the Arizona border.

The land both within and surrounding San Juan County is endowed with mineral wealth: coal, oil, gas, uranium, vanadium, copper, and potash, uplifted as the Colorado Plateau rose above sea level. Lush grasslands surround river basins, ideal for grazing cattle during fall, winter, and spring. In summer the mountains provide forage that can sustain livestock until early fall. Unique communities of plants and animals have evolved to survive in an arid land where temperatures exceed one hundred degrees in summer and dip well below freezing in winter.

The land also contains an irreplaceable archive of human history: of Native peoples who over millennia adapted to this harshest of lands, developing agricultural techniques that yielded abundant crops from an unforgiving desert. Members of the Navajo and Ute tribes in Utah and Colorado and nearly twenty Pueblo tribes in Arizona and New Mexico trace their history in the area to time immemorial, while western archaeologists date the arrival of Native peoples on the Colorado Plateau to approximately 10,000 BCE. Over the next eight millennia, bands of nomadic hunter-gatherers began to domesticate plants and develop distinct cultures, languages, and ceremonial practices.

With the introduction of maize from Mesoamerica around 2100 BCE, agriculture grew in importance, and the people began to live in semipermanent settlements. By 750 CE they were erecting large public buildings on the Colorado Plateau in what is now the Four Corners region. Over the next five centuries they built villages with multistoried structures linked by complex road grids spanning hundreds of miles before suddenly abandoning these settlements between 1250 and 1300 CE, due in part to a prolonged drought and accompanying social unrest. They migrated south and east from the center of the Colorado Plateau to Arizona and the Rio Grande Valley in New Mexico. Their descendants cite stories and prayers that detail an

Salt Creek Canyon

Pictographs, Colorado Plateau

accompanying migration that led the Ancestral Puebloans to their current homes.

Precursors of today's Ute tribes arrived from their homeland east of the Sierra Nevada around the time that Ancestral Puebloans abandoned their homes. Several hundred years later, ancestral Navajos migrated southward from eastern Alaska and northwestern Canada to lands that now comprise the Four Corners region.

Native peoples of the Colorado Plateau see their origin and migration stories manifest in the land, its sculptural forms, and its flora and fauna. The canyons and gulches of Cedar Mesa, the buttes of Valley of the Gods, and the "backbone" of Comb Ridge figure prominently in the creation stories of Native American tribes and pueblos in the Southwest. They view land as a living, breathing entity to be honored and protected, a place where ancestors still walk and where traditional healers still perform ceremonies to heal body, soul, and the earth itself.

Evidence of Native peoples' forebears abounds in abandoned adobe structures built into the sides of seemingly unreachable sheer cliffs; celestial events, animals, and humanlike figures depicted in petroglyphs carved into rock and pictographs painted on protected sandstone walls; a rich trove of baskets, pottery, and jewelry; and the buried remains of those who came before. In San Juan County alone, estimates place the number of Ancestral Puebloan, Ute, and Navajo sites at well over one hundred thousand. Analysis of ancient corncobs and granaries, pottery, and Pueblo villages speak to how both agriculture and urban life arose on the American continent.

The desert's aridity has preserved so much of the past that centuries-old societies feel almost alive in the present. One can visit an adobe dwelling in a canyon alcove and find grinding stones resting near a primitive door, as if the women who used them to make cornmeal centuries ago had left for the afternoon and might return that evening. Parts of pottery kilns are still intact, and the telltale structures of upright stones placed in a wide circle dot the landscape, seemingly ready to fire clay. Pottery sherds are scattered everywhere, and the discovery of jagged pieces of bowls covered in striking painted patterns is a humbling reminder of what endures. Perhaps most powerfully, the painted handprints that adorn rock walls provide a visceral connection to the enigmatic desert dwellers who made this harsh landscape their home.

In the late 1700s the Franciscan priests Francisco Atanasio Domínguez and Silvestre Vélez de Escalante led the earliest European exploration of the Colorado Plateau with the goal of locating an efficient route from New Mexico to the Spanish settlement in Monterey, California. The expedition ultimately reached only as far west as the Virgin River in Nevada and as far north as present-day Provo, Utah. But in the course of their journey, Domínguez and Escalante made the first European maps of large areas of the Colorado Plateau. The Escalante River and the town of Escalante are named after the priest.

John Wesley Powell's legendary 1869 and 1872 expeditions on the Green and Colorado Rivers took him and his men down rivers and through the formidable rapids in Cataract Canyon, on the far western side of San Juan County. Powell meticulously documented his scientific observations of the region's geology and flora and fauna, but he also had a poet's soul, reading Shakespeare and Tennyson to his boatmates as they floated down the Colorado and conjuring evocative names for natural wonders—the Flaming Gorge, the Dirty Devil River—that are still in use today: "The sun shines in splendor on vermillion walls, shaded into green and gray where the rocks are lichened over; the river fills the channel from wall to wall, and the canyon opens, like a beautiful portal, to a region of glory. This evening . . . the sun is going down and the shadows are settling in the canyon. The vermillion gleams and roseate hues, blending with the green and gray tints, are slowly changing to somber brown above, and black shadows are creeping over them below."[1]

The reports from Powell's expeditions gained him national renown and led to his assuming leadership of the Bureau of Ethnology and the United States Geological Survey. He understood, in a way no Washington, D.C.–based bureaucrat could, the folly of trying to apply East Coast principles of land planning and water usage to the country west of the hundredth meridian. His *Report on the Lands of the Arid Region of the United States* outlined a broad conservation plan for water use in the West and served as a prophetic foreshadowing of the water crises that would grip the region in the following century.

The first Anglos to settle permanently in San Juan County were Mormon pioneers. Driven westward from their upstate New York home by those who considered the religion of the Church of Jesus Christ of Latter-day Saints to

---

1. Powell, *The Exploration of the Colorado River*, 148.

be blasphemous, Mormons in 1846 followed the Prophet Brigham Young from Nauvoo, Illinois, to their Promised Land near present-day Salt Lake City, arriving in 1847. Once established in the Salt Lake Valley, Young called followers to settle vast swaths of the West, extending from southern California to northern Idaho. He dreamed of creating the state of Deseret in the Great Basin and Mountain West, where Saints could be safe to pursue their beliefs and to render the land bountiful. (*Deseret* is the word for "honeybee" in the Book of Mormon; it was chosen as the name for the prospective Mormon empire in order to encourage settlers to be industrious in their settlement of the land in the Utah territory. The symbol of a beehive appears on the Utah state flag and on all state highway signs; the state's motto, fittingly, is "Industry.")

In 1879 the church called a group of seventy families to leave a settlement in the southwestern Utah community of Parowan to travel three hundred miles to the banks of the San Juan River near where the town of Bluff stands today. Their little-explored path would take them through some of the most rugged and forbidding territory on the Colorado Plateau. To reach the San Juan, they needed to carve a road into a nearly sheer cliff from fifteen hundred feet above the west side of a canyon, down to the Colorado River, and up the other side, lowering their wagons, livestock, and families through a narrow crevice that today is called the Hole-in-the-Rock.

On Christmas Day in 1879 a team of scouts exploring in advance of the expedition's wagon train, frostbitten and emaciated from a brutal journey that had lasted far longer than expected, caught their first sight of the snow-covered Abajo Mountains and rejoiced. Recognizing a landmark that would orient them toward their destination, they were able to plot a feasible route toward the place where the pioneers would establish the settlement of Bluff. The Hole-in-the-Rock pioneers eventually reached their new homeland in April 1880. (See map on p. 321 for a visual rendering of the Hole-in-the-Rock Trail.)

Over the next century, members of the Hole-in-the-Rock expedition and their descendants, along with other settlers, managed to make a viable living from the land, depending first on ranching and agriculture and later on mining and oil production.

The success of Mormon forebears in surviving their arduous journey and establishing a settlement in rugged country to them served as proof of their strength and the power of the divine. Their century-long efforts to earn a

Redd Cabin, Bluff, Utah (courtesy of Kay and Patsy Shumway)

living and create communities in an unforgiving climate have imbued them with a sense of pride and cultural connection. They profess deep love for and spiritual connection to a land that has long provided sustenance; they believe that they have fulfilled the Creator's will in stewarding it well.

The Mormon pioneers' triumph and success in their new homeland, however, often came at the expense of their Native neighbors, the original inhabitants of the land Mormons sought to claim as their own. In contrast to many other settlers, Mormons' scripture and culture dictated that they treat Native peoples with kindness and fairness while reaching out to bring them into the church for their own salvation. Native peoples did not always appreciate the "generous" attempts at assimilation. As resources became scarce and the newcomers fenced off regions that had been open range, the two groups quarreled over ranchland and, as was the case with most Anglo-Native conflicts over land, Anglos ultimately gained the upper hand. With clear direction from Brigham Young to treat Natives fairly, there has been a degree of goodwill between many Natives and Anglo Mormons. Yet much about the Anglo-Native dynamic was and remains complex and painful. While some Natives have embraced Mormonism, others reject the view that they are in need of salvation. A world evolved wherein Mormons controlled power structures, and, sometimes through words, sometimes through policies, the Navajos and Utes were subject to discrimination. This history and the perpetuation of racism and classism in current-day dynamics infuse conversations about land use with the weight of painful history.

The history of Native peoples in San Juan County is in many ways defined by trauma and tragedy, but above all, their story is one of remarkable resilience in the face of land seizure, armed attacks by Anglo settlers and by the U.S. Army, and government-endorsed attempts to eradicate their indigenous cultures. The People, as they refer to themselves, are still here, their diverse languages and cultures vibrantly, even defiantly, intact.

San Juan County's people, both Native and Anglo, have long depended on the land. They have tilled it, grazed livestock on it, mined it, hunted its fauna, gathered its flora, extracted oil and gas from below its surface, and, in some cases, left it untouched. In this harsh, dry country there has always been a fine line between sustenance and ruin.

Origin of Current Disputes

As travel to the West became more practical, people from around the world began to visit the red rock country of San Juan County. They found a land of unparalleled beauty endowed with unique geological, biological, and cultural riches. To many of them, such land called out for permanent protection so that future generations could experience its wildness and the inspiration that solitude in its vastness brings. They saw as well the competing desires of those residents of San Juan County who wished to drill, mine, and raise livestock in the name of serving both their immediate economic needs and the needs of a rapidly growing world for the natural resources held within the land. And they witnessed the predations of a few who sought riches by plundering ancestral Native sites, robbing graves, and, in the process, destroying a people's history.

By the early decades of the twentieth century, protecting lands on the Colorado Plateau had become a priority for a growing environmental movement. Conservationists looked at maps of Utah and recognized that as a

Hillsides, southwest of Bluff, Utah

condition of statehood, Utah had accepted designation of much of the land within its current boundaries as public land, now administered by various agencies of the federal government: the National Park Service, the Bureau of Land Management, and the U.S. Forest Service. In San Juan County such federally owned and administered public lands comprise 61 percent of the county, with the state owning another 9 percent and Native tribes owning 23 percent. Thus, in the minds of conservationists and their allies, protecting San Juan County's red rock country required curtailing or precluding development on public lands. How to do so while retaining an economic base for the citizens of San Juan County has been a source of controversy and ongoing passionate debate.

An early effort to protect public lands on the Colorado Plateau was advanced by President Franklin Roosevelt's secretary of the interior, Harold Ickes. In 1936 Ickes proposed that a seven-thousand-square-mile area centered on the confluence of the Green and Colorado Rivers be named a national monument, using the president's authority under the Antiquities Act. President Theodore Roosevelt had signed the act in 1906 to provide a tool for the president to protect areas from looting and the desecration of ancestral Native sites and to preserve such land for scientific and historical study. Had Ickes's proposed Escalante National Monument gone forward, not only land but also the ancestral artifacts within the monument's boundaries would have been shielded from development and desecration. However, protests by ranchers and miners eventually led Utah's congressional delegation to oppose the monument, and with the onset of World War II, the monument concept was shelved.

The idea of protection was resuscitated in 1961 by then secretary of the interior Stewart Udall. Again, ranching and mining interests protested designation of a large national monument or park. But after much political maneuvering, a relatively small but essential area containing some of the land for which Ickes had recommended protection was set aside as Canyonlands National Park in 1964.

That same year, the Wilderness Act, designed to protect "area[s] where the earth and its community of life are untrammeled by man, where man himself is a visitor who does not remain," was signed into law. Just five years later, Congress passed the National Environmental Policy Act (NEPA), established the Council on Environmental Quality, and required federal agencies to prepare environmental assessments and environmental impact statements to evaluate the effects on the environment of any proposed federal actions. These acts of Congress marked a transition from the environmental movement's origins in small grassroots efforts to a powerful force on Capitol Hill.

While the tension between conserving land and using it for economic benefit was already high, the passage of the Federal Land Policy and Management Act (FLPMA) in 1976 served as the catalyst for the current fraught, oft-angry debates regarding public land use in southeastern Utah. FLPMA shifted the mandate of the Bureau of Land Management (BLM) to include conservation and recreation in addition to resource management. Moreover, FLPMA required the BLM to inventory public lands that might have characteristics that would merit protection as wilderness. In short, the era of what conservationists called the "Bureau of Livestock and Mining" was over: grazing and mineral extraction would no longer receive de facto top priority.

In response, rural westerners whose economy depended on ranching and mining railed against what they viewed as the federal government's potential to usurp "their" land and threaten their livelihood. Because 41 percent of the land in San Juan County is managed by the BLM, residents feared the economic consequences of withdrawing those lands for conservation. Their protests against FLPMA triggered what became known as the Sagebrush Rebellion, a rejection of federal control of public lands in favor of local control, a movement that has swept through the West over the past four decades. The intensity of the rebellion in San Juan County was amplified by the hostility toward the federal government of many in the county's Mormon majority who know well the stories of Mormon persecution at the hands of U.S. government officials in the nineteenth century. To this day, locals lobby and protest in hopes of returning the BLM's focus to "multiple use," which in their view would restore the priority given to grazing, mining, and oil and gas extraction, all of which locals see as engines of prosperity.

Efforts by environmentalists to achieve the original Ickes vision of an expansive national monument continue, in turn evoking opposition based on cultural and ideological distrust of the federal government and its jurisdiction over uses of the land.

And so San Juan County, the heart of the Colorado Plateau, has become a focal point for this decades-long battle. Within this vast expanse lie the Bears Ears, 8,500-foot-high twin buttes that dominate the landscape for more than sixty miles in all directions. They have come to symbolize two opposing

Bears Ears in winter, sunset

philosophies of public land use: permanent protection by the federal government and a fierce opposition to any federal regulation or control.

For countless generations, Navajos, Utes, and Puebloans from across the Colorado Plateau have come to Bears Ears to hunt, gather firewood, collect plants and herbs, and hold religious ceremonies in a place they all consider sacred. Nearly every canyon, ridge, and wash in San Juan County holds evidence of ancient civilizations stretching back thousands of years. Native peoples of the region believe that the spirits of their ancestors still inhabit these sites. Protecting the land, therefore, is not only about leaving a gift for future generations; it is also about keeping the past alive in the present.

San Juan County's Anglo Mormons perceive their connection to Bears Ears as multigenerational and spiritual as well. The proud descendants of the Hole-in-the-Rock pioneers take seriously their role as stewards of the land bequeathed them by their forebears and promised them by their Heavenly Father.

For both Native tribes and Anglo Mormons, the connection to this land is elemental. It is the key to who and why they are. But despite this shared connection, their relationship both with one another and with the federal government is replete with wounds. Mormons were murdered by agents of the federal government and persecuted for decades. For well over a century they have walked and later driven over these lands, virtually unfettered by regulations until the mid-1970s. They believe they have stewarded the land well, and they believe that the federal government, its regulations and its agents, along with conservationists are taking away both Mormons' freedom and the land on which they depend for their economic future.

Tribes were driven from ancestral lands by Mormons and other Anglos as settlements expanded dramatically throughout the Mountain West. Native children were taken from their parents and sent to Anglo-run boarding schools in attempts to "civilize" them. Multiple treaties have been broken or ignored. Careless desecration and deliberate looting of ancestral sites, some more than a millennium old, have robbed Native peoples of their connection with the past and the spirits of their ancestors.

And then there are the conservationists. To them, this land is one of the last remaining areas within the continental United States where the hands of humans have been relatively light and where natural beauty and cultural history are unparalleled. They see public land as a national treasure, a unique and essential part of who we are as Americans. They believe that the voices of the public at large need to be heard as decisions about the future of *their* land are made.

These multifaceted stories and conflicting passions meet in southeastern Utah. In this book we seek to share with you a unique place with an exceptional history and the people who call it home. Their stories reflect the cultural crosscurrents that roil our times: the struggle to maintain tradition and culture in the face of a rapidly changing world, the lines we draw to define and defend what is ours, the ties that bind us together, and the fears that threaten to tear us apart. Listening to these stories offers us all an opportunity to honor land held sacred by Natives and Anglos—and an opportunity to transform contested ground into common ground.

Over the course of nearly three years of listening, we have come to have deep respect and affection for many residents of San Juan County whose views span a wide range of passionately held positions, as well as for tribal members and conservationists across the Colorado Plateau who have shared stories and offered kindness and hospitality. To honor them, we have endeavored to capture their words so that they can be heard with openness, compassion, and understanding for what they hold sacred.

Comb Ridge (*right*); layered hills (*left*) southwest of Bluff, Utah

CONNECTING TO SACRED LANDS

Voices of Two Cultures

Comb Ridge southwest of Bluff, Utah (aerial image)

JONAH YELLOWMAN
Caring for Ancestral Lands, Leading Prayers for Healing

On a blustery May morning just east of Bluff, Utah, Jonah Yellowman climbs into the passenger seat of our Toyota 4Runner and leads us to a team of stone horses.

The sun has begun its ascent toward the zenith, and the heat from its rays penetrates our skin and hints at the triple-digit temperatures to come. The sky is an intense azure blue, and its brilliant color bleeds into the saturated reds and rusts of the sandstone that surrounds us.

Our guide to Bears Ears country has spent a lifetime seeking the embrace of sun and wind; the creases in his weathered skin map journeys past. His dark-brown eyes are kind and humble; his hands, large and expressive, have a language all their own. He speaks slowly, words carefully chosen, in tones both gentle and deep. The resonance of his voice calls forth a profound connection with the earth and the Colorado Plateau as he shares stories of ancestors who came long before our time, who still inhabit the land on which we walk, and whose eternal presence he and other tribal leaders seek to protect.

Yellowman directs us to a site on the side of U.S. Highway 191, south of the San Juan River, and motions for us to step out of the car and scan the side of the bluff before us.

"You see it?" Yellowman asks, pointing to a place on the left-hand side of the sheer red rock wall. "The tail is right there."

His slow, deliberate speech accelerates as his excitement grows.

"There's another one standing right here, a gray one. Then another one, and another one, and another one."

He draws a quick sketch that we can use as a guide as he moves his hand from left to right. We squint in the sunlight, our brows furrowed in concentration.

Mesa, south of Bluff, Utah

Yellowman's sketch

Jonah Yellowman

Suddenly, we see it: a tail on the bluff's far left side, a downward curve in the sandstone that forms the horse's back, a rounded notch just to the right that is unmistakably an equine head. The sandstone varnish even paints a mane on the red rock.

"Every time I stop I see another one," Yellowman says of the horses manifest in the mesa's cracks and crevices. "It's kind of amazing. I look for . . . amazing things. God's creation."

We have managed to make out a few other horses on Yellowman's team, but we sense that he sees much in the world that surrounds us that we never will. He has been trained as a healer and spiritual leader and has spent a lifetime seeking connection with the voices of the earth: mountains, rivers, plants, insects, and animals. To Yellowman and to Native peoples across the Colorado Plateau, every living thing is sacred, possessing spiritual power and religious significance. The earth itself is a living, breathing being akin to and beloved as a family member, someone to hear and honor through prayer and ceremony.

We drive farther westward to a spot on the Comb Ridge, stopping before the road cuts through the seemingly impenetrable sandstone spine and heads south toward Mexican Hat and Monument Valley.

Over the next hours, Yellowman reflects on the journey he has taken with Utah Diné Bikéyah (UDB), a nonprofit that has given voice to Native concerns for the protection of the Bears Ears region. He describes to us how he was chosen by UDB's cofounder and legendary Navajo political leader, Mark Maryboy, to be one of the group's spiritual advisors.

"[Mark] said, 'You want to be on the board?'" Yellowman recalls. "And I said yeah. Then I asked Mark, 'What are we doing?' He said, 'We're talking about Bears Ears.' I said, . . . 'If we're going to talk about this, I think we should talk to the one who created this land first, the Creator. Tell him what we're going to do. Then we'll go from there.'"

Yellowman speaks to the spiritual teachings that inform his worldview and that have determined his place in the universe. "Way back, in the creation, the Holy People came here," Yellowman says. "This didn't happen in seven days. This happened over millions and millions of years . . . to control how this world was going to be, to have our rituals, to have our songs, [to have] all this.

"This is why I was put here on this world—for this," Yellowman continues. "I thank our maker, and I pray for everybody. Every time they ask me, 'Can you say a prayer for us?' I always do."

As he speaks, his mesmerizing hand movements slowly transport us into a world in which stories are circular.

Another spiritual leader "did a blessing for me, and he said, . . . 'You were told to be [a spiritual advisor].'" His hand points skyward, outstretched and beckoning, while he adds, "'And now you've seen what it means. You are initiated to be that kind of a person now.'"

In a culture where spiritual leaders can have as much or more influence than elected political leaders, Yellowman's words have power and are treated with respect. His humility is manifest in how he speaks about his own need for guidance as he faces challenging situations and uncertainty.

"Even though I might be a leader, I still have to ask my elders for advice," Yellowman says. "I can say I want to do it this way, but still I will go by and ask them, 'Is it OK?' They . . . balance me out. 'This is where you are; don't jump over there yet. Take time. Don't rush yourself. You might not make it.' So I do it that way.

"But it's been moving pretty fast," he says, speaking of the work of UDB and the Bears Ears Inter-Tribal Coalition.

Starting in 2010 UDB provided a voice for Native Americans advocating for the protection of a vast swath of land in southeastern Utah. Most of the organization's staff and board members live in the region and belong to the Navajo and Ute Mountain Ute tribes. They have worked to build relationships with other tribes that trace their ancestry to the Bears Ears landscape and who today continue to gather medicinal herbs and conduct ceremonies at culturally significant sites in the area. In 2015, as an outgrowth of UDB's efforts, an alliance of indigenous leaders formed the Bears Ears Inter-Tribal

Jonah Yellowman evokes the circular world of the Navajo

Coalition, uniting five Colorado Plateau tribes—Navajo, Hopi, Ute Mountain Ute, Uintah and Ouray Ute, and Zuni—to advance a common cause of protecting lands to which they have been connected, they believe, since time immemorial.

Following discussions of the ties of each tribe to the region, Coalition leaders proposed the 1.9-million-acre Bears Ears National Monument in San Juan County to preserve their shared ancestral lands. Their goal is to achieve a historic victory for sovereign tribal nations and a precedent-setting paradigm shift in land policy: collaborative management with federal agencies with assurances of continued access for traditional uses and ceremonial activities.

> For thousands of years, our ancestors lived within the Bears Ears landscape, hunting, foraging, and farming it by hand. They knew every plant and animal, every stream and mountain, every change of season, and every lesson important enough to be passed down through the centuries. We understood this place and cared for it, relating to the earth literally as our mother who provides for us and the plants and animals to which we are related. The Bears Ears landscape is alive in our view, and must be nourished and cared for if life is to be sustained.
>
> —Bears Ears Inter-Tribal Coalition, "Bears Ears: A Native Perspective on America's Most Significant Unprotected Cultural Landscape"

Yellowman recalls the April 2015 gathering that first brought the tribes together at Bears Ears. "I did a prayer meeting," he says. "Different tribes . . . from the coalition . . . lit the fire the old, traditional way, and they put it in the middle of the tepee. Everyone cooked, used the same fire. It started out very traditionally. Everybody shared tobacco. Everybody smoked. No matter what tribe you were.

"Then they shared some stories, old stories. Then they took the tobacco, and they put it in the fire. This [was] our offering . . . to the fire."

His role as a board member of UDB and spiritual advisor to the Bears Ears Coalition has taken Yellowman to Washington, D.C., where he has advocated for the coalition's goals and has prayed for the coalition's success.

"I didn't talk much," Yellowman says. "But [the tribes] asked me to talk, 'Say something for us, too.' I try to make it brief, just to hit the punch line. That's what I do. That's the way I am."

Jonah Yellowman in a ceremonial
tent, Bears Ears gathering, July 2016

To recenter himself in the midst of a challenging and often frenetic political process, Yellowman seeks space for solitude and quiet contemplation in the landscape the tribal leaders are working to save.

"I go out every once in a while, out to Bears Ears, and walk the area out there," Yellowman says. "Look at the land when I'm driving through. I go out in the morning, do my offerings, and sing a song sometimes. They call it Earth Song. So whatever we do, we're doing the right thing. That's what we're told to do when we're young. Go out there and sing the song."

To Yellowman, the idea of land-ownership, so important to Anglos, is antithetical to the Native way of living with and caring for the earth.

"I was told you don't say this is my land," Yellowman says. "This land is not yours. This is everybody's land. We're all God's children. You're just here for a short time, and you're going to be on your way again. So remember and take care of it.

"We talk about healing," Yellowman says. "You stumble, you're going to get hurt on the rocks. Medicine men will gather plants and herbs to heal the wound. That's . . . what they call healing. We're talking about healing the world, the earth, and healing us."

As a medicine man, Yellowman knows where to find herbs and medicinal plants critical to healing ceremonies. Practicing those ceremonies is essential to bringing about the physical and spiritual healing—of land and people—that is central to the coalition's proposal and mission.

He fears that without protection, the tribes' access to vital natural resources will be lost.

"That plant was put there for a purpose, and here you fence it off, and you're going to say no to somebody . . . ready to have a prayer with the Holy

Creator to heal one of the Creator's children, and here you're saying no," Yellowman says. "[A] person asked the medicine man, 'Help me.' And somebody will say, 'Nope, you can't go in there, can't get that medicine.' We can't let that happen."

Once access to resources is gone, there will be no prospect for healing in the future and no connection with ancestors and their wisdom.

Reflecting on what has already been violated or lost, Yellowman speaks mournfully about mining operations that have stripped mountains and mesas for their mineral wealth, left irreparable wounds in the earth, and severed relationships with the past.

"It's a sad thing," Yellowman says. "Who's going to fix it? We don't have the prayers for it. We don't have the songs for it. There's a scar there that we don't know how to fix. We don't want that [any]more. By healing, I think that's how we [can] leave it like this," he says, holding his arms out as if to embrace the land around us, mostly untouched by humans, with no oil derricks or signs of mining activity in view.

But beyond resource extraction, there is desecration wreaked by humans, both determined looters and careless visitors who have robbed graves, stolen artifacts, and damaged ancestral dwellings that in some cases had endured for a millennium or more in the nearby canyons and cliffsides.

"What they did to our ancestors over there, they started digging them out," Yellowman says. "How would they feel if their [ancestors'] bodies were being dug out?

"The petroglyphs. The writing on the walls. Somebody wrote it there. Maybe there's a story. Maybe up to today. Maybe [into] the future. You don't know. People are going in there and trying to take it away. So we would say, no, don't take it. They're there for all of us. Have respect."

Yellowman grew up hearing from some people what many Natives heard and at times still do hear: that he was a simple man incapable of doing much of consequence in a world based on practicalities, hard facts, and competition.

"A lot of people, they say in a lot of different ways, you guys don't know how to do this," Yellowman says. "We've been downgraded."

He, UDB, and the coalition of tribes are eager to prove them wrong, to demonstrate that they can lead a movement that will fundamentally change the way Native peoples are perceived by the dominant culture and to empower indigenous people to advocate for protection of their ancestral lands.

They see strength in combining indigenous and Western wisdom and science and believe that the Bears Ears National Monument can be the vehicle for conjoining the best in each culture.

"I think it's going to open a lot of minds," Yellowman says. "From here on, if we're going to talk about this land, we're going to hear histories. We're going to see and know and understand."

We all believe that . . . there's somebody sitting next to us that we can't see. Maybe multiple folks, helping lead this along. Somebody's prayers, or many people's prayers, or maybe it's the Bears Ears themselves . . . whoever they might be.

—Eric Descheenie, Arizona state representative, District 7, and former cochair of the Bears Ears Inter-Tribal Coalition, January 28, 2016

If you look at the tribes involved, coming together [to protect] a landscape, I don't think people recognize how unique that is. All of them working so well together and looking at their common agenda when they've either fought or had disagreements or people have tried to divide them, and so having them all unite behind [Bears Ears National Monument] is pretty cool. . . . To date, it's the opposite of what Congressman [Rob] Bishop [R-UT] is doing. Congressman Bishop is trying to devolve this to county commissioners. And tribes are trying to elevate this to nation-to-nation dialogue, which is a very different plane of discussion. The county commissioners are interested in near-term elections, and tribes are looking at this landscape through a prism of hundreds and hundreds of years and generations.

—Brian O'Donnell, former executive director, Conservation Lands Foundation, July 27, 2015

From Alaskan mountain peaks to the Argentinian pampas to the rocky shores of Newfoundland, Native Americans were the first to carve out cities, domesticate crops, and establish great civilizations. When the Framers gathered to write the United States Constitution, they drew inspiration from the Iroquois Confederacy, and in the centuries since, American Indians and Alaska Natives from hundreds of tribes have shaped our national life. During Native American Heritage Month, we honor their vibrant cultures and strengthen the government-to-government relationship between the United States and each tribal nation.

—President Barack Obama, presidential proclamation, National Native American Heritage Month, October 31, 2013

INTERLUDE
Native Cosmology and Land Stewardship

We are a spiritual people. However, our holy practices happen right here on earth, not in a church, but in special places like Bears Ears. We sometimes talk to the plants, others sing to the mountains, and we seek out our ancestors, who still roam this land, and we ask them for guidance in a language they can understand. In times long past, the ancient ones sanctified the land and its special places, and the blessings remain in force today.

—Bears Ears Inter-Tribal Coalition, "Bears Ears: A Native Perspective on America's Most Significant Unprotected Cultural Landscape"

To Native Americans in the Bears Ears region and indigenous peoples around the world, the earth is a living, breathing entity, a nurturer, life giver, and beloved family member to be treated with unconditional respect.

In his opening prayer at the 2016 Parliament of the World's Religions, Rupert Steele, chairman of the Confederated Tribes of the Goshute Reservation in northern Utah, articulated his tribe's relationship to the land: "The Earth is our mother. The water is her blood. The rocks are her bones, and the land is her skin. . . . The ground beneath our feet is the ashes of our ancestors. The earth is rich with the lives of our kin. . . . We know the earth does not belong to us. We belong to the earth."

Unlike much of the Western world, which in the modern era has been dominated by consumption-based societies with much of their development and growth driven by natural resource extraction, traditional Native teachings instruct humans to take from the earth only what they need—and to remember their place in the order of nature.

"Just because we're walking and talking and thinking individuals and we [have the power to] take a life, that doesn't make us superior," says Octavius Seowtewa, chair of the Cultural Resources Advisory Committee and a medicine society leader for the Zuni tribe. "There's not this concept of 'this doesn't have a life, and this has a life.' *Everything* has a life. A tree has a life, a rock has a life, even air has a life. Everything that was put here for our use has a reason."

"The basic idea behind conservation is never taking more than you need and always offering something in return," says Carleton Bowekaty, a Zuni councilman and cochair of the Bears Ears Inter-Tribal Coalition. "For ceremonial purposes, when we take certain herbs or visit certain springs [and] take water from there, we always make sure we offer something in return.

"The hardest thing to explain to westerners is that we can't separate our world into different elements," Bowekaty adds. "It's not like a religion where we can set it aside on a Sunday or a Wednesday. We incorporate these prayers almost on a daily basis. It's a way of life. It's a cultural practice that has existed for eons that needs to continue.

"We talk to these higher beings for these blessings that we ask for. The teachings from our ancestors tell us your world's connected."

Eric Descheenie, who is Navajo and the former cochair of the Bears Ears Inter-Tribal Coalition, says that relationships with such beings are at the core of Native spirituality.

"The way I often articulate Native American thought—indigenous thought—is we have intersubjective relationships with what I refer to as 'other than human beings,'" Descheenie explains. "From a [Navajo] religious standpoint, every day we're supposed to get up and communicate with the Diné—most commonly referred to as the Holy People. They rise at dawn, before the sun comes up, before it hits the horizon. And we get up and make . . . offerings. As part of our prayers, there is an exchange that happens. We communicate with them, they communicate with us."

Ancestral lands and archaeological sites considered culturally and historically significant by non-Native visitors to Bears Ears hold more than history for Native Americans; they are sacred to the region's indigenous peoples. Some are religious shrines, places of worship, and sites for ceremonies that have been practiced, according to Native peoples, since time immemorial. Mesas, canyons, valleys, mountains, buttes, plants, and animals—indeed, the entire earth and its flora and fauna—are also held sacred and believed to possess deep spiritual power.

"Wherever you go on this land is sacred ground," says Jonah Yellowman, a Navajo traditional healer and spiritual advisor to Utah Diné Bikéyah. "There are ants that live here. There are animals [and] spiders and flying creatures here. . . . Respect them. Respect where you walk."

UDB cofounder Mark Maryboy clarifies, "There aren't specific places that you can say, 'That's spiritual.' With Navajo, everywhere [is spiritual]."

As Shaun Chapoose, chair of the Ute Indian Tribe of the Uintah and Ouray Reservation, puts it, "Our value system is unique. What you see as a weed, I see as a medicinal plant. It's a living landscape. It has a pulse. It has a heartbeat."

The essence of Native identity is rooted in place: the ancestral and modern-day homelands of American Indians shape and define who they are.

"Everything is all rooted from our mother earth that provides [for us]," explains Regina Lopez-Whiteskunk of the Ute Mountain Ute tribe, also a member of the Bears Ears Inter-Tribal Coalition. "Our strong tie to the earth from a very young infancy helps us to pass along this comfort to our children."

"One of the reasons we are where we're at now is because somehow [our ancestors] knew it was a safe place, and that's where they were directed to go," relates Alfred Lomahquahu of the Hopi tribe. "And it was a spiritual journey, like Moses in the biblical times. We were directed by certain events to eventually come to this place, which we call the center of the universe.

"You have to always remember our spiritual side, because that's where our strength lies: starting from us as different people, going to our tribes and then to the coalition as a whole. . . . That's when the land accepts us as working for them. Basically, that's what we're doing: the land is asking us to work for them."

If one can speak of a shared Native American view of the land, it might be found in the words of Kiowa author, artist, and poet N. Scott Momaday: "To encounter the sacred is to be alive at the deepest center of human existence. Sacred places are the truest definitions of the earth; they stand for the earth immediately and forever; they are its flags and shields. If you would know the earth for what it really is, learn it through its sacred places. At Devil's Tower [in Wyoming] or Canyon de Chelly [in Arizona] or the Cahokia Mounds [in Illinois], you touch the pulse of the living planet; you feel its breath upon you. You become one with a spirit that pervades geologic time and space."[1]

---

1. Momaday, *Man Made of Words*, 114.

Fall, Abajo Mountains

KAY AND PATSY SHUMWAY
Honoring a Pioneer Past,
Continuing a Tradition of Faith

Kay and Patsy Shumway project a warmth and gentle wholesomeness as they welcome us into their Blanding, Utah, home with sincere smiles and a spirit of goodwill that is disarming in today's transactional world. Blanding is an atypical outpost that has some trappings of modern-day America (a Subway sandwich shop, a brand-new fitness center), but otherwise it feels like a rural western town that exists today mostly in people's imaginings of a simpler time.

Kay, age eighty-one and one of eight siblings, is tall and thin and has the suntanned skin of a man who has spent a lifetime outdoors in the near-perpetual sunshine of the desert Southwest. He is well kempt and clean-shaven, with close-cropped hair, a wrinkleless burgundy button-down shirt tucked into khakis, and wire-rimmed glasses that frame his compassionate eyes. He is soft-spoken and articulate, and he exudes the confidence and wisdom befitting a respected member of the Blanding community.

Patsy, seventy-eight, is shorter and round faced, with rosy cheeks and short, curly white hair. Clad in a white T-shirt and blue jeans, she has a no-frills, no-nonsense manner. It's not hard to imagine her herding sheep on San Juan County ranchland or wrangling a classroom of restless high-school students, as she did in her younger years. But she also exudes the kindness of a loving grandmother and great-grandmother, ever ready to provide a home-cooked meal and a hug to children grown and small.

Kay invites us into the living room, a modest space with two easy chairs, a sofa, and a bookshelf filled with binders and spiral-bound books that contain their extensive family histories—a shrine of sorts in a Mormon home and a testament to the importance of family to members of the Church of Jesus Christ of Latter-day Saints.

Kay and Patsy Shumway (courtesy of Kay and Patsy Shumway)

"In our church, we're taught that families are eternal," Patsy tells us.

Mormons believe that they will be with their entire families, including their ancestors, in the afterlife. As such, they are eager to gather as much information as possible about their family members so they can be prepared to greet all of their relatives in what they call the Celestial Kingdom.

"We're taught to keep our family histories and tell our family's stories . . . whether they're good or bad," Patsy says, laughing.

They share their family histories freely and with great pride.

"My grandfather moved from New Mexico into Recapture Canyon fifteen miles from here," Kay says. "They ran cattle there in a place called Fiddler's Green. There was a spring there. They put in a hay field and an orchard. [My family] moved there around 1911. My father remembers the coyotes coming in and eating the peaches. He could hear their teeth on the pits of those hard peaches."

Kay's mother was born in Mexico. In 1885 over 350 families made the trek from Utah to Chihuahua and Sonora and began successful farming colonies. More settlers arrived in the succeeding decades, fleeing persecution from U.S. government officials for their polygamous practices.

In order for Utah to be recognized by the United States as a state, LDS leaders were required to renounce polygamy. Some Mormon communities refused to give up the practice, however, and left their home country to continue living as they had for generations.

The settlers' trials were far from over, however. As emigrant Anglos, they were caught in the anti-"gringo" passions of the 1910 Mexican Revolution and forced to flee back to the United States. Kay's mother was one of the Mormons who left Mexico and started a new life in Utah.

Shumway Cabin, Fiddler's Green (courtesy of Kay and Patsy Shumway)

Kay's parents, especially his mother, who couldn't afford college, instilled in him and his siblings the importance of higher education.

"If you grew up in Blanding [at that time], you had to go away for higher education," Kay recalls. "The closest place was Price, which was two hundred miles away, and if you're going to go to Price, you might as well go over the hill and into the Utah Valley, where there's more available."

Before earning a PhD in plant genetics at Purdue University, Kay studied botany and chemistry at Brigham Young University, where he and Patsy met and fell in love.

Patsy was born in Durango, Colorado, about 125 miles east of Blanding, and she moved with her family to Blanding just ten days after she was born. Her father worked as a ranch hand and "sheepman" for his uncle, legendary stockman Charlie Redd. She and her five siblings spent their childhood summers on the range.

After they married, Kay and Patsy spent the next two decades away from the area as Kay pursued his academic career. They returned to Blanding in 1977, lured by the desire to be close to family and, for Kay, the opportunity

Wedding Picture of

Wayne H. Redd and Caroline Nielson

Caroline Nielson and Wayne Redd, wedding photograph. Caroline came to Bluff with the Hole-in-the-Rock pioneers. Wayne's father was one of four scouts of the pioneering company (courtesy of Kay and Patsy Shumway).

to help build southeastern Utah's first university, the College of Eastern Utah (now Utah State University Eastern, Blanding), from the ground up. "My mother clipped in the *San Juan Record*"—the county's primary newspaper—"that they were getting this thing started, and they needed someone with academic credentials. So we came home."

Kay is proudest of the college's efforts to include Utah Navajos in the student body and to provide educational opportunities that hold the promise of preparing them for success in a world beyond the reservation.

"We [could] actually give . . . bachelor's degrees and occasionally a master's degree right here in Blanding," Kay says. "We had faculty who cared enough about the Navajo people to work with them to face the hard times that they had while coming here. I think that made a world of difference for the future of the Navajo people."

Like their neighbors, Kay and Patsy consider landscapes in southeastern Utah to be sacred not only because of their natural beauty but because the rivers, canyons, and forested mountains of San Juan County are their ancestral homeland.

"I go to these places to pray, to take photographs, to look at stars, to look at the visual landscape," Kay says. "It's just as sacred to me as to a Navajo."

Ironically, it was following his passion for photography that exposed Kay to restrictions on accessing those places, which he used to wander freely.

"This road on Elk Mountain [north of Blanding] I used to run around on had a closure sign on it," Kay says. "This place I used to go on Cedar Mesa is closed," as are a number of places deemed ecologically and culturally sensitive by the Bureau of Land Management. "It made me feel like maybe some person was going to photograph me and write me up.

"It got to be to the point where we would grumble among ourselves," Kay continues. "We [were] thinking, What can we possibly do to show these federal agencies how the local people feel when they're shut out of these places they've always loved for generations?"

The Shumways, along with many Blanding residents, celebrated when their son-in-law, San Juan County commissioner Phil Lyman, formed the San Juan County Public Lands Council in early 2014 to seek input regarding potential uses of federal land in San Juan County. His goal was to present a consensus plan to be included in Utah representative Rob Bishop's (R-UT) Public Lands Initiative, described by the congressman as "a locally-driven effort to bring resolution to some of the most challenging land disputes in the state of Utah."[1]

"We said, 'Great, we've got a spokesperson,'" Kay says.

"Phil grew up with a sense of community and history, and Recapture Canyon is where Phil's grandfather would go hiking," Patsy says. "You see why people have very strong beliefs about people telling them where they can walk, where they can drive, when for four generations, they've just been walking where they wanted to walk."

For many of San Juan County's Anglo Mormons, these beliefs are also inextricably linked to the arduous journey made by their forebears to reach and settle San Juan County. The intrepid Hole-in-the-Rock pioneers who in 1879 made the trek across southern Utah provide inspiration to their descendants—as well as a strong sense of ownership of the land and desire to steward it according to their Heavenly Father's will.

While the Shumways are unfailingly polite, they don't hide their anger at what they see as the federal government's increasing regulation of public land they have called home for generations. Still, they defy the stereotype of rural Utahns as anti-environmentalist. Kay and Patsy are members of the Bluff-based conservation nonprofit Friends of Cedar Mesa. Kay considers the nonprofit's executive director, Josh Ewing, a friend and was invited by Ewing to make a presentation about Kay's family's cabin at the group's annual gathering.

"We have interests in common," Kay says. "I want to preserve the ruins, too."

Their relationship is not without its complications, however, and illustrates the difficulty of bridging the divide between locals in favor of multiple use (mining, oil and gas development, ranching, recreation) and environmentalists, some of whom are dedicated to preserving wilderness in its purest form. For example, Ewing wants to protect a broad swath of land in San Juan County outside the Cedar Mesa area, including the Comb Ridge, and is open to the idea of a national monument designation. Shumway is dubious about both prospects.

"The apostle Paul said, 'I'm betwixt,'" Kay says—torn between "whether to live and to fight with people [he] taught the Gospel to or to go be with Christ. That's the way I am with Josh: betwixt. I want to support the things he does,

---

1. Staff of Bishop, Chaffetz, and Stewart, "Utah Public Lands Initiative."

but some of the things he does are not friendly to the people around here."
(Hear more from Josh Ewing on p. 141.)

"I grew up in a time when federal control of lands in San Juan County seemed to have the multiuse philosophy that they so much tout," he continues, "and it was permissible to use natural resources such as uranium, vanadium, coal, gas, oil, copper, and phosphate. I have seen this change drastically in my lifetime. Just in the last fifteen years, as I have wandered the canyons and mountains of San Juan as a photographer, I have seen area after area, road after road, closed to me.

"Our Heavenly Father put these natural resources and natural beauty here for our use and enjoyment."

My history dates back as far as the Anglo people who settled this county. Jens Nielson, my great-great-grandpa, he came through the Hole-in-the-Rock, and my great-great-grandpa Walter C. Lyman, he founded Blanding. He dug the tunnel through Blue Mountain to give Blanding fresh drinking water in 1915. . . . I hear people coming in and talking about how great it is that they get to rock climb. This is more than recreation to me. This is my home. . . . I'm going to wake up tomorrow, my parents are going to wake up tomorrow, my grandparents are going to wake up tomorrow, and the [Bears Ears National Monument is] gonna be there. . . . I think about America and what it stands for. For the government to come in and make this monument is to take away the freedoms that we enjoy here. It's like taking America away from me.

—Brooke Lyman, Blanding resident and daughter of San Juan County commissioner Phil Lyman, July 16, 2016

I think we could get a whole lot accomplished here if the [LDS] church would just take a stand and say, we don't want any of our people looting sites. I think they're really powerful, and they could do some really cool things with not a lot of effort if they would just address some of those things. I think a lot of people in the Mormon religion would listen if someone said, "This is unacceptable, we cannot support this." . . . But I don't really see them stepping up and [expressing] views on any of those big issues.

—Vaughn Hadenfeldt, founder, Far Out Expeditions, and board chair, Friends of Cedar Mesa, October 27, 2015

One of the purposes of the Hole-in-the-Rock mission was to make friends with the Indians. We believe that we're all God's children. So we have that in the church as one of our tenets, one of the things they need to do in order to return to heaven is to embrace the Heavenly Father.

We believe we're sealed as families, and so we want to understand our ancestors. . . . We know we'll see them again; it's part of the beliefs that we have. We want to know them when we see them, we want to know what they're like. That gives us lots of courage. My great-grandfather, Jents Nielsen, he came over [to Utah] in 1856 with a hand cart, and his feet were badly frozen for the rest of his life, so when I have hard times, I look to him for courage and strength to keep going.

—LaRue Barton, director, Bluff Fort, November 5, 2015

INTERLUDE
Mormon Theology and Land Stewardship

Reverence for nature and a calling to take from the earth only what is needed are enshrined in Mormon theology, and on a personal level, Anglo Mormon residents of San Juan County express a deep spiritual attachment to the canyons, rivers, mesas, and wide-open spaces of their homeland. However, the anti-environmentalist stance of Utah's most outspoken politicians, many of whom also happen to be members of the Church of Jesus Christ of Latter-day Saints, has led many not familiar with LDS teachings to assume Mormons in rural Utah lack strong ties to the land or an ethos of environmental stewardship. Yet as is often the case with religion, the tension lies between doctrine and how its adherents choose to interpret it.

Passages from the Book of Mormon's Doctrine and Covenants read:

> Yea, all things which come of the earth, in the season thereof, are made for the benefit and use of man, both to please the eye and to gladden the heart;
>
> Yea, for food and for raiment, for taste and for smell, to strengthen the body and to enliven the soul.
>
> And it pleaseth God that he hath given all these things unto man; for unto this end were they made to be used, with judgment, not to excess, neither by extortion.[1]

> For it is expedient that I, the Lord, should make every man accountable, as a steward over earthly blessings, which I have made and prepared for my creatures.[2]

---

1. Church of Jesus Christ of Latter-day Saints, *Doctrine and Covenants* 59:18–20.
2. Church of Jesus Christ of Latter-day Saints, *Doctrine and Covenants* 104:13.

Joseph F. Smith, the sixth president of the LDS Church and the nephew of the church's founder and original Prophet, Joseph Smith, was clear with respect to how his followers should treat the natural world. "Nature helps us to see and understand God. To all His creations we owe an allegiance of service and a profound admiration. . . . Love of nature is akin to the love of God; the two are inseparable."[3] "Stewardship is a very strong principle in Mormon theology," says George Handley, a professor of interdisciplinary humanities at Brigham Young University in Provo, Utah, and a member of the LDS Church. The teachings speak to "preserving resources, keeping them healthy," as well as the "idea of being mindful of future generations, not taking more than you need, make sure you are respectful of creation. It's a beautiful, much-needed concept"—and one that was more applicable to daily life when most Mormons were making a living off the land.

"Early Church congregants heard a lot from [church leadership] about conservation," Handley says. "It seemed appropriate to teach about that very directly.

"Stewardship in recent generations has lost more of its environmental implications. The term 'stewardship' is implied to mean development—a lot of Mormons can't understand this need to preserve wilderness: 'God gave us resources on this planet for a reason, they're intended to be used.' The idea of preserving something in perpetuity doesn't make sense, especially when the territory has something that we need."

Brigham Young, the church's second Prophet and the leader of the Mormon exodus from Nauvoo, Illinois, to the Salt Lake Basin, instructed his followers to "always keep in view that the animal, vegetable, and mineral kingdoms—the earth and its fullness—will all . . . abide their creation—the law by which they were made, and will receive their exaltation."[4]

At the same time, says Handley, Young promoted the idea "of redeem[ing] wilderness into a garden" through making the land productive and fruitful in a manner that would sustain generations of Latter-day Saints. "That was a very strong impulse in early Mormon settlements. There was a sense of this is what God wants, this is why He preserved this place."

Stephen L. Peck writes in *Stewardship and the Creation: LDS Perspectives on the Environment*, "Many [Latter-day Saints] assume that the Lord's statement, 'For the earth is full, and there is enough and to spare' (*Doctrine and*

---

3. Smith, "Editorial Thoughts."
4. Nibley, "Man's Dominion."

Covenants, 104:17), is made without qualification. . . . This claim of unlimited abundance is often interpreted by some members to mean that there are no limits set on using and procuring natural resources."[5]

Then there is the intertwining of religion, politics, and history, which complicates the interpretation of scripture and creates barriers between conservation-minded Mormons and non-Mormons and their anti-environmentalist LDS counterparts.

Peck relates his experiences growing up as an LDS youth whose only exposure to the word *environmentalist* was when "it was [used] to degrade or belittle someone. 'Your mother is an environmentalist' was a cutting remark that could only be settled with a fistfight."

Such sentiments are held by a number of Utah's political leaders. In June 2017 Utah state representative Mike Noel (R-Kanab), who is Mormon and represents citizens in rural southern Utah, laid the blame for the rapid spread of the seventy-one-thousand-acre Brian Head wildfire in Utah's Dixie National Forest on the "bird and bunny lovers and the tree huggers and the rock lickers."[6]

His argument: that increasingly conservation-friendly federal land management policies and environmental litigation had prevented large-scale logging in the region, leaving a wasteland of dead trees that provided perfect tinder for a massive blaze. (Environmental groups assailed Noel's statements and pointed out that drought and wind played critical roles in the fire's spread.)

But Peck also acknowledges that members of the church he knows "have a profound love for nature . . . which they speak about with love and passion," as do the Mormons in San Juan County with whom we have spoken. Time and again, members of the LDS Church shared with us their feelings of deep connection to the land, the places in the landscape where they go to pray, and the formative wilderness experiences that have shaped who they are.

So what accounts for the disparity between this love for the land and the anti–"tree hugger" rhetoric?

Peck points to the "don't fence me in" culture of the western United States, in which LDS people are steeped. Handley draws parallels between Mormonism's celebration of freedom and agency and the Sagebrush Rebel ethos.

---

5. Handley, Ball, and Peck, *Stewardship and the Creation*; Peck, "An Ecologist's View," 165.

6. Pestano, "Utah Politician Blames."

"The idea of regulation and imposition from outside" does not sit well with many Mormons, Handley says, especially those living in rural Utah. "It does boil down to a kind of position of distrust toward the federal government."

The discussion about environmental stewardship has been recently addressed by the church's top leaders. In an April 2013 symposium speech entitled "Righteous Dominion and Compassion for the Earth," Elder Marcus B. Nash used passages from Mormon scripture to illustrate Latter-day Saints' calling and duty to protect, preserve, and steward the earth:

> How we care for the earth, how we utilize and share in its bounty, and how we treat all life that has been provided for our benefit and use is part of our test in mortality. Thus, when God gave unto man "dominion over the fish of the sea, and over fowl of the air, and over the cattle, and over all the earth, and over every creeping thing that creepeth upon the earth," it was not without boundaries or limits.
>
> Yes, we have been provided this beautiful and bountiful world, teeming with life and resources to bless and strengthen and enliven mankind, and we are to use them joyfully—but we must do so as careful, grateful stewards over God's handiwork. We are to use these resources with judgment, gratitude, prudence, and with an eye to bless our fellow man and woman and those of future generations, and in that way help Him to accomplish His purpose to help humankind progress, improve, and receive His blessings in time and eternity.

Handley harkens back to Mormon pioneer history to illuminate a more sustainable path forward. "We have a unique opportunity that the early settlers never had," he writes in his essay "The Desert Blossoms as a Rose: Toward a Western Conservation Aesthetic": "We are in a position of comfort, so we no longer have to fight to transform the land; our human signatures on it no longer need to signify our triumph over it. The pioneers may have made their share of environmental mistakes but they also showed the courage to make technological, moral, and aesthetic corrections by returning to the most basic principles of stewardship in the restored gospel. We would be fortunate to be so wise."[7]

---

7. Handley, "The Desert Blossoms," 72.

SHAPING THE FUTURE OF PUBLIC LANDS

Different Visions for San Juan County

Comb Ridge, west of Bluff, Utah, at sunset

MARK MARYBOY

Documenting Cultural Resources, Advocating for Protection of Native Homelands

After a hard rain, the desert releases its secrets. The scent of once-parched plants suffuses the air, and water flows through dormant washes and streaks the sandstone cliffs and bluffs, transforming them from subtle buff to luminous tan. A harsh landscape of drama and extremes is temporarily softened as the sheets of rain subside and the rays of the sun are diffused by the still-moist air. The landscape becomes still, with moisture-laden clay, water pockets, and the fragrance of wet earth the only evidence of the passing torrent.

While we stand mesmerized by the scents and silence, the setting sun breaks through a thick blanket of clouds and bathes the desert landscape outside Bluff, Utah, in golden light. Drinking in the scene with us is Mark Maryboy, who as a young boy would ride his horse on the southern banks of the San Juan River and help his family herd sheep. A self-described "traditional Navajo" whose spiritual beliefs are intimately connected to a land that his ancestors have inhabited since long before recorded history, Maryboy is tall and fit, his short black hair streaked with white. His slow, purposeful gait and serious mien are leavened by a wide smile and a gentle chuckle, which he shares only sparingly.

He asks us to follow his hand as he gestures toward a tree-lined expanse where he and his seven siblings would bring their sheep to drink and where they would swim while their herd grazed. On these shores the course of his life was set.

"In 1968 Bobby Kennedy came, and he met with [Navajo] elders right there," Maryboy says. "I was just a young kid running around all over the place, climbing around on those trees. Then all of a sudden, my dad went like this to me"—he pauses, adopting a stern tone and slower cadence—"'Son, all

Mark Maryboy on the banks of the
San Juan River

of those old people, they're going to be gone pretty soon. Listen to them. Listen to what they have to say.'

"So I sat down for a moment and watched those old people talk, and I noticed that they were talking about the land," Maryboy says, naming sacred places in San Juan County and beyond: the Abajo Mountains, Monticello, Moab, the Great Salt Lake, and Bears Ears.

"They told Bobby Kennedy, 'Those are very important . . . and the land is who we are,'" he says. "'It's something that's sustained us for millions of years. . . . Never, ever forget us.'"

He smiles. "And I guess you could say that was my introduction to politics."

Kennedy's visit inspired Maryboy, as Kennedy's presence on Navajo land demonstrated his respect for Native peoples and engendered hope that their voices might be acknowledged by those in power. The words of Maryboy's elders kindled a passion for working to make Native voices heard and for protecting sacred lands.

In 1986 Maryboy became the first Navajo elected official in Utah's history, beginning a sixteen-year tenure on the San Juan County Commission and a multidecade career of service in the Navajo Nation government. His passionate advocacy for good schools, passable roads, Native voting rights and representation, and protection of public lands for an impoverished and marginalized population placed him in direct conflict with some Anglo leaders who did not want a Navajo on the commission, arguing that Indians "lost the war" and should "go back to the reservation."

Early on, Maryboy clashed with fellow commissioner Calvin Black, the uranium-prospecting politician who inspired the villainous character Bishop Love in Edward Abbey's classic novel *The Monkey Wrench Gang*. Black's pro-industry stance ignored the devastation that Navajos, including Maryboy's father, suffered from exposure to the radioactive uranium-bearing minerals.

Black himself died of lung cancer in 1990 after years of working around uranium mines; Maryboy's father succumbed to lung cancer in 1978.

For many years, Maryboy was the lone representative of Native peoples in San Juan County, where the Navajo and Ute Mountain Ute Reservations comprise nearly a quarter of county land and more than half its population. As such, he bore the brunt of long-festering racial tensions and the weight of his people's painful history: centuries of non-Native groups, from Spaniards to Mexicans to the U.S. Army to Mormon settlers, seizing Navajo land by treaty or force or attempting to eliminate Navajo language, culture, and religion through forced assimilation.

The decades of work on behalf of Maryboy's constituents took its toll, and when he left public office in 2010, he intended to lead a quiet life, free of controversy, and focused on family. But he was called back into service when his brother Kenneth introduced Maryboy to staff from Round River Conservation Studies, a Utah-based environmental nonprofit that works with communities on conservation and cultural preservation projects. The nonprofit had obtained funding to work with tribes of the Colorado Plateau to develop strategies for protecting ancestral lands. They asked for Maryboy's help.

Initially, Maryboy refused. "My biggest hesitation," he says, "was the fights that I had had at every single [commission] meeting" about everything from where to hold a baseball game to how to redraw voting district lines. "I knew that this land issue was full of controversy. But the more I looked at it, I felt like I had more experience than everybody else, and I thought, 'I'll do it again.' Train [other people] so they can do what we want to do, and then step aside."

He accepted the challenge, working with Round River to develop an inventory of sites on the plateau that have past and continuing significance to Navajos and then using these carefully gathered and curated data to advocate for federal protection.

Maryboy was indefatigable in his efforts to interview tribal elders, the keepers of history and knowledge about sacred sites, medicinal plants, bodies of water, and other elements of the natural world that have sustained their people, they believe, since the beginning of time. Persuading elders to share stories and information about sacred sites was a delicate process. Many were wary of divulging any traditional knowledge that might be made public out of fear their knowledge would be used by non-Natives to exploit their land and beliefs.

"Once I explained the purpose, it was very emotional," Maryboy says. "You might say they were talking deep."

Maryboy started by traveling to each of Utah's seven Navajo chapter houses—meeting places where community and tribal political issues are discussed—to encourage participation in an effort to compile a list of cultural resources and tribal history. Members of each chapter house passed a resolution to support cultural mapping activities. They then suggested elders to interview. Maryboy, Gavin Noyes (who was then with Round River), and others began traversing the twenty-seven-thousand-square-mile Navajo Reservation, speaking with elders in far-flung communities, from Aneth on the eastern edge of the county to the westernmost—and most remote—settlement of Navajo Mountain.

Maryboy listened to their stories, working over the course of three years to create maps of cultural resources: ceremonial sites, medicinal plants, and places where wood is gathered. They produced a book, *Diné Bikéyah* (which translates directly as "Navajoland"), that made a case to the public and policymakers for protection of critical portions of San Juan County's public lands as Diné Bikéyah National Conservation Area (NCA), to be managed collaboratively by federal agencies and the Navajo Nation.

Their work was endorsed by Senator Robert Bennett (R-UT) (1933–2016), who hoped to apply to San Juan County lessons he learned from a successful years-long effort to reach a compromise solution in southwestern Utah's Washington County, a solution that both conserved land near Zion National Park and facilitated expansion of nearby St. George. Bennett's 2010 defeat in the Tea Party–dominated Utah Republican caucus ended his nascent efforts. Nevertheless, Maryboy continued to work toward protection of ancestral lands, eventually gaining the formal endorsement of the Navajo Nation. In 2012 the group created the nonprofit Utah Diné Bikéyah (UDB) and formalized its NCA proposal. (See p. 388 for an explanation of national conservation area versus national monument.)

As a result of UDB's meticulous cultural mapping, the Navajo Nation entered into a joint planning agreement with San Juan County in which the two entities agreed to work together on land management issues such as rules for road usage and permitted activities on specific parcels of land. This agreement created an initial optimism that all voices would be included in efforts to shape a final compromise.

In early 2013 Representative Rob Bishop (R-UT) launched the Utah Public Lands Initiative (PLI), an attempt to create long-term plans for land management in Utah's eight eastern counties (Carbon, Daggett, Duchesne, Emory, Grand, Summit, Uintah, and San Juan). He invited groups and tribes from each county to submit proposals outlining their preferred plans for land management. With their cultural mapping effort and the proposal for an NCA already in hand, the Navajo Nation and UDB presented their proposal to the county in April 2013. In response, San Juan County officials said they needed more time to develop their own plan. Toward that end, County Commissioner Phil Lyman established the San Juan County Public Lands Council in early 2014 to develop a plan for Bishop's PLI and invited Maryboy to participate. It was a promising moment.

However, later that year, Lyman led a controversial protest ride into areas of Recapture Canyon that had been closed by the Bureau of Land Management to protect Native archaeological sites and artifacts. Maryboy was deeply offended at the riders' disregard for sites sacred to Natives. In response, he and UDB withdrew from participation in the lands council.

Maryboy and Noyes decided that a different approach was needed. But they knew that a grassroots nonprofit alone could not achieve the result they sought. What UDB needed was additional support from other sovereign tribal nations.

"We decided to invite other tribes because we thought that the government-to-government relationship [tribes have] with the U.S. [would be] an avenue for tribes to speak to the federal government," Maryboy said.

Over the next year, UDB staff and board members traveled to reservations across the Southwest, making the case to tribal leaders that despite their troubled histories and present-day tribe-to-tribe conflicts, they had one thing in common: their cultural, historical, and spiritual attachment to the land in southeastern Utah, which was at the heart of their creation and migration stories and their very identity as a people—and their shared desire to protect it from development and desecration.

The UDB staff and board invited representatives to a gathering in Bluff, Utah, during which they explored the Bears Ears landscape. According to several people in attendance at the April 2015 meeting, it took just two simple but profoundly moving words to bring the tribes together.

Ancestral Puebloan ruin, Cedar Mesa, Utah

"We said to the Pueblos [Hopi, Zuni, and nineteen other tribes], 'Welcome home,'" Maryboy recalls. "You have over 150,000 archaeological sites here.

"We told them that we've done the best we could to take care of those sites, but there are many pothunters, people in the area, who have no respect. We need your help. Instantly, the tribes understood."

In July 2015 the Hopi, Navajo, Ute Mountain Ute, Zuni, and Ute Indian Tribe of the Uintah and Ouray, supported by other area tribes and by the National Congress of American Indians, formed the Bears Ears Inter-Tribal Coalition not only to protect their ancestral lands from the dangers of looting, drilling, and mining but also to preserve a place that is integral to their cultural history and essential for spiritual survival. The coalition was at one point open to protection through designation of national conservation areas as recommended by the PLI, but members came to believe that plans for the NCAs proposed by the Utah delegation provided insufficient protection of antiquities and lacked mechanisms for appropriate tribal input. In October 2015 members of the coalition traveled to Washington, D.C., to present to the Obama administration its official proposal for a Bears Ears National Monument. Frustrated by the belief that their voices had not been heard or respected, coalition members formally withdrew from the PLI process in late December 2015 and subsequently devoted their full effort to advancing their proposal for the Bears Ears National Monument.

As is the case for many conservation campaigns, the coalition's proposal emphasizes the importance of environmental stewardship. But the tribes seek to accomplish much more: to protect and honor their heritage, to ensure that traditional practices that have sustained their people for generations can continue into the future, to educate visitors to southeastern Utah about Native traditional knowledge and its connection to Western sciences, and to preserve the land as a place of spiritual healing.

Critically, the tribes have proposed an unprecedented system of collaborative management in which representatives of each of the coalition tribes would work alongside representatives from federal agencies—the Bureau of Land Management (BLM), U.S. Forest Service (USFS), and National Park Service (NPS)—to make joint decisions about how to manage the monument.

The practical and symbolic implications of this proposal are profound. For the first time, tribes would work as equals with the federal government in determining the fate of their ancestral lands.

Looking west from near Blanding, Utah, toward the Comb Ridge (aerial photo)

PHIL LYMAN

Facilitating Dialogue About Public Lands, Leading the Fight Against Federal Overreach

It is another predawn morning in Bluff, Utah, and in the fading light of a nearly full moon we stumble toward sentience, crunching the red dirt that has collected in the tread of our shoes and spreading it across the tile floor as we gather cameras, notebooks, snacks, clothing layers, and keys—do-you-have-them, yes-I-have-them, here-they-are, okay-let's-get-out-of-here—and load the Toyota 4Runner that has taken us thousands of miles across the Colorado Plateau. We gulp down the last of our coffee, leave the mugs on the counter, and hit the road.

We grumble about the sleep we've sacrificed in our quest to capture the perfect photo, but before we can complain further, our eyes are drawn to the bluffs surrounding us as the first rays of sunlight set the red rock ablaze. Our sleep deprivation becomes a blessing as we stop at every clearing and wide shoulder to capture images of a landscape transformed by the rapidly changing light.

Fortified by another Utah sunrise, we wend our way toward a meeting with one of the central figures in the battle for the future of Utah's public lands: a proud descendant of Mormon pioneers, a polarizing local politician, and a states' rights crusader whose act of civil disobedience catapulted him into the national spotlight.

Several hours later, our trusty Toyota 4Runner bumps down a narrow gravel road just north of Blanding as Phil Lyman shares stories about a landscape that lives in his soul.

"Let's drive down here to Devil's Canyon," Lyman says, pointing on our topo map to a thin black line that weaves its way through mesas studded with piñon and cedar.

There are a surprising number of devils in God's country. Lyman ticks off other favorite spots from his childhood—Devil's Punchbowl, Devil's Heartbeat, Devil's Knoll—where he and his friends would head, sleeping bags in tow, just after the final school bell rang on Friday afternoons.

Lyman exits the car and squints into the sunlight of a crisp, clear April morning, tugging his black suit jacket over his stocky frame. He is the chairman of the San Juan County Commission; he and his two fellow commissioners are the most powerful public officials in the county government. Today was picture day at the county offices, and he is still dressed for business, sporting a starched white button-down shirt, black slacks, and black leather oxfords, which he scuffs as he kicks pebbles down the road. He has closely cropped dark-gray hair with a distinctive streak of white just above his forehead. His intense blue eyes carefully scan the landscape for signs of the past.

We arrive at the edge of a canyon set against the backdrop of Sleeping Ute Mountain, an iconic landmark more than fifty miles away in southwestern Colorado. Lyman points to a site directly across from where we're standing and asks us what we see. He watches as we struggle, then smiles as we make our discovery. Just below the canyon rim lie the remnants of an Ancestral Puebloan cliff dwelling, its open door winking at us like an adobe eye.

"You could pull off anywhere and find ruins," Lyman says. "This is one of the coolest."

He describes its features with the well-trained eye of a desert dweller who has spent a lifetime discovering archaeological sites both by choice and by chance.

His ancestral ties to this land run deep. His great-grandfather Walter C. Lyman was one of the original Mormon pioneers sent by the leaders of the Church of Jesus Christ of Latter-day Saints in 1879 to settle southeastern Utah. In 1897 the elder Lyman foresaw what would become the city of Blanding after a vision came to him of a prosperous community in a rugged expanse of desert. Albert R. Lyman, Walter's cousin, subsequently founded Blanding in 1905 and was its first settler.

"Blanding is here because [the pioneers] were sent . . . to live here at great sacrifice," Lyman tells us.

His appreciation for the Native American ancestral sites that dot San Juan County's public lands seems genuine; there is a touch of wonder in his voice as he shares his thoughts.

Phil Lyman overlooking Devil's Canyon

That impression is at odds with the image of Lyman propagated by the media and held by many locals, that of a prototypical states' rights Sagebrush Rebel determined to "take back" land from the federal government—even though the land has always been under federal control—and transfer it to the states. This image was cemented by his May 2014 ATV (all-terrain vehicle) ride into nearby Recapture Canyon to protest Bureau of Land Management policies, a ride that endangered sacred Native American artifacts—baskets, pottery, tools—near sites like the cliff dwelling he has just shown us.

His protest cost him dearly: ten days in jail, three years' probation, a share of nearly $100,000 in restitution, and permanent association in the public's mind with members of the notorious Bundy family. The patriarch, Cliven Bundy, first made headlines a week before Lyman's ride when he staged an armed standoff at his Bunkerville, Nevada, cattle ranch over his refusal to pay BLM grazing fees. In January 2016 his sons Ryan and Ammon organized a month-long armed occupation of the Malheur National Wildlife Refuge in Burns, Oregon. (The younger Bundys, along with others involved in the

San Juan County commissioner Phil Lyman

Malheur standoff, were acquitted in October 2017; Cliven was acquitted in the Bunkerville case soon thereafter. All have been released from jail.)

Ryan Bundy joined the Recapture Canyon ride in response to Lyman's postings on social media and recruited others to accompany him. Bundy's presence changed the dynamics. By failing to heed belated entreaties by Lyman and others to stay outside the "no trespassing" boundaries set by the BLM, Bundy and his followers transformed a mostly peaceful act of civil disobedience into a chaotic and destructive event.

Local Utes and Navajos, as well as Puebloans from nearby Arizona and New Mexico, believe that the ATVs desecrated land that has deep cultural meaning for Native peoples: a place to pray, to commune with their ancestors, and to gather herbs for medicinal ceremonies. Lyman, however, claims that he never intended to damage antiquities, disrespect Native peoples, or harm the environment. Instead, his primary aim was to protest the BLM's closure of a road that had been traveled by his Mormon ancestors for generations. He wanted to send an unambiguous message to the BLM that decisions regarding access to local roads should be left to local people. But because he tapped into the passions ignited by the increasingly virulent states' rights movement, his assertion of county jurisdiction became a national cause célèbre.

"I feel so misunderstood," Lyman says. "[I'm] put into this box—trespasser, racist, whatever—that I do not belong in."

After we depart Devil's Canyon, Lyman takes us to the scene of the crime. We walk gingerly over a cattle guard next to the gate, taking care to walk with toes facing forward lest we become caught in the wide slits.

"This is not against the law, by the way," he chuckles.

As we walk, he reveals that his principled stand against the federal government was about much more than preserving local access to a road or even protecting Mormon heritage.

"Recapture was just symbolic," Lyman says. "There was nothing about Recapture that was about opening a trail."

He and many others in San Juan County believe that the federal government and the BLM in particular have blood on their hands.

On the morning of June 10, 2009, FBI agents, in coordination with state BLM officials, raided the homes of suspected looters and antiquities dealers in Blanding, arresting sixteen people, including Lyman's close friend, Dr. James Redd, a well-respected and well-loved physician in the community. Redd and his wife, Jeannie, had been charged with felonies in the past for the collection and sale of Native artifacts. Those charges were dropped; the new charges—seven felony counts for illegally selling, trading, and possessing Native artifacts—were more severe.

The raids were the culmination of a two-year investigation into black-market trafficking of Native American artifacts that ensnared twenty-four suspects across the country.

Locals recall the raid as dramatic and terrifying, with armed officers in flak jackets leading away nonviolent citizens in handcuffs and shackles.

"By 7:30 a.m. it's all buzzing around," Lyman says, his speech quickening. "They're beating down people's doors, pulling them out of their beds. . . . One of my friends, a guy who was seventy-eight years old, was awakened that morning, slammed up against the wall, . . . had his hands up in shackles, and [agents] dragged him out onto his front lawn."

While no one was sentenced to jail, the trauma and shame of their arrest may well have led Redd and a Santa Fe resident involved in the trafficking ring to commit suicide. (The FBI informant also killed himself nine months later.)

Redd's death devastated the Blanding community. That it apparently resulted from an operation led by the FBI—and the BLM—resonated powerfully with the long-held narrative of Mormon persecution by the federal government, a narrative that stretches back to the genesis of Mormonism, when both citizen mobs and the U.S. Army strove to annihilate Latter-day Saints.

Residents who witnessed the raids say the agents acted with excessive force.

"You don't do that to people," Lyman says, his eyes narrowing. "Just tell us why it happened. Please explain, Why were these people treated this way?"

House on Fire Ruin, Cedar Mesa

Many residents of San Juan County hold to a different view. Incensed by indifferent or cavalier attitudes toward looting, they believe that those arrested should have served jail time both as punishment and as a warning to would-be lawbreakers that plundering Native ancestral sites has severe consequences.

Lyman dismisses this perspective as a misunderstanding of local culture.

"People who understand who we are and where we live [know that] I can walk out my front door and find pottery out in the cedars," Lyman says. "This is not a crime, this is what it is."

In his mind, the Recapture Canyon protest was essential to giving public voice to those citizens who believed, as he did, that the 2009 raids stripped Blanding of its dignity, eroded residents' sense of small-town security, and reestablished the federal government as their archenemy. Their opposition to the BLM went far beyond states' rights or public lands: it expressed anger welling from the very heart of the community.

Lyman's personal wounds inform his political beliefs. At its core, his philosophy, shared by many throughout the rural West, centers on strongly held beliefs about "freedom." In this context, freedom is defined better not by what it is but by what it isn't: the federal government overseeing land that Lyman and his compatriots feel is theirs; elite, faceless bureaucrats thousands of miles away making decisions about locals' lives without local input, placing restrictions on where they can drive, graze, drill, and mine. To some in the West, the reality of the federal government acting as landlord of public lands—and all the rules and bureaucracy that entails—seems antithetical to what it means to live in the West, in wide-open spaces where people are free to do as they please, worlds away from the suits in New York or D.C.

Lyman and the law-defying members of the Bundy family became folk heroes because they dared to do what many others lacked the courage to do: stand against the federal government by refusing to abide by agency rules. To heck with your grazing fees and wildlife protections, they said; we're claiming this land for the local people.

The definition of "local people" is narrow—Native peoples and the conservation-minded are, for the most part, excluded—and the rallying cry of "take back the land" is factually suspect. Nevertheless, their words and cause spoke to rural westerners who felt left behind or disrespected or who chafed at the rules laid down by the political establishment. Together, they ushered in a new Sagebrush Rebellion at the same time that the establishment-bucking Tea Party Republicans, with whom Lyman proudly identifies, mounted an insurgency and "took back" their government from more mainstream politicians on both sides of the aisle.

The Bundys' presence at the Recapture Canyon ride vaulted a local protest linked to a very personal history into the national spotlight. In the process, Lyman became a polarizing symbol. To Lyman's supporters, he became a hero of sorts: states' rights advocates embossed his face on a T-shirt alongside the faces of Gandhi and Rosa Parks, conflating Lyman by association with icons of civil disobedience. To his detractors (and there are many), Lyman became the de facto face of San Juan County's Sagebrush Rebels.

ATV ride on the Hole-in-the-Rock Trail

Many of Lyman's constituents who shared his outlook were also alarmed by what they perceived as a threat to their financial livelihood: the possibility that public lands adjacent to their homeland would become a national monument through President Barack Obama's use of executive authority under the Antiquities Act of 1906. They were concerned that the law would permanently protect natural, archaeological, and cultural resources within a 1.9-million-acre tract in San Juan County, thereby precluding new mining claims and oil and gas drilling, draining a potential source of income from industries that were once the lifeblood of San Juan County.

Mining royalties, as many locals will tell you, helped to build the county's hospitals and roads and once paid teachers some of the highest salaries in the state. The mining boom did more than bolster the region's economy; it also gave many San Juan County residents a feeling of confidence and pride that their work had an impact on the nation's prosperity and security, particularly at the height of the Cold War. That feeling has long been dwindling, and the possibility of a monument's further depriving residents of their livelihood has ignited strong passions.

Opposition to national monument designation in this region is powerful. Many residents of southern Utah felt blindsided and betrayed by what they perceived as a lack of discussion and due process when President Clinton established the nearby Grand Staircase–Escalante National Monument in 1996. That proclamation instantly protected 1.7 million acres of federal land from further drilling and mineral extraction. When rural Utahns rail against the idea of a national monument, "the Grand Staircase" is inevitably invoked to support their arguments and confirm their fears, despite evidence that the monument may have had a positive impact on surrounding communities— and despite the fact that existing grazing and mining activities were allowed to continue.

The endeavors to find a balance between resource extraction, protection of ancient artifacts, and preservation of natural landscapes are defining issues in the battle for the future of the American West. Many attempts at brokering compromise have ended in failure. Nevertheless, in early 2013 Representative Rob Bishop (R-UT) invited citizens of eastern Utah to participate in what he called the Utah Public Lands Initiative (PLI), the most recent in a series of attempts aimed at devising a solution to a decades-long struggle to shape the future of public lands. Bishop's promise: to use feedback from local people to craft a "grand bargain" that would give all stakeholders a voice. Conservationists would have a chance to secure protection for treasured landscapes, and multiple-use proponents would have a chance to advocate for trails used for motorized and nonmotorized recreation and to keep alive the extractive industry and ranching economy.

The next year, Lyman took on the seemingly unlikely role of spearheading this citizen-led process, inviting a select group of county stakeholders—conservationists, ranchers, ATV enthusiasts, extractive industry representatives—as well as Native American tribal members to serve on the Public Lands Council, tasked with developing a plan for the future of San Juan County's public lands, a plan that would be submitted to Bishop for inclusion in the PLI.

Lyman, however, has a reputation as an unyielding opponent to federal intrusion in what he regards as a local issue. Where in his personal history, we wondered, did he develop his motivation to search for common ground?

At age nineteen Lyman began his church mission in South Africa at the height of attempts to forge a future for the country beyond apartheid. He spent his first year in white Afrikaner communities in Johannesburg and his second in the black townships of Soweto. Like most young Mormon elders (as LDS missionaries are called), he says he felt completely unprepared to provide counsel or guidance to an impoverished and persecuted minority group to whom he looked every bit the oppressor. Yet despite the obvious barriers, he found that he was able to connect with people by simply listening.

"You could tell that there weren't too many people who had ever sat down in a person's living room and asked, 'How do you feel about these things?'" Lyman recalls. "And they would just pour their hearts out. It had nothing to do with the missionary who was sitting there. It was that, 'Nobody's ever knocked on my door and listened to me.'

"It's an essential human thing, to be understood by somebody," Lyman says.

Which is why, at least on this particular day, he feels that the factions warring over the future of public lands should declare a truce and devote their energies to finding common ground. "[The] national monument . . . shouldn't be the big thing on the horizon," he says. "We should be working toward what's taking place right here, between one person and another person."

Yet just weeks after our conversation, Lyman took to Facebook to denounce "lying . . . special interest groups" that support the Bears Ears proposal.

And in his spirited defense of Mel Bundy, who at the time was in jail following participation with his brothers Ryan and Ammon in the January 2016 armed occupation of the Malheur National Wildlife Refuge in Burns, Oregon, Lyman seemed to reject compromise entirely.

"Let's drop the whole facade of trying to work with our enemies and take a stand for our friends instead," Lyman wrote. "They took a stand for us."

Lyman's heartfelt dedication to his community and genuine love of the land is clear, but his past divisive actions and his need to appease his political base make finding compromise difficult.

At the same time, he acknowledges the efforts of the San Juan County Public Lands Council, whose members worked hard, and to a degree succeeded, in crafting a plan for compromise.

"I feel a huge debt to these people who have put in so much," Lyman says.

Utahns have a deep love for our landscapes, communities and resources. Sometimes it is subjugated to a larger distaste for federal control. When we can come together locally over difficult issues, as Utah is capable of doing, we will find lasting solutions for our public lands.

—Ralph Becker, former mayor of Salt Lake City,
as quoted in the *Deseret News*, September 25, 2016

Education's not [going to stop] looters. Prosecution's [going to stop] looters. They know it's wrong. Unless we're willing to truly prosecute them, show that we're willing to do that . . . I'm sure the folks in Blanding would say, well, we lost all our artifacts and were embarrassed and that was enough. Well, I'm sorry, it wasn't enough. . . . I think there needed to be a bit more ramifications.

—Vaughn Hadenfeldt, founder/owner, Far Out Expeditions,
and board chair, Friends of Cedar Mesa, October 27, 2015

There were reports about the way those arrests happened in Blanding. . . . They were criminals, absolutely, who had done something that I think were atrocious crimes. That said, I don't think [there] was any danger that you need to go in with military-like armed SWAT teams to arrest folks. I think that created a bigger backlash that . . . united . . . a small community further against the feds. . . . I don't know when that will heal in Blanding. I think the pain on the side of the Native Americans is a part of the story that doesn't get told in the media when they cover this. I mean . . . can you imagine for white people, if your great-grandmother's grave was dug up to steal her pearl necklace and scatter the bones all over and desecrate the grave and then sell it to some-body? You know, we would want to have congressional inquiries and SWAT teams raiding people's houses, right? . . . The anguish [of] the community of Blanding has been told a lot, but the anguish on the side of the Native Americans hasn't actually gotten out there, so it's a tragedy on a lot of fronts.

—Brian O'Donnell, former executive director,
Conservation Lands Foundation, July 27, 2015

INTERLUDE
A Brief Overview of Native and Mormon
Connection to San Juan County

The tribes that comprise the Bears Ears Inter-Tribal Coalition all have direct ancestral ties to Bears Ears country. While the Ute Indian Tribe of the Uintah and Ouray Reservation, Hopi, and Zuni tribal members do not presently live in the region, members of the Navajo and Ute Mountain Ute tribes still call San Juan County home. To them, Bears Ears remains a landscape that provides physical sustenance in the form of game, firewood, and plants for medicinal and ceremonial purposes. For all five tribes in the coalition, Bears Ears provides powerful spiritual sustenance. But it is also a place of loss and deep pain. This history is key to understanding the passion behind the tribes' efforts to protect these lands.

In the late 1850s competition for land in the Southwest was fierce. Anglo and Mexican settlers and nearby tribes raided Navajo livestock, leading to escalating skirmishes. To quell ongoing battles, in 1861 a treaty between the U.S. Army and the Navajo was negotiated.[1] Nevertheless, small-scale skirmishes continued, with bands of Navajos countering incursions by Anglos with raids of their own.

In 1864 Col. Kit Carson was assigned by the U.S. Army to "solve" the "Indian problem." Aided by Ute allies who knew the territory well, Carson's soldiers set fire to Navajo homes, killed livestock, and obliterated crops. Groups of Navajos in Arizona and New Mexico were rounded up and marched hundreds of miles eastward to Fort Sumner, New Mexico, suffering considerable loss of life. Following what became known as the Long Walk, they remained quartered at Fort Sumner until 1868, when Navajo leaders signed the Treaty of Bosque Redondo, which allowed them to return to their homeland. The

---

1. Lapahie, "U.S. Treaty with the Navajos 1861."

treaty imposed significant conditions on the Navajos, confining them to a reservation far smaller than the lands they had occupied prior to Anglo incursions and ordering compulsory education for their children.[2]

During Carson's scorched-earth campaign, warrior hero Manuelito led a band of Navajos in resisting the Long Walk. Manuelito was born near Bears Ears, and his sacred burial grounds are located there.[3] Chief K'aayelli also resisted and led a group to hide in the mountainous area near Bears Ears.[4] Thus, to the Navajos, the Bears Ears represent not only sacred ground but also a powerful symbol of resistance and resilience in the face of historical trauma. The twin peaks serve as an enduring visual reminder of land they have fought so hard to protect for so long.

While Carson and the Navajos clashed, the Ute Mountain Ute tribe in southwestern Colorado saw their land base drastically reduced both by treaty and by encroachment from settlers and prospectors seeking gold. In 1880, following skirmishes with the U.S. Army, the Uintah and Ouray bands of Utes in northwestern Colorado were removed from an area that spanned millions of acres to far smaller tracts of land in northeastern Utah, where they remain to this day.[5]

The Hopi had been losing land for hundreds of years as the Spanish and Navajos began to occupy areas that had historically been occupied by the Hopi. In response to persistent land disputes, in 1882 President Arthur signed an executive order clearly defining a Hopi reservation.[6] However, some of the land ultimately "deeded" to them by the U.S. government overlapped with the Navajo Reservation, leading to ongoing disputes between the two tribes that continued for decades.

In 1887 plans to divide and purchase remaining Indian lands throughout the United States were formalized in a landmark piece of legislation named after its author, Henry Dawes of Massachusetts. The Dawes Act authorized the U.S. president to survey Indian lands and divide them into allotments. The act also declared a subset of Indian lands as "surplus" to be auctioned off to the highest bidder. Tribal governments and courts were dissolved. The

---

2. Johnson, "Treaty"; Baccellieri, "For Campaign Cash."
3. Siegler, "With National Monuments."
4. Grover, "Bears Ears Region."
5. Kappler, "Indian Affairs."
6. The People, "The First Inhabitants."

the county's residents, would be outvoted by their Anglo counterparts on the county commission and school district board. Shelby ordered San Juan County to redraw its districts; the county complied.[9]

In July 2017, however, Shelby rejected the county's revisions, stating, "San Juan County's remedial plans fail to pass constitutional muster. Specifically, the court concluded race was the predominant factor in the development" of the revised boundaries. He ordered the appointment of an independent monitor to oversee the process of redrawing the districts. San Juan County commissioners Bruce Adams, Rebecca Benally, and Phil Lyman expressed their support for "an unbiased master overseer."[10] Should the boundaries be redrawn in compliance with the Voting Rights Act, the county might for the first time elect two Native commissioners.

Other well-documented and highly visible manifestations of discrimination and social inequality in San Juan County include the substandard living conditions endured by some Utes and Navajos, many of whom lack basic amenities such as electricity and plumbing and access to quality medical care in close proximity to their homes. A number of our Native sources recounted being the target of or witnessing others endure racial epithets. It was not unusual for Natives to be told to "go back to the reservation" even in the relatively recent past.

From Mark Maryboy's perspective, informed by a lifetime of experience as a county resident and elected leader, "San Juan County is racist. Just like the Deep South."

Mormons don't see themselves as harboring any racial bias or patronizing attitudes toward their Native neighbors. If anything, those with whom we spoke stressed the strength of their long-term friendships with Native Americans and their deep commitment, informed by their religious teachings, to respect Natives.

Brigham Young encouraged kindness and conciliation: "I wish to impress [all] with the necessity of treating the Indians with kindness, and to refrain from harboring that revengeful, vindictive feeling that many indulge in."[11]

---

9. McFall, "After Navajo Nation Sues."
10. Winslow, "San Juan Co. Ordered."
11. Young, "Remarks," 290.

"We expect you to feed and clothe them so far as it lies in your power; never turn them away hungry from your door; teach them the art of husbandry; bear with them in all patience and long suffering, and never consider their lives as an equivalent for petty stealing."[12]

Nevertheless, Anglo Mormons are often portrayed, accurately, as colonizers of Native American land and livestock in southern Utah. There are notable exceptions, however, such as LDS Church missionary Jacob Hamblin, regarded as a positive example of an Anglo Mormon who treated Natives with respect and served as a key intermediary between Natives and Latter-day Saints.

But Mormons themselves were not always atop Utah's hierarchy of power. Like the history of Native peoples across the United States, Mormon history is also rife with persecution, violence, and attacks on their religious and cultural beliefs.

The long history of harassment and persecution of Mormons began in the 1840s. The first members of the LDS Church were driven westward from their first home in Palmyra, New York, hounded by those who considered their religion blasphemous and dangerous. After settling in Nauvoo, Illinois, where church founder and original Prophet Joseph Smith became mayor, conflict over reports of Smith's alleged acts of polygamy and his efforts to destroy what he considered a libelous press led to his arrest and murder at the hands of an angry mob in Carthage, Illinois, in 1844.

After some confusion and struggle over the ensuing years regarding the successor to Joseph Smith, the majority of LDS adherents chose to follow Brigham Young, whom they believed to be a divinely chosen prophet. Young articulated a powerful vision: a Promised Land where Saints could start anew and build Deseret, a community and eventual empire that would provide the space to develop the land in accordance with the Heavenly Father's will and fulfill their destiny as Chosen People. It was in Utah's Great Basin in 1847 that the Mormons found the center of their Promised Land, beyond the reaches of their foes and outside the boundaries of the United States. They made a home and established a theocracy that briefly reigned supreme over a huge swath of land.

Autonomy and independence from the federal government were short-lived. In 1848 the United States won the Mexican-American War, gaining

---

12. Hibley, *Brigham Young*, 183.

View from Anticline Overlook, with potash plant on the right

ROB BISHOP

Developing a "Grand Bargain," Defending the Rights of States and Localities

Where does the history behind modern-day public lands disputes in San Juan County begin? Some observers point to Harold Ickes's 1930s efforts to create Escalante National Monument, which encompassed a significant portion of southeastern Utah. Others cite the signing of the Antiquities Act by President Theodore Roosevelt in 1906. Some historians wind the clock back even farther, citing battles that began in the nineteenth century and raged for decades between Native Americans, the U.S. government, and Anglo settlers.

Regardless of when the tensions started, in the years since the passage of the Federal Land Policy and Management Act (FLPMA) in 1976, the battle over appropriate use of public lands has grown ever more intense. FLPMA requires both systematic inventory of public lands to identify parcels that may have wilderness characteristics and a planning process to determine the best uses—current and future—of land overseen by the Bureau of Land Management. Conservationists have taken advantage of the FLPMA process to push for protection of public lands, while others have lobbied for ensuring that public lands can be used to support local economies through livestock grazing, oil and gas drilling, and extractive industry activities.

Congressman Rob Bishop (R-UT) has been at the center of current efforts to resolve this seemingly intractable conflict of competing interests.

Bishop is heavyset, with carefully groomed white hair and an oval face that flushes red when he's animated. He exudes confidence, speaking bluntly with great conviction, at times brash and confrontational, but always collected and in control. (As of 2018, he is serving his seventh term in the U.S. House of Representatives as a Republican from Utah's First Congressional District, and he chairs the House Committee on Natural Resources, a powerful body "tasked with overseeing the nation's public lands.")

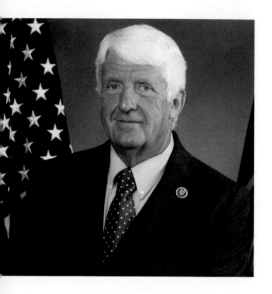

Representative Rob Bishop (R-UT)

Bishop was born in Kaysville, Utah, into a family that he describes as "always political. My father was mayor of our town. I always remember him sitting at the kitchen table on the phone campaigning for other people. The idea of civic service and politics was as much a part of his religion as the other things that he did within the [LDS] church. And he was very active there as well. So I grew up thinking that it was the norm for people to be interested."

Later, Bishop realized, "I had an interest because it was simply part of the family milieu in which I grew up. I was involved in Teen Age Republicans and College Republicans and Young Republicans. I've always had the interest, and it was just natural."

Beginning in 1970, at the age of nineteen, Bishop spent two years in southern Germany on an LDS mission. After returning, he graduated magna cum laude from the University of Utah with a degree in political science. From 1974 to 2002 he taught German and U.S. history and government at Box Elder High School in Brigham City and at Ben Lomond High School in Ogden.

At age twenty-seven Bishop was elected to the Utah State Legislature. During his sixteen years at the statehouse, he served as House majority leader and was later selected as House Speaker by a unanimous vote.

"When I became Speaker," Bishop recalled during our October 2016 interview, "a couple of new legislators who were elected from southern Utah . . . came to me and asked me if I would be willing to help them. I became involved in what they were doing, and I realized that they had been truly abused . . . by a federal government that wasn't looking out for the needs of the people in southern Utah.

"[I learned about] the frustration of those who were living down there who were using the land and the restrictions that were placed upon them, usually arbitrarily, unfairly, and sometimes not necessarily based on statute. Looking out for them to be treated fairly is how I became involved in the entire process of public land. That influenced me. We organized the [Coalition of Western States, which focused on] not just public lands issues but also states' rights and federalism approaches."

In 2002 Bishop was elected to the U.S. House of Representatives, replacing eleven-term congressman Jim Hansen (R-UT). He feels strongly that decisions regarding land use should be made at the state and local levels.

"That is the brilliance of federalism, when you get right down to it," he says. "With federalism . . . you allow people to be able to chart their own decisions."

The strength of his belief is palpable, but despite his strong personal feelings, he looks at himself as a problem solver.

"If we're going to solve the problems of the past, we've got to change the paradigm and change what we have done in the past," Bishop says.

In the mid-2000s Senator Robert Bennett (R-UT) provided an example of such fresh thinking. Bennett and his staff worked for five years to develop a compromise plan that would preserve some public lands in Utah's Washington County, home to Zion National Park, as wilderness and national conservation areas (NCAs) while releasing other parcels to support the growth of the nearby city of St. George. Following extensive on-the-ground meetings with a broad range of stakeholders and residents and a years-long visioning process, Bennett's inclusive bipartisan approach resulted in passing the Washington County Lands Bill in 2009 as part of the Omnibus Public Lands Management Act.

Could the lessons learned in western Utah serve as a model for how to approach similar issues in San Juan County? Bennett was hopeful. He and his staff initiated a dialogue with local residents—Anglo and Native—and sought to use citizen input to develop a vision for San Juan County's future, with a specific focus on the role that public lands might play. However, when Bennett was denied renomination for a fourth Senate term in 2010, efforts ground to a halt.

Bishop envisioned a new process that bore a number of similarities to Bennett's approach in Washington County but expanded the scope of the project to include eight eastern Utah counties in the hopes of reaching a "grand bargain."

Utah's political leadership applauded his efforts to restart debate on public lands use. Environmental groups, though, were dubious, in large measure owing to Bishop's federalist approach to public policy, his advocacy for turning federal lands over to the states, and his criticism of the Antiquities Act. Yet Bishop, working with former Republican congressman Jason Chaffetz (whose district encompassed San Juan County), succeeded at bringing environmentalists, ranchers, extractive industry representatives, motorized and nonmotorized recreationists, and Native American tribes to the table in service of finding common ground.

In 2014 in San Juan County, Commissioner Phil Lyman started and led the San Juan County Public Lands Council to contribute to the PLI effort. The council worked to develop a plan for the county that included wilderness, conservation, and recreation area designations, as well as "energy zones" where mining and drilling for oil and gas would be permitted. Lyman and his fellow commissioners submitted the county's plan to Bishop in August 2015. Some viewed the work of the lands council as a remarkable testament to compromise, inclusive of a multiplicity of voices. But during the planning process, Native-led group Utah Diné Bikéyah (UDB) sought to provide input. Long before the plan was completed or submitted, UDB members felt the council was unwilling to enter into productive dialogue. As a result, they believed the plan submitted to Bishop did not reflect critical and broad-based input from Native voices.

Seeing no path forward with the lands council, UDB appealed to sovereign tribal governments to harness their collective strength and wisdom. After the Bears Ears Inter-Tribal Coalition formed in July 2015, its members began good-faith negotiations with Congressmen Bishop and Chaffetz and their staffs and presented a proposal for a national monument to them and to President Obama. Despite their efforts, in the end they felt that they were neither heard nor respected by those involved in shaping the PLI. In December 2015 the coalition withdrew from PLI negotiations.

Despite vocal and widespread opposition, many locals in San Juan County continued to support the PLI. In their view—one championed by Utah's governor, Gary Herbert, and the state's congressional delegation—the PLI represents the result of a democratic process that gave locals, not "outsider" interests such as environmentalists and out-of-state Native American tribes, a dominant voice in a debate that would shape their future.

In some counties, Bishop's grand bargain succeeded in gaining broad support; in others, including San Juan County, support crumbled. Daggett County withdrew from the PLI process completely.

In our March 2016 conversation, Bishop wastes no time criticizing the groups he saw as most undermining of his efforts.

"Certain environmental groups were disingenuous," Bishop says, quickly adding, "I want you to know that there are certain groups that are still working with us, and I'm pleased with that. [Other] environmentalists criticized the entire discussion draft" of the bill, released on January 20, 2016.

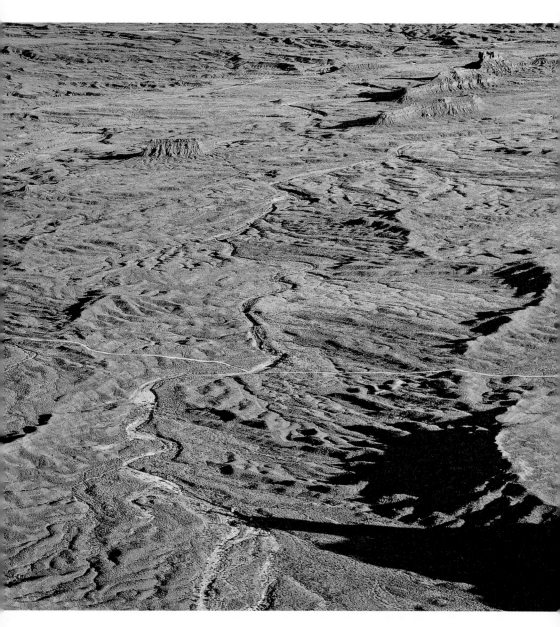

Valley of the Gods (aerial photo)

Were these small, grassroots groups, Bishop might well have dismissed them as insignificant annoyances. Because they were well-funded organizations, such as the Grand Canyon Trust and the Southern Utah Wilderness Alliance, that wield significant influence in Washington, Bishop instead viewed them as a direct threat to his legislation.

"They realize in the back of their mind that if they go into the BLM or the Department of the Interior, [Barack Obama's] Department of the Interior [staff] will back them up," Bishop says. "That's why I was so frustrated the last time I personally talked to [Interior] Secretary [Sally] Jewell. She was parroting the words of some of these groups."

Bishop was a charter member of the congressional "antiparks" caucus, which sought to defund various conservation initiatives, open up protected areas to drilling and mining, and transfer federal lands to the states. His ties to extractive industries are deep—and lucrative. Contributions from key players in the oil and gas industry comprise a key source of Bishop's campaign funds. And despite his focus on federalism and advocacy for his constituents, over 90 percent of his campaign contributions come from out of state—more than any other member of the House of Representatives.[1]

Over time, Bishop escalated his antimonument rhetoric and evoked a storm of criticism after stating at a 2015 public event in Utah, "If anyone here likes the Antiquities Act the way it was written, die." At the same event, he called the law "the most evil act ever invented."

Given Bishop's unabashed opposition to one of the Department of the Interior's core tenets, many of those initially open to compromise lost faith in his ability to deliver a balanced bill. Bishop in turn points the finger at the Bears Ears Inter-Tribal Coalition as the main instigator of conflict and destroyer of compromise.

"The so-called Bears Ears Coalition, they don't want to solve the problem," Bishop says. "They are funded by environmental groups, and they are a front to try and screw everything up. They're the ones that are going to the administration.

"They want to bring the entire process down," Bishop continues. "And they think the [Obama] administration will back them up with that."

Bishop found the coalition's refusal to participate in any further dialogue with the PLI process as particularly offensive to the subgroup of Native

---

1. Baccellieri, "For Campaign Cash."

Americans in San Juan County who believe in Bishop's promise to respect local interests and traditional ways of life.

"We went to the Native Americans who live next to Bears Ears, the ones who are in Utah," Bishop says. "They're the ones who are violently opposed to this idea of a national monument."

A vocal group of Navajos and Utes has indeed spoken out against the proposed Bears Ears monument, contending that such a designation will eliminate their access to plants, herbs, and firewood used for physical needs and spiritual healing. Their concerns are shared by San Juan County commissioner Rebecca Benally, a Democrat who represents residents of the Navajo Nation's "Utah strip" and has forged an alliance with Utah's Republican delegation to support Bishop's PLI and oppose the Bears Ears proposal.

By contrast, UDB, the Bears Ears Coalition, and their allies note that the coalition's proposal clearly provides for traditional uses of the land by Natives. Moreover, land-use policy would be forged by a commission comprised of representatives of five tribes, including the Navajo and Ute Mountain Ute tribes that have residents in San Juan County, and the three federal agencies involved with land management within the proposed monument (the BLM, the U.S. Forest Service, and the National Park Service). Finally, despite Bishop's claims of widespread Native opposition, all but one of the Navajo chapter houses in San Juan County voted in favor of a resolution to support the Bears Ears National Monument proposal.

Bishop viewed the coalition's decision to abandon negotiations as an affront to the spirit and purpose of the PLI.

"We have spent three years talking to virtually everybody," Bishop says. "The overall bill is nothing more than compromise after compromise. The locals have compromised, some of the environmental groups . . . have been very good at compromise, the recreation people have compromised, everyone has compromised, and now there are voices that are coming out of the woodwork saying, no, this is wrong."

Some conservationists cast the plan Bishop proposed in his 2016 bill as a giveaway to extractive industries, while many Natives felt unheard and disrespected. Both groups view his rhetoric deploring the Antiquities Act and supporting Utah's quest to wrest lands from the federal government as offensive, dangerous, and undermining of the very compromise he claims to seek.

But Bishop says that county commissioners "have been the flexible ones. Many of the commissioners with whom we're working are former BLM officials who understand [the issues].

"The higher up I get in the Department of the Interior, . . . the more dog-matic it becomes, the more inflexible it becomes, the more entrenched it be-comes, and the more they insist on me having fuzzy language in there so they have the power to make the rules as they go along," Bishop says. "And I'm not playing that game. That's what's causing the problem in the first place."

Bishop placed a particular emphasis on writing legislative language that is unambiguous and prescriptive—something he found lacking in prior land-use bills, including the Washington County Lands Bill. Like many conser-vative politicians in the West, Bishop wants to ensure that what he and his constituents view as an overreaching BLM is kept in check.

"Washington County was not specific," Bishop says. "It allowed discretion. BLM is picking and choosing which parts of the law they want to obey. I'm not going to make that same mistake. We are telling BLM what they will do, and they will obey the law."

Echoing Commissioner Lyman, Bishop believes that actions by the BLM have played a major role in reinvigorating the Sagebrush Rebellion.

"If the BLM really was people-oriented and wanted to listen to the people, there wouldn't be as [many] negative repercussions and some of the situa-tions we've seen that have developed over the last couple of years here in the West," Bishop says.

"In my view, the BLM people, or the Interior Department people, the For-est Service people . . . they're not evil people, they're not incompetent people, they're simply overwhelmed because the federal government owns one-third of America, and that's just too damn much land to manage.

"You get people in both the Forest Service and the BLM who actually live on the ground and work in the community. Sometimes they are the great-est sources of information [regarding] how you do things the right way. As decisions are pushed further up the line to the regional levels and then to Washington, that's where things screw up."

Bishop's final draft of the PLI bill was presented on July 14, 2016, two days before Interior Secretary Sally Jewell facilitated a public hearing in Bluff to discuss the PLI and the Bears Ears Inter-Tribal Coalition's national monu-ment proposal.

It received many negative comments from the same groups that criticized the January draft, citing the same "poison pills": restricting the president's abil-ity to invoke the Antiquities Act in southeastern Utah; insufficient protection for deserving landscapes; a rollback of protections for lands formally desig-nated as wilderness; and the creation of a commission to manage the proposed

Bears Ears National Conservation Area, with tribes placed in an advisory role instead of as comanagers as articulated in the Inter-Tribal Coalition's proposal.

Bishop says that the discontent regarding the July draft came primarily from conservation activists and tribes outside of Utah whose opinions, in his view, should matter less than those of Utahns.

"There is no one in the Utah delegation that supports Bears Ears National Monument," Bishop says. "There's no one in the state administration, there's no legislative leaders. There are no elected officials who live in and represent this area and [no support from] the Native Americans that live in this area."

But the monument proposal does have support from some Utah politicians. Utah Democratic Party chairman Peter Corroon, as well as a number of other prominent Democrats in the state, have endorsed the efforts of the Bears Ears Coalition. And UDB's board and staff, along with numerous Native Americans in San Juan County, have been outspoken in their support of the national monument proposal.

Bishop sees it as his responsibility to provide a means for rural Utahns to make a living in the extractive industries that in prior decades brought them prosperity. "We've got to open up areas for the chance of creating jobs for the people who live that way," Bishop says.

"What we tried to do with PLI, which has made it so difficult to do . . . and why it's taken so long, is bring together groups into compromise who have never compromised before," Bishop says. "Our goal with PLI was to bring finality to [land-use disputes] by going through the pieces of property and allowing us to designate what would be the primary purpose of those properties. If it's an area that should be wilderness or conservation area, make that the primary purpose. If you can do multiple use within that designation, fine, but there should be a primary purpose.

"You take away a lot of the conflicts if you can designate what is the most significant role for [each] piece of property," he adds. "The reason you need to do that is so the business community knows where they will invest, where they can invest. Right now, the uncertainty is so high, there's no investment taking place. So if you wanted San Juan County to come up with a county plan that is more innovative or different or changed, they don't have the certainty, they don't have the ability of doing that in their land management plans simply because the federal agencies can so arbitrarily and capriciously change it."

In the face of criticism from a wide range of groups, Bishop remained undeterred. In September 2016 the PLI was forwarded to the House floor following a party-line vote in the House Natural Resources Committee. Bishop subsequently introduced language that he hoped would meet the concerns of the tribes advocating for a Bears Ears National Monument, in particular their belief that the original version of the bill did not include language that would grant them a sufficiently strong role in setting policy for a monument.

"I actually like the plans that the administration [is] talking about when it comes to comanagement or correlated management, and I'd like to implement it [in the PLI]," Bishop says. "The language that we have in the bill right now—the origin of that was from the Native Americans who are living in Utah that want to use this particular area."

Bishop still believes that the approach proposed in his PLI bill is far superior to executive declaration of a monument.

"For Bears Ears, if you really want to meet the needs of the Utah Native Americans, who would be the ones who abut this land and would be the ones who really would access it, a monument is not in their best interest," Bishop says. "It would provide restrictions that they don't necessarily want.

"[With a national conservation area] we can put [in the enabling legislation for the PLI] what will and will not be allowed. We can have comanagement as part of it so they have the flexibility that they want to use the land the way they want to use it. That cannot happen if it's a monument designation. The problem with all monument declarations is that you put in what you want as standards, but then you still have to implement them by rules and regulations set by land managers. That's another reason why a monument is a dumb idea."

Bishop remained optimistic that despite the looming end of the 2016 legislative session, some version of the PLI could still be passed.

"The outcome of the [presidential] election will have a major difference on how quickly the PLI could pass both the House and Senate," he says. "I am still confident that there is going to be a whole lot of stuff that's going to be done in the lame-duck session, and this is one of those things that could easily go through.

"I am now more dedicated than ever to pushing this through to finish it," Bishop adds. "If I don't get it passed, I want to make sure it's a good bill, it's written the right way . . . and maybe it can be a template for things that we do in the future.

"But we're going to do it the right way, even if it takes a bit of time." (The PLI passed out of committee in September 2016 but never progressed to a floor vote in the 114th Congress. As of May 2018, a national monument had been declared by former president Obama but was reduced by 85 percent by President Trump. Bishop has not announced any plans to revive the PLI.)

I'm not going to speak for the tribes, because I want them to be able to speak for themselves, but in a perfect world, everyone would rather see legislation than a monument, for a couple reasons. One is that you can get some wilderness areas designated [legislatively]. . . . Second, you can really articulate the level of engagement and management authority that tribes can have in a way that is very specific. Having the protection for that region happen legislatively would give it an acceptance and a stamp of approval by the Utah politicians.

—Brian O'Donnell, former executive director,
Conservation Lands Foundation, July 27, 2015

I applaud [Representatives Bishop's and Chaffetz's] effort to . . . bring together diverse stakeholders to get their opinion and see what we can do . . . to resolve some of these bigger public land issues. We were invited to submit comments three years ago, and we did so because we really saw this as our best hope of mapping the future in [a] way that takes into consideration conservation and development needs. As The Nature Conservancy, we value working with the people in the communities whose lives and livelihoods are connected to the landscapes we hope to conserve, so it fit well within our value system.

—Sue Bellagamba, Canyonlands regional director,
The Nature Conservancy, April 29, 2016

I believe that Mr. Bishop's challenge is that he has a political agenda. He has a statement to make in terms of who's in charge of what. That political agenda is overriding what it takes to create the bargain. Because the bargain's out there. The pieces are out there. We know what the environmental community wants, we know what the recreation community wants. . . . I could name thirty-five people, and if you got five of them and put them in a room with some pizza, they could put together something and show it to the other thirty, and we'd have a deal. The problem is that [Bishop's] political agenda is in the way.

—Ashley Korenblat, executive director,
Public Land Solutions, July 28, 2015

It's now become part of the ideological, "we hate the federal government" [argument]. The Republican Party, the Tea Party types, if the feds propose it . . . it's evil, it's all a big conspiracy by the federal government to take our birthright. That's the Cliven Bundy approach, it makes no sense whatsoever.

—Senator Robert Bennett (R-UT) (1933–2016),
U.S. Senate (1992–2010), April 1, 2016

To play this game of pretending that all the state's problems come from an out-of-control federal government and from a president who's out to destroy Utah has done a great disservice to the people of this state. So what is the future if it's not in [tourism]? It seems to me we have the most choice piece of real estate in the United States of America in southern Utah.

—Jim Dabakis (D–Salt Lake County), minority caucus manager, Utah State Senate (2013–), June 6, 2016

The Bennett process took place in a more fertile climate for collaboration. That climate is gone in Utah now. The rural folks went cowboy and became more strident in their opinion toward land managers.

—Brad Shafer, senior manager, government and public relations, Andeavor; former senior advisor to Senator Robert Bennett, January 7, 2016

I do believe there was a good-faith effort on [Representative Bishop's] part to find common ground. The PLI is an imperfect product of that process, admittedly, but I think it does reflect his genuine attempt to find common ground. The administration plans to act before they leave office, and so that gives us until January 20th of next year [to get legislation enacted]. We still hold out hope that something can emerge in the next two months, but we also recognize that there's not really a clear, obvious path to make that happen.

(As of May 2018, Bishop has not announced any plans to revive the PLI.)

—Cody Stewart staff director, House Natural Resources Committee, former director of Federal Affairs, and former policy and energy advisor to Utah governor Gary Herbert, October 13, 2016

INTERLUDE

History of the Antiquities Act and Background on the Federal Lands Transfer Movement

The Antiquities Act was enacted in 1906 by the Fifty-Ninth Congress and signed into law by President Theodore Roosevelt. The act provides that "the President of the United States is hereby authorized, in his discretion, to declare by public proclamation historic landmarks, historic and prehistoric structures, and other objects of historic or scientific interest that are situated upon the lands owned or controlled by the Government of the United States to be national monuments."[1]

The impetus for the act's creation was the looting and selling of Native American artifacts in the Southwest in the late 1800s and the absence of laws to protect archaeological sites and to prosecute those who pillaged them. Numerous individuals and groups were complicit in the international trafficking of artifacts, but a particularly enterprising and brazen Swede, Gustaf Nordenskiöld, deserves special attention.

In the late 1800s Nordenskiöld conducted several large digs at what is now Mesa Verde National Park in southwestern Colorado and loaded artifacts by the thousands onto railroad boxcars in Durango, Colorado, to be shipped to European museums. Locals grew wise to Nordenskiöld's scheme and, alarmed by what they viewed as his devastation of archaeological sites, had him arrested on September 17, 1891, at Durango's famed Strater Hotel. No matter that Nordenskiöld hadn't violated any laws; local residents simply wanted him held accountable for his illicit activities. He was subsequently released (and chastened), but the incident increased awareness of the dire threat to Native American sites from those who sought to profit

---

1. An Act for the Preservation of American Antiquities. Public Law 59–209.

from antiquities, whether by sending them to museums or by selling them on the black market.

In the next decade, a number of bills were proposed by members of Congress to protect antiquities. In January 1906 Representative John F. Lacey of Iowa introduced the bill that would become the Antiquities Act. On June 8 of the same year Congress passed the Antiquities Act, and President Theodore Roosevelt signed it into law soon thereafter. In addition to bestowing on the president authority to establish national monuments through executive action, the act requires permits to be approved before archaeological investigations can be undertaken on federal land. Since the Antiquities Act was passed, 157 national monuments have been declared.[2]

From 1908 onward large national monuments—including the Grand Canyon—have been the focus of often-rancorous debates and legal disputes. Central to the opposition to monument designation is the argument that restrictions on multiple-use activities will bankrupt communities, shutting down legacy industries (ranching) and extractive industries (mining, oil and gas drilling). Like so many debates in today's politically charged environment, facts are often masked by heated rhetoric.

With that in mind, here is a summary in broad terms of what a monument allows and what it does not. Each monument has a unique management plan, but the plans generally follow the guidelines below.

- A national monument, if kept intact, *does* permanently protect the land within its boundaries.
- A national monument *does* honor and grandfather in *existing* grazing permits. Ranchers who were grazing on public lands before a monument declaration can continue their operations after a monument is established. In some cases, significant restrictions may be placed on grazing in certain sensitive areas—a source of some distress among ranchers.
- A national monument *does not* allow the issuance of *new* grazing permits. If an individual was not ranching on lands within a new national monument before said monument was declared, he or she will not be allowed to do so afterward.

---

2. "Monuments Protected."

- A national monument *does* allow *existing* extractive industry activities to continue; mining and oil and gas leases issued before the monument was declared will be honored.
- As with grazing permits, a national monument *does not* allow *new* mining or oil and gas drilling leases.
- A national monument *does* allow motorized recreation on *existing* roads designated for multiple uses.
- A national monument *does not* allow for the creation of *new* roads for motorized travel.

When President Donald Trump issued an executive order in April 2017 directing Interior Secretary Ryan Zinke to conduct a review of all national monuments created since 1996 and issue recommendations for rescission or reduction, he chose a time period tailor-made to please Utah politicians.

In September 1996 President Bill Clinton designated the 1.7-million-acre Grand Staircase–Escalante National Monument in southern Utah without soliciting input from local communities and other stakeholders. Unlike the establishment of Bears Ears National Monument, which was designated after years of community dialogue, the plans for designating Grand Staircase–Escalante were made and finalized in Washington, D.C., behind closed doors.

In the portrait of Charles Wilkinson (see p. 169), we will learn more about why the establishment of "the Grand Staircase" was so contentious; why many residents of Garfield and Kane Counties, where the monument is located, are convinced, despite evidence to the contrary, that the designation has doomed their communities; and why some in San Juan County equated the Bears Ears designation with that of a monument established in a very different political era in a very different way.

Background on the Federal Lands Transfer Movement

A number of Republican lawmakers condemn "government overreach," which, in the context of public lands disputes, refers to regulations that restrict multiple-use activity on public lands. In particular, the Coalition of Western States (COWS), comprised of legislators and community leaders in Oregon, Washington, Idaho, Arizona, Nevada, Utah, Montana, and New Mexico, "stand ready to oppose continued federal overreach and abuse, support the rule of law and restore management of public lands to the States where it Constitutionally belongs."[3] In early 2016 COWS members traveled to Burns, Oregon, to support the "patriots" leading the occupation of the Malheur National Wildlife Refuge as a protest against the Bureau of Land Management's "abusive" policies regulating grazing and other activities on public lands. Their actions were an overt endorsement and embrace of the beliefs and values of the Sagebrush Rebellion.

A narrative of persecution is strong: the unassuming, hard-working denizens of rural America are underrepresented and at times even mocked by elected leaders more focused on meeting the needs of their urban constituents than the needs of those residing in "the sticks."

In a November 2014 blog post entitled "Why Rural America Must Fight!" COWS member Jim Beers points to "a gang of nefarious characters"— including "National Radical Organizations" such as Greenpeace and "rich computer executives attached to a 'cause' like global warming"—dead set on destroying rural communities by "treating Rural Americans and their interests like the Soviets treated Eastern European countries or European powers treated 'their' Colonies hundreds of years ago." The only solution, Beers concludes, is to strengthen local government to stand up to the "tyranny" of federal bureaucrats, including the state directors of federal land agencies like the BLM. Then and only then will rural Americans be able to "stop the federal oppression . . . and have any hope for a better tomorrow."

The COWS ideological stance underpins the federal lands transfer movement: an effort by politicians at the national and local levels to transfer public lands from federal to state control. In their view, the federal government cannot be trusted to steward public lands: What do bureaucrats thousands of miles away know about the needs of rural landowners? Lands transfer boosters believe that state and local leaders know best how to manage lands for the benefit of their rural constituents, especially where multiple-use rules are concerned.

Utah has led the charge on lands transfer issues. Its state legislature in 2012 passed the Utah Transfer of Federal Lands Act, demanding that the government transfer ownership of federally controlled land to the state of Utah by 2014. Unsurprisingly, the bill did not achieve its stated goal, but some of the state's elected leaders persisted, commissioning in late 2015 a

---

3. Coalition of Western States, http://cowstates.com/.

nearly $500,000 study that recommended Utah sue the federal government.[4] Such an undertaking was projected to cost upward of $14 million and was roundly criticized by a variety of groups, including sportsmen, conservation organizations, and others who believed the state's true intent was to accelerate drilling and mining on public lands. Additionally, critics asserted that the state could not bear the costs of services currently provided by the federal government, such as fire prevention. As of July 2017 the state legislature had not filed a lawsuit.

In February 2017, facing stiff opposition from sportsmen's groups, former Utah congressman Jason Chaffetz withdrew a bill that sought to transfer three million acres of federal land to the states of Utah, Montana, Arizona, Wyoming, Colorado, Idaho, Nebraska, New Mexico, and Oregon. But the debate over federal lands transfer rages on, fueled by the passions of Tea Partiers and Sagebrush Rebels.

---

4. Maffly, "Republicans OK $14M Land-Transfer Lawsuit."

Valley of the Gods (aerial photo)

GAVIN NOYES

Elevating the Vision of Native Peoples, Protecting Culturally Significant Lands

On an unusually warm morning in June 2016, Gavin Noyes arrives on a bicycle for our 8:00 a.m. meeting at a Salt Lake City café and greets us with a warm smile and improbably calm demeanor, given the intensity and high stakes of the work in which he is immersed. Clad in a muted, lightly patterned button-down shirt and dark jeans, a satchel slung over his shoulder, Noyes is tall and rail thin, with short brown hair, a boyish face, a gentle, soft-spoken manner, and a habit of appending a soft laugh to his sentences. As we talk over breakfast, it becomes apparent that, at least this morning, Noyes has a seemingly endless capacity for coffee.

"You're keeping me full," he says to our waiter, chuckling as the man pours a third round into Noyes's mug. This much coffee could be a lifelong habit, or it could have evolved as a way for Noyes to survive an astonishing pace of travel and meetings. Since 2010, when he embarked on the venture that eventually led to the founding of Utah Diné Bikéyah (UDB), Noyes estimates he has logged 225,000 miles traversing Utah from San Juan County to Salt Lake; making trips to Native American reservations in the Four Corners region; accompanying tribal leaders to press conferences and legislative hearings at Utah's state capital and in Washington, D.C.; organizing community meetings to engage citizens in dialogue about protecting land and ancestral sites; and dispelling persistent rumors and misinformation proffered by those who oppose UDB's efforts.

When stories are told of the battle to protect ancestral lands in southeastern Utah, the role played by the Bears Ears Inter-Tribal Coalition inevitably takes center stage. But five years before the coalition took form, a grassroots movement started by a small group of Utah Navajos began laying the

Utah Diné Bikéyah executive director
Gavin Noyes

groundwork for what would become the coalition's proposal for the Bears Ears National Monument.

In 2010 Mark Maryboy, a Navajo activist and former politician, cofounded UDB with Noyes and led the group's efforts to interview tribal elders, gathering documentation of sites in southeastern Utah that have cultural significance to Navajos. Behind the scenes, Noyes and UDB board members began to develop strategies for seeking federal protection for those sites.

Noyes's training in natural resource management and conservation was essential to UDB's success, but it was his personal journey, from the sandstone canyons of Utah to pottery kilns in Japan and back again, that provided him with the patience and sensitivity essential to intercultural communication.

His groundedness and lack of pretense speak to his fundamental humility, his patience with people and process, and his quiet perseverance. Noyes understands that fundamental change cannot happen in the span of a congressional cycle; instead, change happens over many years as trust is developed and movements take hold.

Noyes's temperament was honed during the two years he spent in Japan, where he studied ceramics, apprenticing with a master ceramicist and traveling to towns with ancient kilns where artists had been producing traditional pottery for well over a thousand years. During his travels, he spoke with many people, trying to understand the reasons behind the accelerating decline of traditional Japanese culture among young people and their growing attraction to U.S. pop culture and materialism.

"I was really interested in place-based art and the tie between local resources that predate transportation," Noyes explains, "and how people would weave those and establish an art tradition."

Like so many people with whom we've spoken, Noyes's life path has been defined by formative experiences in the wild beauty and harsh terrain of Utah's canyon country.

"My story really begins here in Utah," Noyes says, "falling in love with Utah landscapes and eventually deciding to major in natural resources at the University of Michigan." Noyes graduated with a BA in environmental science and Japanese language and culture and secured a grant that allowed him to travel to Japan and pursue his budding interest in ceramics.

"I visited all the pottery towns in Japan, all the ancient kilns that have been around thirteen hundred years or more," Noyes says. "Eventually, I studied my favorite one of those, which makes pots which look a lot like . . . the landscape of southern Utah," with texture reminiscent of Utah sandstone and colors created by dripping wood ash onto high-fired clay pots.

Imbued with a desire to make place-based art of his own in a landscape he loved, Noyes returned to Utah, choosing to build a cabin and a kiln not in his hometown of Salt Lake City but in Hanksville, Utah, a town of about two hundred people located in the rugged landscape of south-central Utah.

"Japan was crowded, so I wanted to get as far away from people as possible," Noyes recalls, laughing.

While in Hanksville, he spent time assisting with a wilderness field survey for an environmental campaign and discovered a passion for land conservation policy that connected to his undergraduate work. In 1997 he started working for Save Our Canyons, a small nonprofit that focused on conservation efforts on the Wasatch Front. His work as the organization's first employee and later as its executive director focused on protecting the landscapes around Salt Lake City during the building frenzy leading up to the 2002 Olympics.

"It was just madness for five years," Noyes says. "We had four or five lawsuits going at the same time."

The endless battles drained Noyes, and he returned to Hanksville to refocus his energy on pottery. It didn't take long for him to return to the world of community-driven conservation.

"After a little break from the trenches, I missed the trenches," he says.

In 2005 he developed a proposal to initiate conservation efforts in Wayne County (home to Hanksville) and its adjacent eastern neighbor, San Juan. He presented the proposal to Round River Conservation Studies, a nonprofit that uses its expertise in conservation biology to provide communities and governments with a scientific basis for conservation efforts. Noyes envisioned exploring how to include the voices of Native American tribes in shaping the future of public lands. Round River obtained funding for the project in 2007, and work began in earnest in the following year.

From the outset, Noyes and his colleagues were confronted with the complexities of intercultural relations in San Juan County. The most formidable barrier in approaching environmental issues was the divide between Mormons and non-Mormons in both Anglo and Native communities.

"When I met with people, everybody would be totally open, and we'd walk away with some great ideas that we were going to pursue and then . . . I don't know," Noyes says. "They look into the handbook of who's Mormon and who's not, and I can't ever get a call back. That just happened again and again. I don't know why that was. Because I think there's a lot of common ground."

Noyes made some progress with rural ranchers, whom he calls "as radical of environmentalists as I am" because of their concern for maintaining ecosystems that benefit their livelihood. It gave him hope that Round River could find a way to create a plan for conservation that reflected the values of local people.

"You listen for long enough and then you can start to really piece together where are the opportunities for shared progress," Noyes says.

The conversations petered out in the fall of 2008 due in part to the upheavals following the onset of the Great Recession. Funding dried up, and Noyes was left without many resources to continue the project. Even in the face of diminishing resources, Noyes nevertheless continued to invest time with the tribes.

"It was so hard to get a meeting scheduled," Noyes says. "You just have to keep showing up. I just showed up, and I'd listen at every meeting. I'd get up and talk for a few minutes, respectfully, and just try and limit how much I said.

"None of them had any interest in public lands," he adds. "Except one," who, ironically, belonged to a Great Basin tribe that didn't fit into Round River's Colorado Plateau project.

Over a period of years, Rupert Steele, a member of the Goshute tribe and a Bureau of Land Management employee, had prepared maps of the Goshute Reservation land on which he delineated a comprehensive inventory of his tribe's ancestral sites. In August 2008 he told Noyes that these sites were in jeopardy because the city of Las Vegas wanted access to the Goshutes' groundwater to supply the rapid expansion of housing, casinos, and fountains. (A similar battle between the Standing Rock Sioux tribe in North Dakota and a Texas oil company building the massive Dakota Access Pipeline led to a multimonth standoff near Cannon Ball, North Dakota, in the latter half of 2016.)[1] Instantly, Noyes recognized that Steele's fluency in both the bureaucratic language of the BLM and the traditional culture of his tribe could be the key to developing a strategy to protect the Goshute sites. Together, Noyes and Steele prepared a presentation comprising the testimony of tribal members, Steele's meticulous maps, and an overlay that delineated the threats presented by Las Vegas's groundwater proposal.

"We interviewed every tribal member out there and then some," Noyes says. "I testified on our mapping before the state water engineer . . . and we won."

The combination of personal testimony and data was persuasive. After many challenges to an initial ruling favorable to the tribes, in May 2015 the Nevada Supreme Court finally affirmed a decision protecting seven hundred thousand acres of Goshute ancestral lands.

Noyes saw in the Goshute process a possible template for working with tribes on the Colorado Plateau. Freshly energized by the Goshute victory, Noyes and Round River resumed work in eastern Utah.

For over a year, they struggled to make inroads.

"It was like a black box," Noyes said. "We had no idea where to start."

So he did what he had done with the Goshutes and, years before, with Japanese potters: he showed up, talked little, listened much, and waited patiently for tribal members to decide he was someone who could help in efforts to protect ancestral sites.

"Like a lot of cultures, their initial reaction is no and then it warms to a yes," Noyes says. "They didn't recognize that they had any rights on their ancestral lands unless it said so in their treaty. Everywhere people said, 'We have very deep interests on public lands, and we do not talk about them to white people, because if we do, we know what those white people are going to do. They're going to take them.'"

---

1. For an update, see "Standing Rock Is Everywhere: One Year Later," *Guardian*, February 22, 2018, https://www.theguardian.com/environment/climate-consensus-97-per-cent/2018/feb/22/standing-rock-is-everywhere-one-year-later.

Nearly two years after he began his work with the tribes, Noyes conducted his first interview: a memorable drive with a Paiute elder who pointed out sacred places from the passenger's side of Noyes's car. As they drove, the elder would point out one site, then another, with enthusiastic exclamations— "Sacred! Sacred! Sacred!"—that underscored not only how much of the landscape he considered spiritually significant but also the depth of his connection to the land.

"He was incredible," Noyes recalls. "There were just so many wonderful people like that that I eventually got to know, but it took forever . . . [and] the way that we got started was I just listened."

Another breakthrough came in June 2009 at the annual Paiute powwow. The Utah Tribal Leaders Association was discussing a recent move by the state legislature to build a commuter rail station on an ancient Indian sacred site near Draper, a Salt Lake City suburb. The proposal stood in direct violation of a 2000 mandate by the state legislature granting the site permanent protection.

In the midst of heated exchanges regarding how best to address the problem, Kenneth Maryboy, Mark Maryboy's brother, stood up and spoke about his people's connection to the Draper site: how the Navajo would travel from their homeland in southeastern Utah to the Salt Lake Valley to collect salt and trade with the Utes.

Following Maryboy's lead, "every tribe went around, and they talked about . . . how strong their ties are to this place," Noyes says. "And as usual, I was the only white guy in there."

He shared with the tribes the model that had worked for the Goshutes and urged them to come together as a coalition of sovereign nations to articulate their case for protecting the lands they all considered sacred. They all committed, and Noyes started collecting stories.

"They cared so much about this spot that they . . . pulled out all the stops," Noyes says.

As his first act in office in August 2009, Governor Gary Herbert signed an order permanently protecting the site.

The Draper victory provided Noyes with evidence that cultural mapping represented a critical first step in building a case for protection of tribal ancestral sites. That approach would be central to UDB's work. The concept of uniting multiple tribes to assert their sovereign rights, critical in the

Draper fight, presaged the approach eventually adopted by the Bears Ears Inter-Tribal Coalition. The relationship with Kenneth Maryboy forged at the powwow proved essential to initiating work with the Navajo Nation tribal members and their political leadership.

"[Kenneth] said, 'Come on down, you've got to meet my brother Mark,'" Noyes recalls.

At their first meeting, Mark Maryboy was not receptive to Noyes's vision for protecting Navajo ancestral lands. According to Noyes, Maryboy considered him yet another well-meaning white person with big ideas and no follow-through. Noyes was undeterred.

"I had had so many cups of tea with Japanese pottery senseis that I knew exactly what he was doing," Noyes says. "In Japan that's what you do. You tell people 'no' three times, and then if they keep showing up, you say, 'Okay, you've got the perseverance to make this work.'" On their third meeting, Maryboy agreed to work with Noyes and Round River.

Noyes proposed the creation of a catalog of traditional indigenous knowledge of the environment using a method that the data-driven world of Western science would understand and respect. It was a radical approach based on his work with the Goshutes: combining hard data with the voices and stories of Native peoples, amplifying their voices so that they could be heard by a government that had ignored or denigrated them for well over a century.

"Mark is really the key to all of this," Noyes says. "He's an extremely talented politician."

Maryboy related stories of painful encounters during his years as a member of the San Juan County Commission and told Noyes how difficult it would be to change attitudes regarding public lands use given San Juan County's challenging and often hostile political climate.

"He said, 'We can't just *meet* the standard,'" Noyes says. "'We have to do everything twice as good. If it's not twice as good, nobody's even going to give it a second chance.' So we did that. That's been our mantra ever since."

Over the course of several years, UDB, guided by traditionalists, created maps of cultural resources and presented a case for protection of the most culturally significant parcels of San Juan County's public lands as either a national conservation area or a national monument. Their efforts gained the endorsement of Senator Robert Bennett (R-UT), who had started to work

Spire, Anticline Overlook

with San Juan County residents before he was succeeded by Senator Mike Lee (R-UT), who did not continue Bennett's work.[2]

"Bennett gave Navajos and Utes hope that they could be part of something," Noyes says. "He was the first person ever to ask Natives what they thought."

After Lee's election, Noyes, Maryboy, and their Native collaborators moved forward with their efforts. In 2012 they formalized the group carrying out the cultural mapping as a nonprofit, naming it Utah Diné Bikéyah.

As a result of UDB's work, in 2012 the Navajo Nation entered into a joint planning agreement with San Juan County in which the two entities would work together on land management. UDB presented its proposal to Representative Rob Bishop (R-UT) for inclusion in his Public Lands Initiative (PLI), a process for designating land use through compromise that was similar to Bennett's efforts. When San Juan County commissioner Phil Lyman established the San Juan County Public Lands Council in early 2014 as part of the county's participation in the PLI, he asked Mark Maryboy to participate. But when Lyman led his ATV protest ride into Recapture Canyon several months later, Natives felt disrespected by what they perceived as a direct attack on their cultural heritage.

"I don't think Mark has ever forgiven [Phil]," Noyes says, a statement that is corroborated by Maryboy's account. "I don't think anyone else on our board ever wanted to work with him again." So Maryboy and UDB withdrew from lands council participation, deciding that a different approach was needed.

Building on Kenneth Maryboy's and Noyes's success in uniting tribes in service of a common cause in the Draper fight, Mark Maryboy and Noyes decided to seek the support of other sovereign tribes that had shared interests in protecting ancestral sites located in San Juan County.

Over the next year, UDB staff met with tribal leaders in New Mexico, Colorado, and Arizona and elsewhere in Utah whose peoples shared common cultural, historical, and spiritual attachment to the land in southeastern Utah. In April 2015 representatives from more than twenty tribes and pueblos met in Bluff, Utah, just north of the Navajo Nation's "Utah strip," to discuss approaches to protecting their ancestral lands.

---

2. Utah Tribal Leaders Association Letters.

At the beginning of the gathering, Maryboy welcomed the tribes back to their ancestral home. The invitation paved the way for the formation of the Bears Ears Inter-Tribal Coalition in July 2015. That fall the coalition presented a formal proposal for the Bears Ears National Monument to the White House. As sovereign nations, the tribes were able to elevate discussions from a county to a national level. (For a discussion of tribal sovereignty, see p. 177.)

As the Bears Ears Inter-Tribal Coalition moved ahead with its efforts, UDB continued to mobilize grassroots support for the monument proposal, holding community meetings on the reservations of the coalition tribes and accelerating its media campaign. Celebrities from Leonardo DiCaprio to Robert Redford penned op-eds expressing support for Bears Ears. The momentum for monument designation increased as the campaign received extensive national recognition.

UDB's claim that tribes as sovereign nations were united in their support of the monument is accurate. But that does not mean all members of those tribes favor monument designation. A small but vocal group of Navajos and Utes, led by San Juan County commissioner Rebecca Benally and supported by the Utah congressional delegation and Republican governor Gary Herbert's office, waged a campaign in opposition to the monument proposal. They argued that a national monument would place ancestral lands under greater control of a federal government that in their view has abused and betrayed Native Americans for many years. Like UDB, the coalition, and its allies, the monument opponents among the Native population in San Juan County wanted to protect land from desecration and maintain their access to firewood, plants and herbs, and other sources of physical and cultural sustenance. Unlike monument supporters, however, they saw the federal government not as the entity that would afford protection but as a grave threat to the land and their freedom to access its resources. Moreover, they claimed that a monument would remove lands from further mining and oil and gas development, crucial in their view to sustaining well-paying jobs. Their voices were amplified by the state's politicians, who used the groups' opposition to paint a portrait of a divided county whose future might be determined by "outsider" tribes and elitist environmentalists.

On July 16, 2016, over a thousand people attended a public hearing in Bluff, Utah, one of San Juan County's southernmost towns. Then secretary of the interior Sally Jewell and the heads of the Bureau of Land Management, the National Park Service, the U.S. Forest Service, and the U.S. Department of Agriculture listened to arguments pro and con regarding designation of Bears Ears as a new national monument.

Noyes, the Maryboy brothers, UDB board members, leaders of the coalition, and hundreds of supporters from across the West donned sky-blue "Protect Bears Ears" T-shirts and held signs asking Secretary Jewell to #ProtectBearsEarsNow. Comments from monument supporters and opponents alike were riveting and heartfelt, each communicating passionately their love of the land and their desire to keep it safe from intrusion, whether by "outsider" environmentalists and tourists, oil and gas developers, or mining operations. Their conflicting views reflected the cultural struggles that have raged in San Juan County and the rural West for generations. The testimony offered at the meeting underscored how difficult it would be for opposing groups to achieve consensus and to develop policy for stewarding the land.

As the coalition and its many allies continue their efforts in support of the monument, Noyes is also taking the long view. Having worked in San Juan County for nearly a decade, he knows well the economic and cultural challenges facing the county.

"My view is that we need to get the national monument first, and then we need to talk about nothing but economic development," Noyes says.

Given the strong disagreements among all sides about the merits and liabilities of ranching and mining, wilderness and tourism, it will take all of Noyes's considerable patience to find paths for polarized parties to arrive at common ground.

"There's a lot of territoriality," Noyes said. "There's a lot of mistrust. What I'm doing . . . is trying to think of ways to break through some of those barriers. Because if we don't, we all lose."

Noyes recognizes the entrenched multigenerational issues that have led to cultural and political impasses. He also places some of the blame squarely on the shoulders of local and national leadership.

"It's baffling to me that we've got leaders that are driving things as far apart as they are," Noyes says. "We need to get everybody together. . . . Don't we need to be talking to each other?"

Perhaps the most fruitful and revolutionary conversations about bridge building and solidarity are taking place at the international level. Noyes says that there is a powerful movement among indigenous peoples around the world to protect their ancestral lands and practices from the incursions of onrushing industrialization and globalization. They are beginning to find ways to use the power granted to them in the United Nations Declaration on the Rights of Indigenous Peoples. Noyes sees tremendous potential for tribes across the United States to connect to the global community to advance their rights.

The coalition and UDB have a role to play in presenting to other groups a model that harnesses the grassroots support of people locally and nationally to foster change and indigenous self-determination. They also can learn from the success of groups in other countries.

"There's a movement that's going to be trickling down and will hit tribes on every level," Noyes says. "The indigenous community sees that it's worth it to get everybody talking and sharing information about what's happening elsewhere.

"We do need to share the story of what's going on here and then ask people what's working elsewhere," Noyes says. "I think it's an area where we can make a lot of progress."

He returns to the concept of healing that the tribes have placed at the heart of their efforts to protect their sacred land and educate the wider world about its cultural and environmental significance. Noyes believes that a national monument comanaged by the federal government and American Indian nations has the potential to foster intercultural understanding and a shared appreciation of a unique landscape.

"This is not a political proposal," Noyes says. "This is a fundamentally human proposal [that envisions] a new era of recognizing that we're all human, we all have values, we're all connected to each other, and we respect each other. That's what [the tribes] are looking for: they're looking for respect, for a recognition of the diversity of their cultures."

Gavin is the right guy. He's got the right temperament, he's got a tough job, he's done a great job with it. Would it be better if he were Navajo? Maybe.

Mark [Maryboy] and Gavin went to all the chapter houses. They thought people weren't going to talk about [ancestral sites], but to Mark's and Gavin's credit, they spent a lot of time, built trust, and got people to start talking about what mattered to them.

It's funny, people are asking, "Is this OK?" And I'm like, are you kidding me? You've got a proposal [for Bears Ears] from five tribes saying they want to protect it? I couldn't have even imagined that happening. Then people say, "Well, what's going to happen?" And I say, if we've got to choose between the Monticello [BLM] office making a decision and the Hopi making a decision, I know who I'd pick.

—Scott Groene, executive director, Southern
Utah Wilderness Alliance, July 28, 2015

[The lands council] wasn't perfect. We can always look back in hindsight and say, "Well, we could have done more and better or had an even broader representation on the council." We tried to get a representation of Native Americans on the council, and we probably could have had more, working with [the] Diné Bikéyah group, who supposedly represented Native Americans. But maybe [the tribes] weren't willing to come to the center with the county on a lot of things. [They] kind of splintered off. We didn't get as good representation and voice from Native Americans as we could have.

—Nick Sandberg, public lands coordinator,
San Juan County, November 9, 2015

INTERLUDE

Attempts to Forge Compromise in the Use of Public Lands

Battles over the future of public lands in Utah have raged for more than eighty years. Conservationists have long urged enhanced protection for lands that are unique in their stark magnificence, while mineral extractors and ranchers have lobbied persistently for increased access to those lands and the economic benefits they may yield. The push and pull between these forces have led to heated conflicts, with moderate voices often drowned out by strident claims, counterclaims, and propaganda from advocates on each side.

In 2006 Senator Robert Bennett (R-UT) initiated an effort to seek consensus regarding a particularly contentious dispute in Washington County, home to the rapidly growing city of St. George and Zion National Park. St. George needed access to public lands in order to expand its boundaries to accommodate rapid growth, while conservationists fought to protect nearby areas adjacent to the national parks. Together with Representative Jim Matheson (D-UT), Bennett encouraged the county's leadership to develop a multidecade vision for Washington County that took account of the seemingly incompatible needs for growth and conservation.

In response, the county initiated Vision Dixie, a process that brought together a diverse group of local stakeholders and gave each a voice in recommending how best to use public lands. Following several false starts, Bennett, with the help of Matheson, Senate Majority Leader Harry Reid (D-NV), and Senator Richard Durbin (D-IL), was able to include the Washington County Growth and Conservation Act (known locally as the Washington County Lands Bill) in an omnibus bill that was signed into law by President Barack Obama in 2009. The bill was hailed by many as a model for balancing competing claims on public lands.

Bennett hoped to replicate the Vision Dixie process in San Juan County. He was particularly concerned that representatives of the Ute Mountain Ute and Navajo tribes be given a strong voice in the stakeholder-driven effort aimed at reaching a consensus vision for public land use. However, soon after he and his staff initiated on-the-ground conversations and surveys in the area, Bennett lost his seat as the state Republican Party caucus coalesced around Tea Party favorite Mike Lee, who has represented Utah in the U.S. Senate since 2011.

Three years later, Representative Rob Bishop (R-UT) launched his Public Lands Initiative (PLI), a process aimed at emulating and, in his view, improving upon the efforts of Senator Bennett. Bishop hoped to reach a "grand bargain" that would settle the decades-long battle over public land use in eight counties in eastern Utah. The stories of Rob Bishop, Mark Maryboy, Phil Lyman, and Gavin Noyes illustrate the promise and pitfalls of the PLI process and what ultimately led to its failure.

The years-long effort among tribes, San Juan County officials, Representatives Bishop and Jason Chaffetz and their staffs, the Department of the Interior, and the Obama administration's Council on Environmental Quality (CEQ) to achieve a viable compromise revealed many areas of agreement regarding both land protection and how best to incorporate the voices of tribes, conservationists, and local citizens. In the end, however, the PLI failed to achieve the grand bargain envisioned at the start.

Some blamed the tribes and their supporters in the environmental community. Others believed the language in the PLI hewed too closely to the wishes of the oil and gas and mining industries and that a parallel bill aimed at undermining the president's powers under the Antiquities Act revealed Bishop's ideological biases.

Had the discussions regarding the PLI taken place at a less politically polarized moment, they might well have achieved the vision articulated by Bennett. Instead, what seemed so tantalizingly close to a viable compromise has devolved into ideologically driven recriminations that resonate to this day.

With the PLI not reaching a floor vote, President Obama used the powers granted to him in the Antiquities Act to protect 1.35 million acres in southeastern Utah as Bears Ears National Monument. After President Donald Trump took office in January 2017, there was considerable uncertainty about whether any significant changes to the monument would be made—and utter certainty that any alterations proposed by the Trump administration would be met by a robust legal challenge from the tribes, the outdoor industry, and environmental groups. When Trump signed a proclamation on December 4, 2017, calling for an 85 percent reduction of the existing Bears Ears National Monument and the establishment of two much smaller monuments on the remaining 15 percent of land, San Juan County residents celebrated and protested in equal measure. As predicted, nonprofits, outdoor-recreation companies, and tribes that supported Obama's monument filed suit. The age-old battles between familiar rivals continued; the high stakes intensified the rhetoric and attacks from both sides.

What Bishop ostensibly set out to achieve—to develop long-term land management plans that support a robust economic future for San Juan County and rural Utah writ large—will need to wait.

Time Line of Land-Use Planning: Twin Visions Evolve

2010
Senator Bennett begins land use planning in eight counties in eastern Utah and invites Natives to join the process, then **Bennett** loses bid for 4th term.

2012
Congressman Rob Bishop begins informal meetings with stakeholders about land use in the eight eastern counties of Utah.

2014
San Juan County Public Lands Council is established by **Commissioner Phil Lyman** to make recommendations to **Bishop** for inclusion in the **PLI**.

2015
SJC commissioners forward recommendations from **SJC Public Lands Council** to **Congressman Bishop** for inclusion in the **PLI**.

Representatives **Bishop** and **Chaffetz** and **Senator Mike Lee** invite the tribes to reengage in the **PLI** process.

2016
Bishop and **Chaffetz** release the first draft of the **PLI** in January and the final draft in July, days before Interior **Secretary Jewell's** visit.

2009
Washington County Lands Bill: Senator Bob Bennett leads compromise between protection and growth in Washington County, Utah.

*Daggett County was originally part of the PLI process but withdrew.

SUMMIT · DAGGETT*
DUCHESNE · UINTAH
CARBON
Seven PLI Counties
EMERY · GRAND
SAN JUAN

2013
Bishop's Utah Public Lands Initiative (PLI) launches. The Navajo Nation, working in conjunction with UDB, is invited to participate.

2016
Interior Secretary Sally Jewell visits San Juan County and holds public meetings in Bluff.

PLI bill presented to Congress and moves from House Natural Resources Committee to the full House.

2010
Mark Maryboy and **Gavin Noyes** begin interviewing Navajo elders to develop cultural mapping of ancestral lands.

2012
Utah Diné Bikéyah (UDB) officially forms as a nonprofit.

2013
UDB presents Bears Ears land conservation and co-management proposal to local, state, and federal officials, then the Navajo Nation submits it to **Bishop's Public Lands Initiative**.

2015
Leaders of 5 tribes with ancestral connection to the Bears Ears region found the **Bears Ears Inter-Tribal Coalition (BEITC)** and assert their right to negotiate as sovereign nations.

At year's end, **BEITC** abandons the **PLI** process.

2016
BEITC and environmental groups reject the **PLI** first and final drafts and direct all efforts towards a **Bears Ears National Monument** designation.

Mesa near Bluff, Utah, at sunset

REBECCA BENALLY

Pursuing Prosperity for Utah's Tribes, Opposing a National Monument

Duke's Bistro is a recent addition to Bluff's culinary landscape, which makes it the town's fifth restaurant and one of two that are open in late October. With its glass tabletops, cloth napkins, and servers clad in starched shirts, Duke's is either a welcome fine-dining addition to Bluff or evidence to some locals that the yupperati are stealthily conquering the town. The earnest young waitstaff take breakfast orders with expeditious aplomb and deliver elegant yogurt parfaits and blue-corn pancakes to early risers.

Into this tranquil atmosphere walks San Juan County commissioner Rebecca Benally, a petite, well-dressed Navajo woman with an agenda: a typed document, replete with bullet points, visible in a meticulously organized binder, ready for her next meeting with the U.S. Forest Service. Her fitted red jacket and beaded black jewelry are all business, as is her demeanor: professional, intense, and singularly focused on driving home her message.

Benally can shift her facial expressions in an instant. She smiles warmly as she describes her connection to her homeland, "that spiritual connection to what we call Mother Earth and Father Sky, how we fit and how others fit." The next moment, her eyes narrow and her smile disappears, conveying a simmering anger at what she sees as a misleading attempt by a group of Utah Navajos—specifically, the staff and board of Utah Diné Bikéyah (UDB)—to convince her constituents to support the Bears Ears National Monument. She has her talking points at the ready and deploys them with a seasoned politician's skill, even though at our October 2015 meeting she has only been in office for nine months.

"I don't support the monument designation," Benally says. "I have yet to be assured that a national monument designation will bring any economic development."

San Juan County Commissioner Rebecca
Benally (courtesy of San Juan County)

Instead, she believes that a monument will limit the ability of her constituents to make a living, and she is particularly unimpressed with the argument that tourism will be the economic boon that monument boosters predict.

"You have to realize that San Juan County is the poorest county in the state of Utah," Benally says. "And they say when Cedar Mesa and Bears Ears . . . is designated as a national monument, that will bring tourism money. If that is true, why isn't that happening now?"

She points to Monument Valley, forty-five miles to the south on the Arizona-Utah border, as an example of a nearby international tourist draw that, from her point of view, fails to deliver sufficient jobs and income to her constituents on the Utah portion of the Navajo Reservation. But some data challenge her claims.

While not focused on Utah Navajos, a 2011 Navajo Nation visitor survey notes that approximately 50 percent of the nearly six hundred thousand visitors to the Navajo Nation stop at Monument Valley, with a 32 percent increase in economic impact from 2002 to 2011. The report concludes, "The total economic impact of visitors to the Navajo Nation area is therefore substantial, and contributes significantly to the greater regional economy."[1]

However, like her fellow commissioners, Benally must answer to citizens who have made a living in the oil fields and see efforts to protect public land from mining and drilling as a threat to their future.

Benally reserves particular contempt for what she regards as an aggressive and disingenuous campaign led by supporters of UDB aimed at convincing

---

1. "2011 Navajo Nation Visitor Survey."

Utah Navajos that seeking protection for the Bears Ears region as a national monument is both consistent with Native values and economically beneficial.

"They have come on so strong, so negative, and so aggressive, and they want to speak for all Native Americans," Benally says. "I feel that they've misled some of the Native American people. The elders think that if this gets designated as a national monument, they'll get to live there. That's what they're told: they will have full access, they will have their land again. Some of these Bears Ears board members, when they go to [chapter house] meetings, they're bullying people to support them. And that's . . . unethical. And the Navajo people are divided because of that.

"What confuses me," she adds, "is that's not the Native American way. We're supposed to be in harmony and balanced, spiritually connected and respectful. But that's not what I've seen."

Yet Benally is viewed by many as one of the most divisive figures in the Bears Ears debate, stoking the fears of some Natives in San Juan County who worry that the federal government will take away their land much as it did in centuries past through broken treaties and backroom deals. She has unleashed scathing critiques of the Bears Ears Inter-Tribal Coalition and UDB in particular as engaged in a "cynical divide-and-conquer campaign" and dependent on private foundations and "magazine environmentalists" for success.

"I go to every chapter house monthly in my [constituent areas], which are Aneth, Red Mesa, and Mexican Water. I go to Oljato and Navajo Mountain every other month, and they were not aware of [the proposal for a Bears Ears Monument]," Benally says. "None of those chapter houses were informed when a new delegation from the Navajo Nation administration passed a resolution for a national monument [in March 2015]." Several sources, however, dispute her account.

She sees it as her job to give voice to the voiceless and the poorest of the poor, many of whom she believes have been deceived. Benally also condemns what she feels are personal attacks on her as a female leader—attacks she might have expected from Anglos but not from Navajos.

"The non-Native people, the white people, have been good mentors to me," Benally says. "It's the Navajo men that have been pushing back. . . . I once heard somewhere that Native Americans can be like crabs in a bucket, trying to pull each other down," Benally adds. "It really disappoints me, but I see that happening."

Benally, who is Mormon but maintains ties to traditional Navajo culture, says that upon taking office, she was warned by former Navajo commissioners to beware the malevolence of San Juan County's Anglo residents. But she says her experience doesn't jibe with theirs.

"I was always given the impression by my predecessors that the white Mormon people just hate Navajo people, they're not coming to help. I was a teacher in San Juan School District"—which is 54 percent Native—"and I never really saw that. My eyes were opened as a commissioner, and I realized that what they were saying was not really true." She sees her willingness to work with non-Navajos as a political strength, even if some of her Navajo detractors see it as a betrayal of her people.

"Phil [Lyman] and I had a little disagreement about Recapture Canyon," Benally says, referring to the May 2014 ATV ride Lyman led to protest a road closure by the BLM. They also don't see eye-to-eye on politics: she's a member of the San Juan County Democratic Party, while Lyman is a proud Republican. "But we were mature and smart enough to know that while we may disagree, we have bigger issues to work on together. He knows my position, we talk about it, he's respectful. I respect him, you know?

"I believe that people need to work together, put their differences aside, define our mission and our objectives and . . . see how you can give and take, because you're not always going to get what you want," Benally says. "So what are we willing to compromise to get to that point?

"This whole process is not about my agenda, what I believe," Benally says. "It's what the greater percentage of people believe needs to happen. If it is designated a national monument, then we'll just have to sit down and work together and see how this works for the people. Because we didn't get what we want doesn't mean we should give up. We should come back to the table and say, 'This is what it is. How do we come together to find common ground, commonalities, and continue to move forward?'"

For now, Benally's focus is on practical issues, like paving some of the county's eighty-seven miles of dirt roads used by school buses to transport Navajo children to schools on and off the reservation. She counts as a success the county's recent hiring of a lobbyist to advocate in Washington for the allocation of Navajo school bus route funds to the county. She hopes this will be the first step toward improving services and infrastructure for Utah Navajos.

"I'm here to speak for my constituents, who are Native Americans, and find a way to get them to the table anytime there's planning for this county, because they have a right to help plan things in this county," Benally adds. "I don't think we should divide people or diminish any way we can work together."

In the year following our conversation with Benally, she became a larger-than-life figure in the debate over Bears Ears. Her opposition to the monument has been seized upon by Utah's local and national Republican elected officials, who point to her cohort of "grassroots" Utah Navajos as proof that the Native people of San Juan County do not want a monument. The Aneth chapter house came out against the national monument, while the remaining six of the seven Utah chapter houses of the Navajo Nation voted to support it.

Benally has intensified her rhetoric around the potential dangers of allowing federal agencies to assume a greater role in managing local land. She and her fellow commissioners reference the fallout from the National Park Service's designation of Canyon de Chelly and Navajo National Monuments, noting that in their view the agency pressured Navajo families to move off their land in service of making the monument more tourist friendly and in doing so drastically diminished local Navajos' access to land and resources. They claim that a monument designation for Bears Ears would prevent Navajos and Utes from collecting wood, herbs, and piñon nuts and from performing traditional healing ceremonies at sacred sites, even though the Bears Ears National Monument proposal explicitly states that all of these traditional uses would be allowed in the monument.

Benally's words have galvanized a small but vocal group of Utah Navajos and Ute Mountain Utes who reject a national monument and embrace Representative Rob Bishop's Public Lands Initiative (PLI) as representing the product of a democratic process that honored all voices and strove for a compromise designed by and for local people. Much like many of their non-Native neighbors in San Juan County, they believe that the Bears Ears Inter-Tribal Coalition represents the interests of "outsiders" with little understanding of what the county's people want and need. They made their opposition known at the July 2016 public hearing in Bluff attended by Interior Secretary Sally Jewell and other federal officials when they interrupted the testimony of pro-monument speakers, including the president of the Navajo Nation, Russell Begaye, with loud jeers and boos.

In her September 14, 2016, testimony at a House Committee on Natural Resources hearing on the Public Lands Initiative, Benally stated that the "Bears Ears National Monument campaign is a cynical political stunt that, if successful, will deny grassroots Utah Navajos access to their sacred and spiritual grounds. Trusting the federal government, especially agencies within the Department of Interior, has not worked out well for the Navajo people. If history is our guide, we would be crazy to do so again and expect a different result. Two hundred years of broken promises should tell us all we need to know."[2]

---

2. Rebecca Benally's official testimony from House NRC hearing on PLI, September 14, 2016, http://democrats-naturalresources.house.gov/imo/media/doc/testimony_benally.pdf.

There needs to be a balance. We need tourism. If we have jobs in energy, they're very well paying jobs. This area will always be worth seeing and recreating in. So we can have the tourists, but we would like to be able to sustain ourselves economically with energy resources. In the fifties and sixties San Juan County was the second wealthiest county in the state. That's when all the buildings were built, that's the way to pay for things we all depend on.

—Merri Shumway, chair, San Juan County
School Board, January 28, 2016

The worst possible decisions are being made, capped off by the greatest dumb-ass move in the history of government in this state as far as I'm concerned: doubling down, tripling down on coal. It is a vicious boom-and-bust cycle that no one would want their children to experience. Even when it's at its optimum, it ain't working all that well.

That's where leadership comes in. That's where county commissioners, that is where governors, that is where state legislators come in and honestly and fairly explain to the public what the options are. Not just feedback and rhetoric and . . . fear. These are not inconsequential, not unsubstantiated fears. These are honest-to-goodness fears. They're losing their jobs. Their children are moving away because there's no opportunity. Things are drying up. I mean, there's ghost towns all over.

—Jim Dabakis (D–Salt Lake County), minority caucus
manager, Utah State Senate (2013–2018), June 6, 2016

The Navajo are the majority of citizens in San Juan County. You're going to have more BLM, Forest Service, Park Service employees to write a management plan, to do signage, interpretation, to build a visitor center . . . for a monument or conservation area. So I think there should be a preference for Native Americans when they develop this. . . . They've been economically disenfranchised by the federal government, no doubt about it. There is absolutely nothing wrong with the federal government using some of its powers to help enfranchise and help them and alleviate poverty in those nations. . . . So it's not just [that the tribes] do all the heavy lifting to get it designated, and then someone else makes the buck.

—Brian O'Donnell, former executive director,
Conservation Lands Foundation, July 27, 2015

Cattle grazing in a meadow in the Abajo Mountains

HEIDI REDD
Working Toward Compromise, Seeking Balance
Between Preservation and Development

Dugout Ranch is where the archetypal red rock country of the Southwest meets the iconic cowboy imagery of the Wild West. Nestled on fifty-two hundred acres near the Needles District of Canyonlands National Park, the ranch is surrounded by towering mesas. Lavender Canyon is nearby, named after David Lavender, a rancher turned writer who wrote prolifically about the American West and was known to stay at the ranch from time to time. Looming over the landscape are the Six Shooter Peaks, a pair of sandstone towers that resemble the pistols used by real-life and Hollywood cowboys of yore to enforce or evade the law.

Heidi Redd, with whom we're scheduled to meet on this gloriously clear October afternoon, is the longtime owner of Indian Creek Cattle Company, whose livestock graze both on Dugout Ranch, which she sold to the Nature Conservancy in 1997, and on more than 250,000 acres of Bureau of Land Management land that surrounds the ranch.

We have seen her photo in magazines and on "Heidi Redd: Democrat for State Senate" billboards that feature a headshot of Redd adjacent to a photo of her astride a horse, driving cattle. We just can't seem to find her on her own ranch.

While searching for Redd, we walk around the grounds and take in an idyllic scene: a crystal-clear creek meandering through a shady glen; cows grazing on lush, green grass beneath cottonwood trees; birds chirping and taking flight against the quintessentially southwestern red rock backdrop.

Weathered wooden stables, tool sheds, and homes for ranch hands, workers, and researchers extend for a good half mile from where we begin our search for Redd. We first peer into the windows of a small, wood-shingled

Heidi Redd at Dugout Ranch

building, then investigate a pair of modest cabins designed to house scientists who work at the ranch in partnership with the Nature Conservancy's Utah office.

After a time, we spot Redd bouncing along a dirt path in a golf cart, small dog in tow. With a smile and a friendly greeting, she invites us to hop on and then proceeds to drive us back to her house, a light-filled space with an expansive covered porch affording a panoramic view of grassland and mesas. The house is filled with classic western décor. A leather saddle sits atop a wooden saddletree just outside the kitchen, and an eclectic collection of wall art features subjects both cheeky and tasteful, ranging from coyotes in a variety of poses to cowboy hats of many vintages.

Redd looks the part of the western cowgirl: she is wiry, with tanned skin weathered from a lifetime of hard work in the intense sun of canyon country and her long silver hair wound into a tight braid that reaches her waist. A wide-brimmed white Stetson is positioned squarely atop her head, her light blue button-down shirt with white pearl snap buttons is tucked into dark-blue Wrangler jeans, and her real-deal cowboy boots are creased from wear. She projects the grit of John Wayne and the grace of Katharine Hepburn, mixing physical toughness with effortless composure and understated elegance.

She has called Dugout Ranch home for nearly half a century, moving there in 1967 with her then husband, Robert, a member of a Mormon family with deep roots in San Juan County. She relishes the ranching life; her vibrant blue eyes dance as she waxes poetic about her passion.

"[Ranching] isn't an easy occupation," Redd says. "If you don't love it, if you don't love being out there on a horse in the heat and the cold and all that goes with this, you won't do it."

As a longtime rancher and a well-known and respected local resident, she was asked by San Juan County Commission chairman Phil Lyman to serve on the San Juan County Public Lands Council he formed in early 2014 as part of the county's participation in Representative Rob Bishop's (R-UT) Public Lands Initiative. She accepted Lyman's invitation because she recognized an opportunity for the county to have a voice in policy decisions that could not only ameliorate long-standing disputes regarding public lands use but also shape the economic future of San Juan County.

"My first loyalty is to this land and how I'd like to see it protected," Redd says emphatically. "I also realize that if I want to play a role in future land decisions that are made, I have to be a team player, I have to build bridges. We need to get in the game, or all the touchdowns are going to be made by somebody else. This is our chance to be a part of it. There aren't many places like this left. We cannot squander [our opportunity].

"Every year there's always a threat to these undeveloped parts of nature, these places of beauty," she adds. "To get on top of that and make legislation . . . is very, very difficult."

Redd is credited with helping to move the lands council beyond abstract, sometimes ideological conversations to more substantive discussions, decisions, and compromises.

"I said, 'Do you think the county could get a great big map of each area we need to talk about, and we'll stand around the map, and then we'll vote on our ideas?'" Redd says. "And that's how we finally got to things."

She advocated for protection of some public lands while also allowing designation of other parcels for historically lucrative economic activities such as mining and oil and gas drilling. When she shared her rationale for supporting protection of some areas with her more conservative Mormon friends, they were suspicious.

"I went around to a lot of different people and [explained] what . . . I would like to see happen," Redd recalls. "At first they didn't want anything: 'This is our land; leave us alone.' But slowly, they started understanding.

"We've gone past the era that this is just your playground," she says. "Sadly, even I want to go back to fifty years ago, [but] that's not gonna happen."

In the end, Redd was satisfied with the work she and her fellow council members did to balance the needs and desires of a diverse group of stakeholders and to bring everyone to agreement that certain areas were significant enough to merit protection via congressional action.

Six Shooter Peaks, west of Dugout Ranch

"I was very pleased that we finally had enough trust in one another to say, 'All right, let's have wilderness,'" Redd says.

"It was our goal to try to protect areas that were scenic and beautiful, which all the county is, which is very hard!" she says. "And at the same time have areas [where] the county could pay its bills with [revenue from] mining."

Redd echoes a narrative we have heard from many San Juan County residents.

"I'm not a big fan of mining, but I recognize that this is a huge county, and you have to pay the bills," she says. "There's miles and miles of road and infrastructure to take care of, and it's always been done through mining. Mining built us our libraries in the sixties, built us our high school, built us our hospital. In the sixties San Juan County had the highest-paid schoolteachers in the state due to uranium. So there's always the double-edged sword about these things. I do know that the county has to have a way to pay its bills."

Another recurring theme is the promises and pitfalls of tourism as a means of creating jobs for locals and generating tax revenue for the county. Redd is dubious of the tourism-as-panacea argument.

"Tourist dollars come at a high price," Redd says. "If you look at the tourist businesses that pay [their employees] minimum wage, people act like that's a godsend. If you can get tourism, man, that saves everything. Well, it doesn't. It's very demanding on the land. You drive your car down here, you use gasoline, you stay in a motel, you use water. It just amazes me how environmental groups will go after cattle ranchers for a cow using water when they're probably staying in a motel using twice as much.

"Once you decide it's a park or a monument, you then advertise worldwide—'Come on in, the door is wide open,'" Redd says. "Part of the beauty here has always been that you could walk out and say to yourself, You know, I might be the first person to ever have seen this. But we're losing that. And the more activity you promote, the more you lose. Some of the most beautiful areas [in San Juan County]—the Bears Ears, Dark Canyon Plateau, Beef Basin, Cedar Mesa, which is just a treasure trove of antiquities—would absolutely lose [their] spiritual quality if it was wall-to-wall tourists like it is in Moab," an outdoor recreation mecca forty-five miles to the north. "So how do you say, 'You can be here and not here'? How do you keep it so that everybody in the United States, every person that wants to, doesn't come to these areas? To me, the answer's always been wilderness."

Once protected by an act of Congress, areas designated as wilderness can never be logged, mined, or traversed by motorized vehicles, with rare exceptions. While a national park, monument, or conservation area precludes residential and commercial development along with extractive industry activity, it will typically provide a visitor center, parking lots, paved hiking trails, and other highly visible footprints on the landscape.

Redd bristled when the BLM in 2010 built a parking lot to accommodate the ever-increasing crowd of rock climbers who scale a cliff adjacent to Dugout Ranch, and she has watched with unease as Highway 211, the paved road to the Needles District of Canyonlands National Park that passes by her home, grows busier every year. She shudders to think of the development that would accompany declaration of a monument and prefers a legislative approach like the PLI that could designate many of her treasured landscapes as wilderness.

Redd realizes that her stance may be unpopular with multiple-use advocates, including some members of the lands council.

"I think if more people could have [fewer] toys out here on the land and just enjoy the scenery, it'd be great," Redd says.

She laments the fact that Commissioner Phil Lyman undermined his own efforts at compromise with his May 2014 ATV protest ride into Recapture Canyon to draw attention to the BLM's closure of a road used by some locals for motorized recreation. From Redd's perspective, the ride was an act of rebellion that exemplified an unwillingness to put aside ideological principles in service of the broader goal of leading a multivoice dialogue that could have created an imperfect but livable outcome. Worse still, in Redd's view, Lyman inspired states' rights advocates across the West to join him, including members of the notorious Bundy family, whose proclivity for leading armed standoffs against the federal government has made them Sagebrush Rebel heroes and anti-environmentalist villains, depending on one's allegiances.

"I think [for] Phil, it was kind of a fluky idea," Redd says. "But then the press pushed him, and up until the very day of the ride he was trying to back out of it. But then the Bundys showed up . . . and said, 'Oh, no. You've gotten yourself this publicity, and now you can't just [back out].' I really think Phil recognizes in his heart what a blunder that was."

Nevertheless, the lands council continued its work and in June 2015 presented a plan to the county commissioners. Two months later, the commissioners forwarded an amended version of the plan to Bishop and Jason Chaffetz, the latter of whose district includes all of San Juan County.

"[Representative Bishop] has the onerous job of figuring out how he's going to give each stakeholder some reward," Redd says. "I would hate to have his job."

Despite her sympathy for Bishop's challenging task, she chastises him for allowing the county governments the option to withdraw from the process if they are unsatisfied with the ultimate legislative proposal. Redd joins a chorus of many PLI participants and outside observers who perceive this aspect of Bishop's strategy as fundamentally flawed.

"He's repeated time and time again, 'If at the end you decide this process isn't something you want to be a part of, you can pull out,'" Redd says. "Well, anyone can be a spoiled child and say, 'I didn't get anything!' So that is a real worry to me."

Regardless of the ultimate fate of the PLI, Redd believes that San Juan County citizens and their leaders need to envision a realistic plan for economic growth.

"We are not going to have the jobs in twenty years that we have now," Redd says. "They're going to be different jobs. I don't think that there's one kind of industry, whether it be tourism, mining, windmills, whatever. I think we do need tourism, but I don't think that should be the only egg in the basket or that we should exclude other possibilities. I think we have to diversify as much as we can and look for every possibility for new jobs and technology."

Redd doesn't believe that the county should focus its energies on courting large-scale employers from outside. Instead, she thinks it would do well to foster entrepreneurship among its current residents.

"Maybe we should stop looking for these industries that would employ one or two hundred [people] and start looking for little things that you could do yourself with the Internet," Redd says.

She mentions as an example a saddle maker in Monticello who produces handcrafted pieces for clients around the world, people who have come to know his work through successful promotion on his website. Redd thinks that with the right training and incentives, more San Juan County residents could do the same.

"I think it's going to take some very, very creative thinking to figure out how we're going to salvage this economy," Redd says.

She has engaged in some creative thinking of her own about how to keep her ranch solvent and sustainable in the face of a changing climate. From

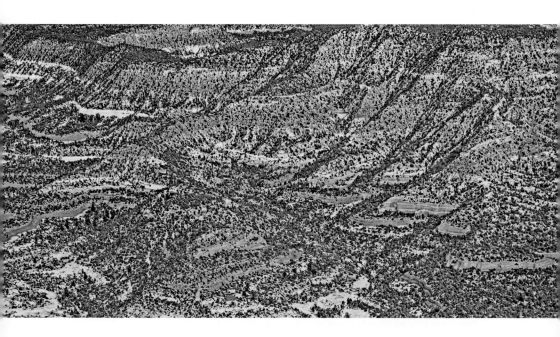

Posey Canyon (aerial image)

her perspective, the survival of both the cattle industry and the land that she loves depends on innovative approaches to land stewardship that rely on sound science and place-based research. Toward that end, she developed a partnership with The Nature Conservancy that has turned Dugout Ranch into a vast outdoor laboratory.

"In the early nineties, as I would be out cowboying I'd run into these researchers [and] scientists," Redd says, referring to the times she would check on livestock on BLM land surrounding Dugout Ranch. "They had their study plots, and I'd ride up and ask them what they were finding. I was kind of curious: How can . . . this research translate into something that would benefit ranchers?"

Redd learned that a host of researchers were carrying out a variety of studies independent of one another, and she saw the opportunity to coordinate their efforts and pool resources.

"Nobody knows what the other person's doing out there," Redd remembers thinking. "So we [at Dugout Ranch] would meet with the BLM and the Park Service, the Forest Service . . . for three or four years. We had a lot of good ideas, but it didn't really gel into what we wanted."

At the same time, Redd, her ex-husband, Robert, and her two sons, Matt and Adam, were faced with a dilemma precipitated by the couple's divorce: whether to sell or divide the ranch. Redd feared that if they did not negotiate a favorable arrangement in short order, developers could court investors to fund the building of subdivisions that would fragment the ranch and destroy the integrity of the landscape.

In 1995 Redd contacted the Nature Conservancy's Utah office to gauge the nonprofit's interest in purchasing Dugout Ranch to support research that would focus on helping ranchers develop strategies to manage their land in the warmer and drier world that climate scientists predict for the American Southwest. There was one caveat: Redd wanted reassurance that her property would remain whole and that she could stay there and continue to ranch.

In 1997 the nonprofit bought the ranch, and the fledgling Canyonlands Research Center began operations. For the past two decades Redd has continued to live in the main house and graze cattle both on a portion of the Dugout Ranch on which she holds a life estate and on land she leases from the BLM. Scientists conduct experiments from bases either on-site or in the towns nearest to the ranch.

One of the key programs initiated by the center's researchers involves a series of investigations aimed at understanding how both subtle and dramatic changes in climate patterns can affect grass and tree growth.

"Usually we have our spring rains and then our fall monsoons," Redd says. "What happens if that changes and we get our rain in the summertime? What grasses will survive? In the past few years, . . . instead of having both warm and cool season grasses, I have either/or. Not both."

"We have four thousand cottonwood trees that we've planted," Redd says. "One thousand from Arizona, one thousand from New Mexico, one thousand from Colorado, and one thousand from here. So which of those species, as climate changes, will be the healthiest and live?"

Redd hopes that in the future the Nature Conservancy will establish partnerships with other educational institutions in San Juan County such as the Four Corners School of Outdoor Education in Monticello and Utah State University in Blanding. In her view, such partnerships could help change the perception of many San Juan County residents that environmental organizations are unconcerned with their lives and hostile to their culture.

"What I'll tell you about the Nature Conservancy is that they respect communities," Redd says. "They respect that people have to make a living. They own this place, but they pay taxes. They wouldn't have to pay taxes on all this if they didn't want to. They try to work with the local communities." Unfortunately, she has seen some environmental groups do just the opposite.

"If you wonder why the local people dislike the SUWA [Southern Utah Wilderness Alliance] so much, if you've ever been to meetings where they demean the local people . . . it's disgusting," Redd says. "They could have had far more [wilderness] than they have right now had they come in here and treated the local people decently."

Redd is equally dismayed by the current animosity between many locals and BLM employees. She thinks the mentality fostered by the Sagebrush Rebellion has strengthened in recent years in part because many staff members at the BLM's Monticello field office are now choosing to live outside San Juan County, a change from two decades ago. She cites as examples BLM and Forest Service employees who work in Monticello but live in Moab and Cortez, Colorado, as opposed to Monticello, Blanding, or Bluff as they have in the past.

"This is one thing that I think is not good . . . for the BLM," Redd says. "If you aren't bumping into people in the grocery store and visiting, then you have this separateness, and you are the guy from out of town telling the guy in town what he can do. If I were the BLM director or [Interior Secretary] Sally Jewell, I would change that immediately."

In days past, Redd says, "A person would come in and spend their career here. They weren't job-hopping. Now they come in, they're there for [only] three or four years."

Some believe that the choice to live outside the communities where they work results from the harassment of BLM employees and families by Sage-brush Rebels. There have been reports of bomb threats at regional offices throughout the West, coupled with the still-vivid reminder of the January 2016 armed occupation of the Malheur National Wildlife Refuge in Burns, Oregon.

"I just keep thinking that a lot of these problems that are [caused by] people butting heads, it's because there isn't that sense of community anymore," Redd says.

"I've just seen so much strife, when really, working on the lands council . . ." she trails off, shaking her head. "Compromise. We all can't have exactly what we want. The dinner plate has to be split."

I think landscapes pick their protectors, and I think Dugout Ranch picked Heidi Redd. . . .

Right now there's multiple things going on, but two of the projects are being run out of Northern Arizona University. It's called the Cottonwood Gardens. They have picked three places to plant Fremont cottonwoods that have a variety of genotypes to see as we go into a warmer and drier future, which ones are going to be the best to survive. When we were thinking about doing the research center, Dr. Mark Miller with the [National] Park Service said to me, "You know, everything we learned about restoration we learned in a wet period. Now we're facing a dry period. We need to learn how to restore these landscapes in a drier period." So this Cottonwood Garden is going to really help people that are interested in restoring riparian areas to know what's going to be most successful into the future. Also [in] the same vein [the United States Geological Survey] is doing some work on grasslands. Which grasslands are going to be able to survive a hotter and drier climate?

As you know, climate models for this area really show the Southwest to be the bull's-eye for climate change.

—Sue Bellagamba, Canyonlands regional director,
The Nature Conservancy, April 29, 2016

They don't want to let go of what they've experienced in the past: mining and ranching and all those things. Now the new generation changed their mind—let go of that, let's go with tourism. It's worse! It's so much worse than ranching ever was.

I want wilderness designation. Not a national park. You [designate] a national park, they build more roads, more everything, you [lose] everything you want to protect. What is it that—what do people want? The land is still going to be there, blah, blah, but what is it that they really want? I want wilderness. I didn't want these national parks. [They attract] more people.

—Ken Sleight, environmental activist, wilderness guide,
and inspiration for Seldom Seen Smith in Edward Abbey's
The Monkey Wrench Gang, November 13, 2015

In truth there are some of the extremists in the environmental groups that don't want that [development based on tourism] either. But they won't say it. They don't want tourists there. They want it to stay this prim, proper, unexplored, complete wilderness, pristine place, and they don't want to do studies about tourism. They don't want to enhance the infrastructure. They don't want the hordes there. They see what's happening in the national parks, and they don't [like] that.

—Jim Dabakis (D–Salt Lake County), minority caucus
manager, Utah State Senate (2013–2018), June 6, 2016

San Juan River looking southeast toward Navajo Mountain

JOSH EWING

Building Bridges Between Diverse Groups;
Protecting Endangered Landscapes

Wiry and bespectacled, wearing a Patagonia fleece and rope sandals, Josh Ewing embraces a cup of coffee with both hands as he greets us at Bluff's venerable Twin Rocks Café. Despite the early hour, the executive director of Bluff-based nonprofit Friends of Cedar Mesa sports a five o'clock shadow, testimony to the long days he often spends advocating for protection of archaeological resources in southern San Juan County. As the caffeine begins to take effect, Ewing's eyes dart, and he becomes increasingly animated. A fast talker with an abundance of energy, Ewing is both politic and blunt, both cerebral and impassioned—in short, the ideal leader of an organization that prides itself as being collaborative but isn't afraid to take a stand against politicians with opposing views on land stewardship.

Somewhere between moving to Bluff in 2012 and our April 2016 meeting, Josh Ewing became a key conservationist voice in the Bears Ears battle.

Ewing grew up on his family's ranch in Nebraska, where he learned firsthand the grueling work required to care for livestock and land and the challenges of keeping an agricultural business healthy and sustainable. His personal experience allows him to speak and understand the language of ranchers in San Juan County. Even though the climate and terrain are vastly different from the midwestern plains of his childhood, many of the economic and cultural issues are the same.

After graduating from the University of Pennsylvania, Ewing eventually moved to Salt Lake City, drawn by his passion for rock climbing. Ewing admits that he "didn't really know much about Salt Lake, other than I'd read in climbing magazines [that] there's decent climbing there. A career where there was some climbing is what I was looking for."

Josh Ewing, executive director of Friends of Cedar Mesa, at an Ancestral Puebloan ruin (courtesy of Josh Ewing)

He landed a job as communications director for the Salt Lake City mayor's office and instantly was immersed in the world of high-level public relations. Ewing worked on the city's 2002 Olympics planning committee and later became involved with a variety of environmental and conservation projects.

Following an unsuccessful run for the Utah state legislature and a decade-long life in politics and public relations, Ewing came to the realization that the passion he'd moved west to satisfy was missing—or, rather, it lay several hundred miles south in the red rock country of southeastern Utah. In 2012 he moved to San Juan County with his partner, Kirsten, to live in a landscape they loved and had been visiting for years. Kirsten found work at a school in Monument Valley on the Navajo Reservation; Josh cobbled together consulting gigs, hoping to avoid the burnout from his fast-paced city life and "work twenty hours a week and adventure eighty hours a week."

During his climbing sojourns into the canyons of Cedar Mesa, Ewing became fascinated by the ubiquitous Ancestral Puebloan ruins and other indications of civilizations past. He quickly learned that such sites and artifacts were threatened by looters, antigovernment activists, and well-meaning but uninformed visitors who unwittingly did irrevocable harm to thousand-year-old structures.

"I [wanted] to have an impact," he says.

He started volunteering with Friends of Cedar Mesa, a nonprofit formed in 2011 by former Bureau of Land Management employee and river guide Mark Meloy. The mission of the organization is to "effect good stewardship that protects the natural and cultural integrity of public lands in San Juan County, Utah." The nonprofit's leadership recognized Ewing's passion for protecting cultural resources and his experience as a public spokesman and communications strategist and recruited him to be its executive director. Ewing evaded their entreaties for several months.

"I had no desire to be running nonprofits," he says. "I made the excuse, 'Look, I don't have any interest in trying to raise my next paycheck.' That was my big mistake." Friends found a donor that funded his salary, calling Ewing's bluff. By January 2014 he was heading up Friends of Cedar Mesa.

As he dove into his work, building Friends a robust website and raising money for on-the-ground activities, he began to foster relationships with members of the Pueblo tribes in Arizona and New Mexico who recognized their cultural connection to sites on Comb Ridge and Cedar Mesa. Over time they became invested in working with Friends in advocating for protection of ancestral sites.

"Pueblo people are very passionate about where their ancestors came from," Ewing says. "When you have a connection to the land that's far deeper than a white guy like me has . . . it's so much [more] than, 'I want to go hiking here.'"

Ewing became involved with Representative Rob Bishop's Public Lands Initiative (PLI) and in 2014 was invited by San Juan County commissioner Phil Lyman to serve as a member of his newly formed Public Lands Council alongside Friends board chair Vaughn Hadenfeldt. The council, comprised of stakeholders from the recreation industry, longtime ranchers, extractive industry representatives, and a representative from the Navajo tribe, was tasked with developing a land-use proposal that the county would submit to Bishop, who would then integrate it along with proposals from seven other eastern Utah counties into a congressional bill.

The first few meetings were devoted to moving council members past their entrenched differences about how San Juan County's public lands should be managed. Some expressed harsh views about the role of the federal government in their lives. Some favored the status quo, with the federal government providing minimal protection and regulation. Others favored opening public lands to energy development and extractive industries, while still others sought protection of both landscapes and Native ancestral sites via wilderness designation or declaration of a national conservation area or national monument. Long-standing cultural and ideological disagreements surfaced. Members of the Native-led nonprofit Utah Diné Bikéyah (UDB) soon came to believe that their voices had not been heard, and Mark Maryboy, UDB's cofounder and Navajo Nation representative on the lands

Josh Ewing rock climbing in Bears Ears country (courtesy of Mikey Schaefer)

council, stopped attending meetings. Gradually, the remaining members of the lands council came to an understanding of one another's perspectives and discovered a surprising amount of common ground.

"A big part of this [process] is just getting the same people in the same room," Ewing says. "You can agree on a lot, but if you don't meet together often and don't normally talk eye-to-eye, you'll never know that you'd agree."

Ewing is credited with helping advance compromises that would both protect certain areas that everyone agreed deserved protection, such as Cedar Mesa, and allow for more traditional uses like ranching to continue in others. The lands council developed three alternatives, each of which designated some level of protection for selected land parcels, outlined possible "energy zones" where oil and gas drilling and mining could begin or continue, and indicated areas where livestock grazing could continue. The council also delved into the contentious issue of what constitutes a road on public land and how many roads should be open to residents and visitors.

Ewing felt that the lands council could craft a proposal with the potential for lasting change; indeed, the official proposal forwarded by the San Juan County Commission to Bishop in August 2015 was based in considerable measure on input from the lands council and proposed far more protection via specified national conservation and wilderness areas than many stakeholders and observers thought possible. However, the proposal, which was modified somewhat by the county commission before it was submitted to Bishop, also included language that would prevent future presidents from designating national monuments in San Juan County using the Antiquities Act—"despite the fact that the cultural resources in San Juan County are exactly the types of antiquities the Act was created to protect," Friends noted on its blog in August 2015.

By the time San Juan County submitted its proposal to Bishop, one county—Daggett, roughly 350 miles north of San Juan—had withdrawn from the process. In the fall of 2014 Daggett County was the first to provide Bishop with a proposal, but a newly elected slate of conservative politicians rescinded the proposal after being sworn into office. Bishop and his staff issued a draft bill in January 2016 based on the proposals from the seven remaining counties. Ewing and others in the environmental community ultimately concluded that the Bishop draft failed to protect a large number of culturally significant sites and created "energy zones" reserved for oil and gas drilling that were far more extensive than those proposed by the lands council, thereby putting cultural resources at risk.

During our April 2016 conversation, Ewing still held out hope for a legislative solution—"There's so much more you can accomplish through legislation and so much less controversy"—but shortly after Bishop introduced a new version of his bill in mid-July, Friends issued a statement saying it could not support the bill as written. The nonprofit noted its willingness to compromise and stay at the negotiating table after many environmental organizations declined further participation, and it lamented the failure of the legislative process, which "could have been and should have been the best solution" to protecting Cedar Mesa and the Bears Ears landscape.

The same week that Bishop's second draft was released, Interior Secretary Sally Jewell visited San Juan County along with key representatives from the BLM, the U.S. Forest Service, and the National Park Service. Their goal was to hear voices from local communities and tribal leaders on both sides of the PLI versus monument debate. Ewing and Hadenfeldt accompanied Jewell on a hike on Cedar Mesa, visiting some of the area's most striking and threatened cultural resources and explaining their cultural and archaeological significance.

In October 2016 Friends threw its unequivocal support behind the proposal advanced by the Bears Ears Inter-Tribal Coalition to create a national monument, feeling that a monument was the only viable option for protecting archaeological sites, absent last-minute major changes to the PLI legislation.

Though the Friends board and staff joined a large chorus of grassroots citizens, prominent environmental organizations, and celebrities in advocating for a national monument, their decision was not made without significant ambivalence.

"Even if there is a monument [declaration], there's not going to be a plan for the monument for five to ten years," Ewing notes. "Something in the meantime has to happen. We've kind of publicized the heck out of this [area] to show people that it's of international quality and needs to be protected. But that's resulted in even more people coming to visit without any resources or any plans [for protecting the land]. It's a really big problem."

In response to the likely prospect of increasing numbers of visitors, Friends has sought partners among government agencies and citizens to help protect archaeological sites until a firm management plan and adequate resources are in place. As a first step, Ewing and Friends have started to work with the BLM both to offer rewards to individuals who provide information that leads to prosecution of vandals and grave robbers and to develop initiatives aimed at educating tourists to "visit with respect." Marcia Simonis, a Friends board member, was the nonprofit's first site stewardship coordinator and focuses on developing visitor education programs in conjunction with the BLM. (Simonis's husband, Don, works as an archaeologist with the BLM's Monticello field office; read his story on p. 215.)

But partnering with federal agencies comes with its own baggage—many locals' strong antigovernment sentiments. This could make the bridge building Ewing champions far more difficult.

The challenge of finding common ground in the context of uneasy relationships—between locals and government, and locals and tribes—speaks to what Ewing calls "a hundred-year emotional issue": the deeply entrenched cultural beliefs and values that keep San Juan County, and the town of Blanding in particular, from acknowledging, if not embracing, the idea of a prosperous future that looks different from the past.

"There's endless entrepreneurial opportunity around here, and there's plenty of resources for people," Ewing says.

Evidence provided in recent studies by the nonpartisan think tank Headwaters Economics seems to confirm his optimism. Headwaters, whose research focuses on economic development and the value of public lands, concluded that in most cases, a national monument declaration can produce steady growth as tourism replaces ranching and mining as a primary economic base.

But Ewing notes, "The reality is, you're not going to have a successful tourism economy in a town (such as Blanding) that you can't even buy a 3.2 percent beer in. It's a cultural thing." (Devout members of the LDS Church, in accordance with their religious teachings, do not drink alcohol.) "As soon as you start . . . changing the rules and allowing a brew pub to open, that changes the demographics and the makeup of the town, and I don't get the sense that's what the town wants. They want it to stay the way it is."

In that sense, the conservationists in Bluff and the religious conservatives in Blanding have something in common: many long-term Bluff residents don't want to see their world change either.

"People who want to keep it the way it was thirty-five years ago . . . are the people who see where it's going and want to at least try to keep it the way it is now," Ewing says. "This whole Bears Ears thing has the potential to really change our town in a way that a lot of us moved here to avoid."

Where can conservationists championing a monument and defenders of traditional economies find common ground? Ewing sees an opening for collaboration through preservation of shared heritage. He describes a first step along this path: working with Blanding resident Kay Shumway to preserve his family's hundred-year-old cabin in lower Recapture Canyon.

"It's that anti–federal government thing that we kind of disagree on," Ewing says. "But . . . people working together bridges gaps. We may never agree on certain things, but we can agree to work on others."

Such connections and mutual trust must be established over time, an effort that requires patience and a commitment to the often-thankless work of achieving compromise among people with strikingly different worldviews and values.

"This is a generational-type change, not a five-year-type change," Ewing says. "In fifteen years Blanding will go, 'Holy cow, the sky didn't fall when that Bears Ears monument happened, our economy's done great.' . . . But before that time, there's just so many generational, philosophical, political, demographic things that come into play that if people think one way or another some dramatic change is going to happen . . . [it's] probably not."

(As it turned out, Bears Ears National Monument was established in December 2016 by former president Barack Obama but was reduced in acreage by 85 percent as part of President Donald J. Trump's proclamations slashing the boundaries of both Bears Ears and Grand Staircase–Escalante National Monuments. Within the 15 percent of land that remained from Obama's monument, Trump established two noncontiguous units, Shash Jáa and Indian Creek. See map on p. 329.)

What made the lands council meetings work as well as [they] did in the end is I'm a tree-huggin', long-haired whatever, [but] both Josh and I were born on farms and ranches. I grew up hunting, I got a closet full of guns. . . . I can easily talk [that] lingo all day long. And that doesn't hurt. A lot of the environmentalists that I've worked with don't have any of that. But these aren't local lands; we all own these places. [Locals] really shouldn't have so much say about it that you nix out everyone else. And that's what I'm worried about with this Native American proposal, kind of adding another thing like that on top. So you've got the local thing, then you've got the Native American thing, and you know, I'm just hearing more and more people get concerned about, what is that going to do to what I want to do here?

—Vaughn Hadenfeldt, founder/owner, Far Out Expeditions,
and board chair, Friends of Cedar Mesa, October 27, 2015

It was going pretty good. We went [into the lands council] . . . everybody's not trusting the other guy. By the end, we were all buddies. There were a few things we didn't agree on, but . . . we liked each other, we kind of tried to see the other side, "maybe you oughta take this, we oughta preserve that. . . ."

Then toward the end, some of the tribes started coming, unofficially . . . and they'd spend half an hour, each of them talking. They were being used, I thought, by environmental groups and lawyers. One of them was sitting there, telling him what to say, directing him. Finally, after about two hours . . . I got up and left, and I say, "It's hijacked now. Who's gonna listen to me when you've got a tribe?"

—Shane Shumway, rancher, Blanding, Utah,
and member of the San Juan County Public
Lands Council (2014–15), January 28, 2016

It actually got a little scary for me for a while when I realized how much I liked some of the SUWA [Southern Utah Wilderness Alliance] staff, you know, people that I thought were just so diametrically opposed to my beliefs. But you spend a couple days with them on the road, and you find out that they're just like you, and they have families and interests and hobbies and passions, and you like them. And so . . . I think that there's been a lot of bridge building and relationship building over the past several years, and I just don't know where that goes if things play out how I think they probably will.

—Cody Stewart, staff director, House Natural Resources
Committee, former director of Federal Affairs, and
former policy and energy advisor to Utah
governor Gary Herbert, October 13, 2016

Lockhart Basin from Needles Overlook

BRUCE ADAMS
Representing Rural Utahns, Championing Local Land-Use Solutions

Paint a mental portrait of a cowboy. Weathered, leathered skin. Boots, Wranglers, and a button-down shirt. A laconic and stoic disposition. Looks like he belongs on a horse—in fact, he looks like he'd *rather* be on a horse instead of confined to a conference room in a county courthouse. Combine these features and add a soft voice and a science-teacher sensibility, and you have Bruce Adams, fourth-generation rancher, retired educator, proud Mormon pioneer descendant, and, for over a decade, one of San Juan County's three commissioners.

Adams has a background similar to that of many county residents. His family tree includes members of the legendary Hole-in-the-Rock expedition and other early settlers; he was born in Monticello and raised in San Juan County; he belongs to a large Mormon family (including six children, twenty-four grandchildren, and countless cousins); and he has long been active in civic life, serving on the Monticello City Council and the county's Economic Development Committee. As a rancher and a politician, Adams knows intimately the rules and regulations of the Bureau of Land Management, the technical definitions of wilderness and multiple use, and how the laws of the land impact local people economically, culturally, and spiritually.

In 2010 Adams participated in the effort by the late Senator Robert Bennett to devise a stakeholder-driven compromise to long-standing land-use issues in the county. He recalls traveling with representatives from the Wilderness Society to lands they proposed setting aside for protection. Bennett was attempting to replicate in San Juan County what had been a successful multistakeholder process in southwestern Utah's Washington County. There, a diverse group of citizens developed a plan for balancing development and conservation in one of the United States' fastest-growing areas.

San Juan County commissioner Bruce Adams (courtesy of San Juan County)

"People are pretty attached to extractive industries, because extraction has been the way that the people in this county have been able to survive here," Adams says during an October 2015 interview at the San Juan County courthouse in Monticello. "People in this area who live here really have not wanted to designate any part of the county as wilderness."

But while he preferred that not all of the county's public lands receive wilderness designation, Adams recognized that there was a need for protection both for the natural landscape and for the Native American and Mormon ancestral sites that are an integral part of the county's history.

"I wanted to be involved at some level in helping decide how [land] protection would come to pass," Adams says. "After the Bennett process fell apart, I thought [the Public Lands Initiative] was a good opportunity for the county to engage on a grassroots level . . . with [Utah congressmen] Rob Bishop and Jason Chaffetz and see if we couldn't come up with a way that the local people could be involved.

"Citizens who live here had never come up with a proposal [for public land use]," Adams says. "And that to me was a great need. We left the door open for a proposal to be accepted by Congress with us having nothing to do with that proposal. I thought, well, we can't let that happen. We, the people of San Juan County, need to make a decision, need to come up with something. And believe me, it was not well accepted by citizens," says Adams, laughing as he shakes his head. "They wanted status quo, they wanted no change."

Only 8 percent of the land in San Juan County is privately owned.[1] Many residents of the county fear that changes to land-use policies will eliminate any possibility of future extractive industry jobs, which many see as the county's best opportunity for a more prosperous future. In the collective memories of San Juan County residents, the 1950s and 1960s are recalled as glory days. In those years, money from mining helped build hospitals and schools and provided high-paying jobs for rural residents who otherwise would have eked out a living on the land or might have left the county to seek more lucrative work elsewhere. Even as mining activity has slowed dramatically and oil and gas prove less lucrative, there are still those in southeastern Utah who hold out hope that an economy based on extractive industries may once again fill county coffers.

Adams shares their hopes and concerns.

"We're stuck here trying to make a living, and a layer of designation that is put on public land here diminishes the ability of us to survive," he says.

In early 2014 Adams's fellow commissioner, Phil Lyman, formed the San Juan County Public Lands Council, a group comprised of a diverse array of stakeholders tasked with developing a plan for the county's public lands that would be submitted to Bishop for inclusion in his larger PLI bill, an ambitious attempt at land-use compromise.

Adams feels the proposal the lands council agreed upon after nearly eighteen months of meeting and mapping struck a healthy balance between preservation, recreation, and energy development. From his point of view, there was just one problem.

"An environmental group"—he declines to identify the specific organization—"got itself too attached to a group of Native Americans calling itself [Utah] Diné Bikéyah," Adams says. "And in my opinion, that environmental group polluted the process with their own agenda . . . and convinced [a] group of Navajos that their agenda was the *right* agenda."

His view is shared by some with close knowledge of the PLI process and dismissed by those who have worked with and supported the tribes for years.

Adams felt blindsided when Utah Diné Bikéyah ultimately announced their withdrawal from the lands council process.

"We've *always* wanted to include the Navajo people," Adams says. "We absolutely wanted to listen to them."

---

1. "San Juan County Resource Assessment."

But at a certain point, he felt the areas of disagreement created a divide that was impossible to bridge—a view shared by UDB, though its board and staff reached very different conclusions regarding what was responsible for the divide.

Nonetheless, Adams is proud of the proposal the lands council submitted to the Utah delegation and feels it reflects the interests and input of the stakeholders who chose to participate in the process.

"It's the citizens' proposal," Adams says. "It's not the three county commissioners' proposal."

"We have gone through a very arduous process, and we represent those citizens who are on the ground in this county," Adams says. "That's not discounting the fact that citizens outside the county and the state, citizens of the United States, want to have a say in what everybody views as public land. . . . But I'm hopeful that they will weigh our citizens' proposal [more heavily] than they will somebody who was making a proposal [from outside the county]."

Bishop released an initial draft of the PLI in January 2016. It included a partner bill that exempted application of the Antiquities Act to public lands in eastern Utah, in effect preventing declaration of a national monument via executive action. Adams, his fellow commissioners, and many of the state's rural citizens and politicians applauded Bishop's attempt to preclude use of the Antiquities Act. However, it immediately came under heavy criticism by environmental groups, as well as by the Bears Ears Inter-Tribal Coalition, which in October 2015 submitted its proposal for a national monument to the Obama administration.

Unlike others in San Juan County, Adams seemed less agitated by the opposition of the tribes and the environmental community. When we spoke with him again just after Bishop released his initial bill, the realist in Adams seemed resigned to the possibility that in the end, local input may have minimal impact on the outcome of the public lands debate. He viewed a national monument as the likely outcome but believes monument boosters will be sorely disappointed.

"The national monument is not going to give people what they think it is," Adams says. "Especially Native American people, who have been told that the president will make special concessions to them to gather wood, to do their ceremonial things, to gather herbs. I don't see the president using his executive powers just to do that for one group of individuals. It's too

Bruce Adams herding cattle on his ranch (courtesy of Bruce Adams)

discriminatory to everyone else. There are a hundred groups of other individuals who would want special considerations."

Adams points to a place that many Utahns consider a poster child for the pitfalls of national monuments created by presidential proclamation.

"We have the Grand Staircase–Escalante [National Monument] over in Garfield County, right next to us," Adams says. "And the county commissioners are telling us that it's had a pretty negative effect on their economy, so much so that they're looking at closing a school in Escalante."

The anecdotal views from Garfield County commissioners seem at odds with analysis from a 2017 study by the nonpartisan think tank Headwaters Economics. Their data suggest that the communities in Garfield and Kane Counties surrounding the monument have experienced strong economic growth since the monument was established in 1996, with a real per capita income growth of 17 percent.[2]

Regardless, the message that the Grand Staircase experience represents a cautionary tale of what can happen when a national monument is declared is widely believed in San Juan County.

---

2. "The Economic Importance."

No matter what comes to pass, Adams sees the need for an economic plan that looks beyond mineral extraction and oil and gas development and toward new sources of revenue. The creation of this plan will require county leaders and residents to acknowledge the inevitability of tourism as the main economic driver.

Investment in infrastructure projects such as the Latigo Wind Park, which began operation in Monticello in the fall of 2015, can be another part of the plan. Adams is proud of his role in bringing about the wind park, which was the culmination of a fourteen-year joint effort by county leaders and *San Juan Record* publisher Bill Boyle. A robust economic future in the county will also require a commitment from county leadership to adopt and enact a coherent economic plan. Adams's experience in the trenches suggests it will be a tough job.

"We haven't been that judicious at planning for the future," Adams admits. "For me as a commissioner, I've been jumping from one fire to the next the past eleven years. You just have a hard time catching your breath and saying, 'What are the things that we should be doing, looking to the future?'"

While a lack of time and resources for planning represents a major impediment to designing a sustainable economic model for San Juan County, Adams suggests that the largest barrier to change may well be the citizens themselves.

"There's a reluctance on the part of the commission to do anything," Adams says. "Just leave it alone so we don't get blamed."

Despite this seeming pessimism, Adams sees the potential for entrepreneurs to start profitable businesses linked to the tourism-based economy that he sees as a key part of the county's future. That could inject new life into the area and perhaps stem the exodus of young people leaving the county in pursuit of education and career opportunities.

"Most people who live in San Juan County don't live here because they make big money," Adams says. "They live here for other reasons. So somebody that wants to live here and make enough money to make a living and enjoy the vastness of San Juan County, they'll figure out a way to do it. But nobody will come here to make a million."

We're very much old cowboy West. We may be the last giant pocket of it in America. In southern Utah we're talking about the biggest tract of land without roads in America, exclusive of Alaska. There is this kind of pioneer independence. There's kind of a direct descendancy from those Mormon pioneers right to where they are. Their belief is that [the land] is theirs.

—Jim Dabakis (D–Salt Lake County), minority caucus
manager, Utah State Senate (2013–2018), June 6, 2016

We just need access to the land. We just need it for jobs and energy and way of life. Any place that is worth living has access to the land. . . . [When] it's privately owned . . . it can sustain itself. And here, the public lands, if there's true multiple land use, then it would be able to sustain that kind of living.

—Merri Shumway, member and former chair,
San Juan County School Board, January 28, 2016

The county recognizes that tourism is . . . part of our portfolio. We want to diversify. Even though minerals and energy have been the biggest tax base for revenue for the economy, that can be a boom-bust economy, too. So the county just wants to keep all options open. . . . Now let's say Cedar Mesa was either a monument or an NCA. It does not have a high-known energy and mineral potential. It has a high concentration of cultural resources, antiquities, and the recreation that's associated with that. It's got some good livestock grazing. It's also a source of fuel wood, primarily for Native Americans. And it's just an area people want to explore, whether on trails that are within the area or on foot. Those are the things that Cedar Mesa might have, and that's the reason both the county and the lands council agreed, yeah, let's make it a national monument, we can live with that.

—Nick Sandberg, public lands coordinator,
San Juan County, November 9, 2015

View from the Moki Dugway at sunset

BILL BOYLE

Providing San Juan County with Balanced News,
Guiding the County Toward a New Future

On a frigid January morning in Monticello, Utah, *San Juan Record* publisher Bill Boyle's blood is boiling. Seated at his desk in the newspaper's office, the short, bespectacled editor in chief launches into a full-throated takedown of the latest development in the Public Lands Initiative saga.

"The PLI was just released this morning, and every [environmental organization] had their prepackaged press releases ready to discount a remarkable effort to bring everyone to the table, give everybody a voice, and give everybody an opportunity to have input into this," Boyle says. "And it pisses me off beyond my ability to express. They didn't even have time to read it." He pounds the table with his left fist.

Years in the making, Representative Rob Bishop's (R-UT) PLI was supposed to bring certainty and resolution to long-standing land-use conflicts in Utah by giving local stakeholders in eight counties the chance to develop their own plans for how best to use and protect public lands.

Many in San Juan County view the PLI as a success. Many others, however, see the bill as a disaster for the environment, filled with giveaways to the oil and gas industry and to the motorized recreation community.

Boyle sees the immediate condemnation of the PLI by environmentalists and Native Americans and their intent to abandon the process completely in favor of a national monument designation as antithetical to the democratic process.

"A unilateral designation . . . that's not democracy! That's not the way a government works!" Boyle exclaims. "That's going to be done in a back room by a bunch of people who don't know the details and don't care about the details."

Bill Boyle in his office at the *San Juan Record*

To Boyle, the reactionary messaging by conservationists and tribes is reminiscent of past efforts when diverse stakeholders came together to forge a compromise—only to have a carefully constructed plan overridden by powerful environmental groups. In his view, should the monument proposal succeed, it could spell the end of tenuous cooperative efforts among county residents holding widely divergent views on land use.

"I gained a tremendous amount of respect during the PLI process for people who were hard-liners, who compromised, who did an admirable thing," Boyle says. "But as they come out of this process, hell no, they're never going to compromise again."

His allegiance to the wisdom of local people in San Juan County working together for the common good springs from his deep roots in the region.

"My tie to this land goes way back, to the earliest days," he says.

Born and raised in Monticello, Boyle grew up with stories of his great-grandfather, one of the original Mormon settlers and the first mayor of the town. His father was both chairman of the San Juan County Democratic Party and a county commissioner in the 1970s, serving alongside Calvin Black—the same Calvin Black whose antigovernment fervor and anti-environmentalist capers earned him the moniker "Father of the Sagebrush Rebellion."

In southeastern Utah, where everyone is a legend, or knows someone who is, it can sometimes be difficult to discern where fiction ends and fact begins.

After high school, Boyle moved north to attend Snow College in Ephraim, Utah, where he studied before serving a two-year LDS Church mission in South Dakota. He spent significant time on the Sioux Reservation, a transition eased somewhat by his experiences growing up in a county where half the population is Native American.

George Adams, Bill Boyle's great-grandfather, first mayor of Monticello, Utah (courtesy of San Juan County Historical Archive)

"Native American interaction and cooperation and development is a part of who I am," he says.

Following his mission, Boyle completed his schooling at Brigham Young University. But his most formative college experiences took him far from the Provo, Utah, campus to Jerusalem, where he worked for BYU's Middle East program, helping to establish and develop a study-abroad program. He found himself immersed in a region that witnesses ongoing tumultuous political struggles.

"Forget western land issues. *That* is [a region] with entrenched issues!" he says.

During his time in the Middle East, Boyle gained "an intense love and feel for people on all sides of the spectrum," a view that informs his perspective on public lands issues in Utah and provides insight into his desire to bring contending factions together to achieve compromise.

After returning to U.S. soil, Boyle earned an MBA at Stanford Business School and then moved to Seattle with his wife, Lynda, and worked for a bank. But he felt a call to come home and in 1994 moved back to Monticello with his then small family, which has now grown to include five children. He bought the *Record* with the goal of injecting positivity and pride into his community. As he puts it, "I want to be upbuilding, I want to help people, I want to help this county be what it wants to be."

Housed in a small building near the center of Monticello, the *Record* shares the building with a bookshop that provides an extensive collection of local and Mormon literature, both popular and scholarly. Boyle and his staff move among towering stacks of paper, filing cabinets, and copies of recent issues. Navigating to his office requires moving carefully among the stacks.

San Juan Record building in Monticello, Utah

The *Record* itself is the main source of the county's news and provides a fascinating reflection of the county psyche as manifest in passionate letters to the editor and feisty op-eds from engaged locals. Discussions of land use and notices of upcoming events mingle with full-page features on high-school football teams and down-home recipes from loyal readers.

Since returning to his hometown, Boyle has focused not only on the *Record* but also on developing a vision for San Juan County. In his view, the county has the potential to transform itself into an economically prosperous and highly desirable place to live, an area that attracts private investment, talented entrepreneurs, and young people who, like him, grew up in San Juan County and left the area to seek an education but want to return home to raise their families.

Working with a small committee alongside county commissioner Bruce Adams, Boyle has spent the past fourteen years promoting two major projects: a wind farm and a center for hands-on, place-based education.

The Latigo Wind Park and Canyon Country Discovery Center, both of which are located in Monticello and opened in the fall of 2015, have (as of 2016) brought in a combined $140 million in private investment, created nearly thirty new jobs, and have the potential to bring significant, ongoing tax revenues and tourism dollars to the state's poorest county.

"[These projects] have seeded the entire community with positive things and have helped restructure who we are and what we're all about," Boyle says animatedly.

But while many locals support both projects, some longtime residents view the new projects with skepticism and even outright scorn, casting both as favoring and furthering an environmental agenda.

"This is the western creed of the highest possible use of their land!" says Boyle about the wind farm project. "Extractive industries are not well, the uranium industry's in the tanks, you [can] hardly get anything out of copper, and ranching and farming continue to struggle. Here's a $125 million infrastructure project that will help educate kids, and feed senior citizens, and pave some roads, and pay the secretary to lick stamps at the courthouse. How is this a bad thing?"

The Canyon Country Discovery Center is a particular source of pride for Boyle. Run by the Four Corners School of Outdoor Education, the center is a place where students and teachers from schools across the Colorado Plateau and visitors to the region can learn about the natural and cultural landscapes of southeastern Utah through hands-on exhibits and activities.

As Boyle sees it, "The [center] is one piece of the puzzle" of economic development in San Juan County.

"[We can] stop some of the traffic coming through with a pretty good message—a message of education, of wonder, of appreciation for what we've got here, not to just show it off, but educate people on what it's all about," says Boyle. "It creates jobs, it builds infrastructure, it increases education. That's pretty good economic development . . . if it works."

Boyle sees the center and the wind farm as first steps toward improving county infrastructure—from increasing cell phone coverage, bringing high-speed Internet to remote parts of the county, to perhaps even providing reliable airline service. All would increase the chances for county economic growth based on a far more diverse range of economic activity.

Boyle's vision and hope for the county's prosperity—economic, cultural, and otherwise—are challenged by a seemingly insurmountable obstacle: the entrenched feelings local residents have toward the federal government, feelings that breed resentment and that threaten to erupt with as much fervor as the hostile takeover by the Bundy family of the Malheur National Wildlife Refuge in Burns, Oregon, in January 2016.

"How they want to deal with that"—through standoffs and destruction of government property—"is just so counterproductive," Boyle says. "You damage your cause, and you strengthen the other side when you pursue extreme ideology."

In fact, the situation on the ground in San Juan County is still tense years after the FBI raided the homes of Blanding residents targeted in a Native American artifacts trafficking sting in 2009. The residual fear and anger make it difficult, if not impossible, to accept any federal efforts to effect change with respect to public lands in the county.

"Blanding has again and again been in the crosshairs," Boyle says, "and I think the federal government is looking to send messages to communities throughout the West that it's not okay to plunder an archaeological heritage"—a message he feels the community needs to acknowledge.

But Boyle thinks that there may be a path toward reconciliation.

"There is a portion of the culture that looks the other way or winks at the plunder of archaeological treasure, which is entirely unacceptable," Boyle says. "Blanding ought to stand up and say, 'We agree, there are difficulties here, and we have to stop it.' And guess what: the federal government will turn their attention somewhere else."

Boyle, champion of compromise, holds little hope of hearing words of reconciliation from either federal agencies or local citizens in this politically polarized climate. He worries as well that a national monument declaration will once again inflame long-held antipathy. Then again, he notes, the real San Juan County is much more complex than the loudest voices that fill the papers might suggest.

"An outsider will come in, and there's a supposition that [San Juan County] is a monolith," Boyle says. "They think you can carve a single San Juan County resident and replicate him fourteen thousand times. But there's pretty remarkable diversity, I think. A broad spectrum of views."

The history of the public lands fight for many years has been very, very akin to World War I fighting styles. It just struck me at the time, and it continues to be something I keep in the back of my mind as I see how people literally get back in their trenches and just start lobbing bombs at each other. There's this vast no-man's-land in between that—we just kind of stop talking and really engaging, and it's sad, and I'm afraid we're on the verge of doing that again.

Overall, I think Utah's done a pretty good job, but the rural economies haven't kept pace, and it's sometimes harder for them to do that. But in order for it to work, it's got to be something where the people on the ground, multi-generational families, recognize, "In order to preserve our way of life, we want to diversify, and here are ways that would make sense." If that's how it's approached, and that's how they feel about it, you can move forward. But if they feel like it's forced or crammed down their throat, and they were not involved in the discussion about how and why, I think sometimes they're reluctant to really dive in and accept that premise.

—Cody Stewart, staff director, House Natural Resources Committee, former director of Federal Affairs, and former policy and energy advisor to Utah governor Gary Herbert, October 13, 2016

In Monticello, there's a lot of anger. [The PLI hearing] felt different than other public lands hearings because people were really angry. These are people who aren't doing well economically, and this is giving them a chance to show up and express their anger. Many people [said], "*You're* rich and have . . . land, but our kids can't afford to buy a house." There are no jobs for kids with high school degrees. There's a lot of anger that I think is what we're seeing in the public lands arena. It feels misplaced.

—Scott Groene, executive director, Southern Utah Wilderness Alliance, July 28, 2015

Somebody needs to say to the . . . people in southern Utah, you know what, those traditional ways of earning a living through extraction, fossil fuels, are simply not going to make it in the next century. They're from the nineteenth century. Not the twenty-first century. It's not going to be there. It isn't a matter of any outside conspiracy trying to wreck the lives of people, or it's not President Obama who's got it out for the coal industry or for Utah in particular. It's a tidal wave of economic change that's coming. To put our heads in the sand and ignore the tidal wave of history is to guarantee that the next generation of Utahns is not going to be prepared for what is to come.

—Jim Dabakis (D–Salt Lake County), minority caucus manager, Utah State Senate (2013–2018), June 6, 2016

Metate (grinding stone) and mano (handheld stone), Cedar Mesa, Utah

PROTECTING ANCESTRAL LANDS
Exercising Tribal Sovereignty

Mesas, Fry Canyon

CHARLES WILKINSON
Advocating for a National Monument, Promoting Indigenous Self-Determination

If you want to understand a man, take a glance at his bookshelf. The spines of novels, nonfiction, and scholarly texts provide a window into his personal and professional passions, knowledge, even values. The books that populate Charles Wilkinson's office reflect the tastes of a western outdoorsman fluent in the classics of the region—Edward Abbey's *The Monkey Wrench Gang*, Wallace Stegner's legendary biography of John Wesley Powell, *Beyond the Hundredth Meridian*, and, unsurprisingly, a copy of *Federal Indian Law: Cases and Materials*, which Wilkinson coauthored with Felix S. Cohen and Rennard Strickland in 1979.

Yes, Wilkinson literally wrote the book on federal Indian law and has contributed considerably to the literature and scholarship of public land and water statutes. A longtime distinguished law professor at the University of Colorado at Boulder, he is widely regarded as one of the leading scholars and practitioners in his field; he has also been one of the strongest advocates in the United States for the rights of Native peoples.

Starting in the 1970s, when he worked for the Native American Rights Fund, Wilkinson has devoted his professional life to helping tribes use their rights as sovereign nations to regain what has been denied or wrested from them through treaties or trickery: water and mineral rights, access to quality education, and tribal lands. The powerful language in the Bears Ears Inter-Tribal Coalition's national monument proposal reflects Wilkinson's work with tribal leaders not only to articulate their wishes but also to assert their right to meet and work with the federal government as equals to develop a plan for collaboratively managing the Bears Ears landscape.

Wilkinson strides into his office a few minutes after his final class of the day and greets us with a strong handshake and a generous smile that crinkles

Charles Wilkinson (courtesy of Tim Peterson)

the crow's-feet behind his thin-rimmed glasses. He then issues a hurried apology as he sprints back to the classroom to grab his coat, his mind still on the prior hour's discussion. When he returns, he eases into a large armchair draped in a vividly colored and intricately patterned Pendleton wool blanket. His neatly tucked, camel-colored button-down shirt defies rumpled professorial chic. From the waist down his attire is insistently, proudly western: burnt-orange leather boots, well-worn jeans, an expansive belt buckle shaped like a bear's head with the eponymous buttes for ears. His outfit, perhaps subconsciously, evokes the two aspects of his life: a man dressed for the classroom and a lifetime explorer of the plateau's remote canyons, rivers, and mountains.

As he begins to speak, Wilkinson's deep baritone is muted. His passion for the land and its first inhabitants soon emerges, his voice rising as he narrates stories of Native-Anglo relations in San Juan County, where he spent many years working with the Navajo and Ute tribes to seek justice on cases ranging from gerrymandered school districts to tribal water rights.

"San Juan County may have the most radical politics in the United States of America," Wilkinson says with barely contained rage. "To their everlasting credit, the [leaders of the Bears Ears Inter-Tribal Coalition] have not used the word 'racist' in public. But I do think that it is important for fair-minded people who believe from a lot of data that they have seen racism to use that phrase sometimes. That's the first time I've used that. I believe it is baseline racism."

Wilkinson acknowledges that there are other pertinent issues at play.

"There is a deep devotion to a way of life, a religion," Wilkinson says—the Mormons' faith and their pride in their ancestors' journey to settle the land.

"They go back five, six, seven, eight generations. That's something they're proud of, and anybody would be.

"But there are, without question, racist attitudes here that are very prevalent," Wilkinson says. "It's hard being a Native American in the county," even though Natives make up the majority of San Juan County's population.

"In the [1970s] I was lead counsel in major school discrimination litigation [in San Juan County]," Wilkinson says. "Since both of the county's high schools were up north, in Monticello and Blanding, the Navajo children had to endure bus rides of several hours a day just to go to school. One route was over 150 miles round-trip.

"The prevailing attitudes have changed shockingly little since then. I will say there's one difference: it's not quite as much in the open. Most basically, in downtown Monticello and Blanding, you don't hear as often, 'Go back to the reservation.'"

While Wilkinson defended Native rights in San Juan County, another movement erupted that would sweep across the West, one that continues to define the battle over land use in the states west of the hundredth meridian: the Sagebrush Rebellion.

When the Federal Land Policy and Management Act (FLPMA) was passed in 1976, it shifted the Bureau of Land Management's mandate to include conservation and recreation in addition to management of ranching and extractive industry activities. It also required the agency to do a complete inventory of all areas within its purview that contained wilderness characteristics such as "outstanding opportunities for solitude" and "ecological, geological, or other features of scientific, educational, scenic, or historical value."

Locals whose economy depends on ranching and mining view the expanded mandate of the BLM as a threat to their livelihoods, fearing the economic consequences of withdrawing lands for conservation. Many demand more state and local control of public lands, and a militant few urge acts of defiance to what they perceive is an overreaching federal government.

In addition, the specter of a new national monument managed by the BLM, possibly in partnership with Native Americans, adds to the multigenerational history of racial division and discrimination, creating a toxic brew of anger and resentment.

"Certainly, there will be some violence [should a monument proclamation happen]," Wilkinson says. "Some of it is likely to be right after the proclamation, if not before. But we've now made some arrests with these Bundys" following the antigovernment armed standoffs at Cliven Bundy's ranch in Bunkerville, Nevada, in 2014 and at the Malheur National Wildlife Refuge in Burns, Oregon, in 2016. "It really says, 'You will go to jail if you get into this stuff,' and that's going to help." (As it turned out, there was outrage but no violence when the monument was declared in December 2016. Against all odds, the Bundys and many of their acolytes involved in the standoffs were subsequently acquitted and released from jail.)

Wilkinson strongly believed that the Public Lands Initiative (PLI) legislation proposed by Utah representatives Rob Bishop and Jason Chaffetz would fail. To him, the PLI was a disingenuous, extractive industry giveaway masquerading as a conservation bill.

"Putting legislation through is purely hypothetical," Wilkinson says, his voice rising. "It's a joke. There is no possibility of legislation. There's no point in talking about how much more flexible legislation is.

"There is one way to get this monument, and that is through a presidential proclamation. Period," Wilkinson continues. "And that's why the Antiquities Act is a hundred thousand times better. It's infinitely better than legislation because there can be no legislation.

"You can't do 'the right thing to do' on land issues in Utah!" Wilkinson exclaims. "You just can't do it."

Wilkinson then relates work he was called to do during the summer of 1996, when he was tapped by John Leshy, then solicitor for the Department of the Interior, to join a small group of individuals "to create a large national monument that would begin to revive the impetus that [Interior] Secretary Harold Ickes had with the effort in the 1930s."

In 1936 the famously ambitious Ickes laid out a vision for the Escalante National Monument that comprised most of southern Utah, including areas that later became Canyonlands and Capitol Reef National Parks, Natural Bridges National Monument, and Glen Canyon National Recreation Area, which lies on the western border of the proposed Bears Ears National Monument. That proposal died amid opposition from local residents and state politicians.

Wilkinson worked for two months on a draft proclamation for Grand Staircase–Escalante National Monument to protect a Delaware-sized landscape spanning southern Utah from just west of the Colorado River to the eastern boundary of Bryce Canyon National Park. The proclamation, a counterproposal to the Utah congressional delegation's 1995 Public Lands

Management Act, was kept under wraps until just before the September 1996 ceremony, when President Bill Clinton declared the monument. The signing ceremony was held not in Utah but at the rim of the Grand Canyon, much to the chagrin of Utah's already incensed congressional delegation and political leadership.

"You can't keep a secret in Washington, but this secret got kept," Wilkinson says. "It was something that had to be kept completely confidential because of fears that the Utah delegation would grind anything to a halt. And I believe it would have, and I believe we would not have a Grand Staircase today if it had been a public process. And I am one who believes in public input."

The behind-closed-doors creation of Grand Staircase–Escalante National Monument and the very public campaign to designate the Bears Ears National Monument appear to present a study in contrasts. But Wilkinson says the difference between the two goes far beyond simple classifications of open and closed processes.

"The Grand Staircase came about clearly as a conservation matter," Wilkinson says. "This [Bears Ears] is a combination of conservation and tribal sovereignty and tribal culture. It's a great conservation monument, and it's a great tribal cultural monument. It's a movement that is really gathering steam, and is very broad, and has very human and intellectual appeal to it. [The Grand Staircase] was . . . an uprising of a very small group of people."

Wilkinson knows well the power, conviction, and occasional aggressiveness with which environmental organizations and coalitions pursue their conservation goals in the Southwest—and the pride they take in their victories. Because of their decision to take a background role in the Bears Ears campaign and to let tribes take the lead, he is "so proud of the environmental movement. This is their ground, [advocating and campaigning for] monuments."

Starting in 2012, a coalition of environmental organizations had in fact begun advocating for a proposal for the Greater Canyonlands National Monument encompassing up to 1.8 million acres, including much of the land in the Bears Ears proposal, which was finalized in 2015. But according to Wilkinson, the leaders of those organizations soon recognized the value, not to mention the political advantages, of supporting a tribally led proposal.

Both before and during the efforts to establish the Greater Canyonlands National Monument, "I think the tribes felt that they were not being taken seriously by the environmental movement," Wilkinson says. "And then the tribes came forward with this coalition, which is so vibrant, and the environmental movement decided to step back and say, 'The tribes are taking the lead on this. Talk to them; we support them.' And I just think it's so beautiful."

Wilkinson believes the work of the coalition will inspire other tribes across the nation to pursue collaborative management of tribal and ancestral lands.

"Every acre of land in the United States is former tribal homeland," Wilkinson says. "There are many areas on the public lands that have sacred sites, have special meanings, like the Bears Ears does. I know that the idea of collaborative management has been a topic in Indian Country that's increasing steadily. I think it's a certainty other tribes will come forward. If they can make a compelling case, we will see some more comanagement. It's not precedent in the sense that people can casually walk in. This coalition has spent a hell of a lot of time on this. It won't be easy. Other tribes will have to work hard."

Wilkinson hopes eventually to see more widespread local acceptance and acknowledgment of federal land protection and how it can benefit surrounding communities, from Escalante to Blanding.

"Everything [in the Grand Staircase area] is motels, new gas stations, new office buildings in towns that are picking up with activity," Wilkinson says. "Cattle grazing's still allowed in there, and I would like to see those family [enterprises] continue. I have no trouble with that. I respect families who work the lands and graze it. It's not land that really should be grazed from any biological standpoint, [but] I still have sympathy and intellectual and policy support for those families continuing to stay there. I do not think that the Grand Staircase or Bears Ears is going to interfere with that."

In particular, Wilkinson sees potential for well-paying jobs that don't rely on drilling, mining, or ranching, jobs that could keep future generations in San Juan County.

"I think that the fact that kids are moving away is because kids don't want to go into ranching," Wilkinson says. "But it isn't the Grand Staircase, and it isn't the threat of the Bears Ears, and the truth is those places offer opportunities. You have forty-five employees at Grand Staircase. Most of them are scientists of different kinds. There are some local jobs where kids could stay in their homelands and not have to ranch."

Is there an opportunity for Anglos and Natives to collaborate and prosper in ways that benefit both groups? Wilkinson thinks it comes down to long-held beliefs and whether influential Anglo leaders will embrace a new paradigm or cling to a states' rights / Sagebrush Rebel mentality.

"They think they own the land," Wilkinson says. "They don't think it's federal land. And in my view . . . I think it's important to acknowledge that that's their worldview, and you want to try to respect that. It's just that they make it hard to do because it traces into racism and intolerance that is firmly held."

Should the monument designation succeed, Wilkinson looks forward to seeing local representation on the eight-member commission—one representative from each of the five leading tribes, and one employee each from the National Park Service, the Bureau of Land Management, and the Forest Service—that will manage the monument.

"We'll have two of the five be from San Juan County," Wilkinson says. "One from Navajo and one from Ute Mountain Ute. [San Juan County] got [two] local people, just like they wanted."

(As we now know, the monument designation did succeed; former president Barack Obama established Bears Ears National Monument in December 2016. But the monument was gutted a year later by Obama's successor, Donald J. Trump, who signed a pair of proclamations reducing Bears Ears by 85 percent and reducing the long-contentious Grand Staircase–Escalante by nearly half.)

The [Obama] administration is taking action to strengthen Native American communities through education and economic development. These initiatives build on the significant progress the President has already made in partnering with tribes on a nation-to-nation basis to promote prosperous and resilient tribal nations.

Underlying this progress is President Obama's firm belief that tribal leaders must have a seat at the table. To make this commitment a reality, the President has hosted the White House Tribal Nations Conferences with tribal leaders every year he has been in office, and last year, he established the White House Council on Native American Affairs to ensure cross-agency coordination and engagement with Indian Country.

—White House press release, "Strengthening Tribal Communities through Education and Economic Development," June 13, 2014

The county did agree to include comanagement of parts of the Cedar Mesa National Conservation Area because that was an original proposal that Diné Bikéyah had. It has never really been defined. There's probably going to be some sort of an advisory committee set up for any designation, a monument or NCA. The county would like to have more county representation than you'd see with a monument or NCA. . . . But there may be more opportunities for concessionaires or other economic development where Native Americans are given a preference and invitation to bid. Maybe more Native American staff on the agency management team and that sort of thing. That could be one interpretation of comanagement. —Nick Sandberg, public lands coordinator, San Juan County, November 9, 2015

INTERLUDE
Tribal Sovereignty Explained

The first governments in the Western Hemisphere were those of Indian nations that exercised sovereignty over their peoples well prior to the formation of the United States. Upon the arrival of Europeans, their sovereignty was explicitly recognized through the negotiation and signing of treaties between tribal nations and the Netherlands, Spain, France, and Great Britain.

During the Revolutionary War, the nascent United States entered into its first Indian treaty, negotiating a formal military alliance between the Delaware Nation and the colonies. The sovereignty of Indian nations was later enshrined in Article 1, Section 8 of the United States Constitution and affirmed by a series of decisions in the early 1830s by the Supreme Court under the leadership of Chief Justice John Marshall. The court ruled that Indian tribes are "distinct political communities, retaining their original rights as the undisputed possessors of the soil from time immemorial. . . . [T]he very term nation, so generally applied to them, means a people distinct from others, having territorial boundaries within which their authority is exclusive, and having a right to all the lands within those boundaries, which is not only acknowledged but guaranteed by the United States."[1]

Tribes thus possess powers of self-government with the notable exceptions of those relinquished by government-to-government treaty with the United States and those that Congress has explicitly removed. Tribes have the right to form governments, levy taxes, establish citizenship, and administer justice. The U.S. government has a trust responsibility to protect tribal lands and resources.[2]

---

1. Marshall, opinion in *Worcester v. Georgia*.
2. "Tribal Sovereignty."

All that said, a cultural commitment to Manifest Destiny and resulting federal policies led to what might best be called inconsistent adherence to the notion of Indian nations as sovereign entities with well-established borders. A series of treaties, many broken and then renegotiated, led to drastic reductions of Indian lands and frequent relocation to ever-shrinking reservations.

Following the Civil War, passage of the Dawes Act in 1887 by the Forty-Ninth Congress committed the federal government to a policy of assimilating tribes into the dominant culture. The act authorized surveying of Indian lands in service of dividing reservations into allotments that could then be sold by individual "owners" of land that had long been considered communal by the tribes. Some tribal lands were declared "surplus" and auctioned off to the highest bidders. Tribal governments and courts were disbanded; reservation lands were diminished; governments were weakened to the point of impotence; and, perhaps most tragically, children were forcibly removed from their homes, taken to federally operated boarding schools, and robbed of their language and culture.

Attitudes toward Native Americans began to change in some ways following World War I. American Indians fought valiantly alongside American citizens, and in recognition of their commitment to the United States, they were granted citizenship by the Sixty-Eighth Congress in 1924, over fifty years after the passage of the Fourteenth Amendment to the Constitution had granted citizenship "to all persons born or naturalized in the United States."

In 1934, as part of what has become known as the "Indian New Deal," the Seventy-Third Congress passed the Indian Reorganization Act, which reversed the push for assimilation and allowed tribes to once again organize their own governments and manage their own assets, including tribal lands, some of which were returned. Over the following decades, Congress has enacted a variety of statutes aimed at supporting and enhancing tribal self-government. Notable among them was the Indian Tribal Justice Act of 1993, which supports the authority of tribal governments and the independence of their judicial systems.[3]

The accelerating recognition of tribal rights paralleled decades of American Indian activism, culminating most visibly in the 1970s, when demands for enforcement of treaty rights and respect for sovereignty resulted in

---

3. H.R. 1268 (103rd).

clashes with the Bureau of Indian Affairs. (See p. 363 for a brief history of the BIA.)

More recently, tribes have worked through the legal system to assert their sovereign authority to reestablish fishing rights, establish the right to tax corporations operating on tribal lands, seek the right to try nontribal members in tribal courts, demand funding for adequate schools and infrastructure, and ensure fair representation in local and state governing bodies.

Over the past decade, the conservative bent of the Supreme Court has led to decisions that appear to diminish tribal sovereignty by ruling that tribal rights exist solely because Congress has passed statutes protecting those rights. If history is a guide, the federal government's support of tribal sovereignty will continue to ebb and flow. But the commitment of tribes to assert their rights will continue unabated, supported by an increasing cohort of sophisticated Native lawyers, government officials, and grassroots activists.

Abandoned hogan, hillsides west of Comb Ridge near Bluff, Utah

NATASHA HALE
Connecting Grassroots Activists and Tribal Leaders, Supporting Native Entrepreneurship

Natasha Hale insists on calling herself a minion, a behind-the-scenes worker bee whose jobs as coordinator and cat herder for the Bears Ears Inter-Tribal Coalition are neither glamorous nor remarkable. According to numerous sources, however, Hale has been taking charge and managing even the strongest personalities with her unique blend of directness and tough love. Through a combination of tenacity, political savvy, and commitment to an ambitious vision, she helped catalyze a movement that could usher in a new era of tribal self-determination and set in motion the campaign for the Bears Ears National Monument.

To hear her tell it, Hale has no interest in glory or public recognition. Instead, her tireless "minion work" is a manifestation of her "total loyalty to the cause. I am going to do what it takes to get this done."

Tall and confident, with waist-length dark hair and large, expressive brown eyes, Hale is as comfortable in stiletto heels as she is in sheepskin boots, as authentic in Capitol Hill business wear as she is in a T-shirt and jeans. Whatever her attire, without exception she sports beautifully crafted Navajo jewelry: a large silver armband with turquoise inlay, intricately beaded earrings and necklaces, and other striking pieces that showcase the artistry of Native jewelers and speak to Hale's appreciation of her Navajo heritage.

Hale possesses an almost frenetic energy, which makes her preternaturally effective in her work for the coalition and for the nonprofit Grand Canyon Trust, where she manages the Native America program, working with communities to create economic development projects that draw upon traditional Native culture for success in entrepreneurial ventures. Each time we meet with her, she is either just returning from a coalition trip to Washington, D.C., or on her way to a conference somewhere in the Southwest.

Natasha Hale at the Bears Ears gathering, July 2016

Even when deeply engaged in conversation, Hale seems ever ready to jump to the next topic, we suspect because her rapidly firing synapses have just generated a new idea.

Hale, whose mother was born and raised on the Navajo reservation and whose father is from Mecca, Saudi Arabia, is fiery and thoughtful, with limited patience for equivocation or shading opinions. Her professional career has spanned journalism, politics, film, and the nonprofit sector. Her starring role in the 2007 film *Turquoise Rose* made her a familiar face to many Navajos. In the film, Hale's character relinquished the chance to vacation in Europe to return to the reservation and care for her ailing grandmother, a story that endeared her to Navajo elders everywhere. We have heard that when traveling with Hale on or near the Navajo reservation, it is not unusual for her to be delayed by acolytes hoping for a picture with their favorite movie star.

On a chilly evening in early October 2016 we sit down to dinner with Hale and her husband, Jordan, in a cozy Indian restaurant in Flagstaff, Arizona. Animated and sharp as always, Hale shares her personal story and the story behind the formation of the Bears Ears Inter-Tribal Coalition, both of which have seen unexpected turns but are anchored and unified by a passion for social justice and a drive to empower indigenous communities.

The focus of Hale's work is to understand, in her words, "who is doing what, and how do we bring people together for a conversation? How do you navigate within different spaces so everything can be functional? How do you uplift the people around you so that this work can be successful?"

Hale began to hone her political skills at a very early age. Growing up in Twin Lakes and Gallup, New Mexico, she was the oldest of six children and learned quickly how to understand and navigate relationships, work with people of varied personality types, and develop the thick skin that allowed her to be the "no" person who kept the coalition focused on achieving its primary objective: successfully petitioning President Obama to declare the Bears Ears National Monument. The tribes' vision is to protect 1.9 million acres in southeastern Utah sacred to the five tribes—Hopi, Navajo, Ute Mountain Ute, Zuni, and the Ute Indian Tribe of the Uintah and Ouray Reservation—that constitute the coalition.

"My role within my family is pretty similar to what I'm doing now," Hale says. "Just calling people out when they f*ck up but also telling them they can still be awesome."

Driven by her competitive nature and interest in academics and leadership, Hale was an honors student in high school and served in student government, but she also lived in a world where social inequality and racism were constants.

Gallup has a sizeable Native population—around 40 percent of its residents identify as Native American—"but there [were] only a few of us that were Native American in the honors/AP courses," Hale says. "It was the same four or five of us that took classes together."

Hale recalls self-selecting seats with the three other Navajo students in one of her classes and hearing the story her teacher told them about how a visiting New Mexico School Board officer questioned her seemingly segregated seat assignment system.

"It kind of caught her off-guard," Hale says. "[She told the officer], 'I don't seat the students; they arrange themselves.' But . . . they wanted to address it, so she brought it up to us.

"You see those race relations come out," Hale adds. "I was really acutely aware of that. I would bring them up during class, and you could tell . . . people just did not want to enter into that space. Everyone got super stressed."

But for Hale, calling attention to injustices was second nature. She would channel her passion for advocacy on behalf of disadvantaged Native populations in a number of different ways.

After graduating from the University of Arizona in 2005 with a degree in family studies and a minor in American Indian studies, Hale returned home to New Mexico to help her mother and younger siblings find stability in the wake of an untidy divorce.

"I wasn't even thinking about what my . . . next move was," Hale says. "I just knew I had to come home and help pull things together."

She landed a job as a reporter for the *Gallup Independent* and freelanced for the *Navajo Times*, where she reported on a wide variety of issues impacting communities on the Navajo Reservation. Hale focused on stories that humanized and demystified complex issues, and she didn't fear challenging the narratives and talking points of politicians and institutions in service of revealing a less rosy reality.

Hale remembers being assigned to report on an event at Chaco Culture National Historical Park in northern New Mexico. The press release billed the event as a celebration of the center's groundbreaking work over the years. But Hale ended up writing a very different story.

"I interviewed family members, community members from Chaco Canyon who were removed from the canyon so that it could become a park," Hale says. "My whole story was about how they weren't able to collect herbs" for medicinal and ceremonial use—a key element of tribal life that the Bears Ears National Monument would aim to protect.

"I remember the park superintendent called my boss," Hale says. "He was really angry about it. But I was like, 'This is the story about the community there. I'm sorry I didn't write your press release [story] the way you wanted.'"

Her work interviewing community members and learning more about the inner workings of legislation sparked her interest in politics. She was hired by then Navajo Nation Speaker Lawrence T. Morgan's office and served as his public information officer.

"When I worked for the Speaker's Office, a lot of what I was trying to put into my work [was], how is this relevant to communities? How is this empowering the communities?" Hale says.

She soon found herself doing work for her boss both behind the scenes and in front of a microphone.

"The Speaker [would say], 'Okay, I can't go to this meeting; speak on my behalf,'" Hale says. "Which offended a lot of people, because I was this twenty-four-year-old with braces and bangs."

Hale discovered just how central a role the Navajo Nation's political staffers play in providing stability in an environment where frequent leadership churn is the norm—a lesson she would apply years later as she was helping to organize the sometimes tumultuous Bears Ears Coalition. She also built a strong working relationship with one of her colleagues in the Office of the

Speaker, Eric Descheenie, whom she would recruit to play a central role during the coalition's initial phase.

In 2011 Hale made the leap from politics to the nonprofit sector, joining the Grand Canyon Trust's Native America program, where she continues to work. As an offshoot of her work with the trust, Hale is the associate director for the Colorado Plateau Foundation, which funds groups working to protect natural and cultural resources—also twin missions of the coalition.

Through her work in journalism, in the Office of the Speaker, and in the nonprofit sector, Hale built an intricate web of professional connections and gained a unique understanding of the intersection of political maneuvering and grassroots advocacy.

Also in 2011 Hale reconnected with Mark Maryboy, whom she knew from her days in the Office of the Speaker. He introduced her to the work of the group that would officially become Utah Diné Bikéyah (UDB), work that focused on finding a path toward protecting Navajo cultural resources and maintaining access to land that provided physical and spiritual sustenance.

Hale saw the enormous potential of UDB's work to transform tribal land management and recognized the power of forming a coalition of sovereign nations to advocate for protection of a landscape that connected them all.

"[Utah Diné Bikéyah] was not getting in the door to convince [Navajo] political leadership of why they needed to take ownership of this," Hale says. "So that's where I came in . . . to build that [connection] between UDB and the elders from other tribes. It was mapping relationships and mapping where the power is within the communities, seeing, what is their motivation? What is their focus? And also just knowing the process of getting in front of the right people."

Hale realized that UDB needed the support of other sovereign tribal nations to achieve the land protection they sought. She also saw the perils of having respected but polarizing figures from the region's largest tribe pitch their cultural mapping work as something that other tribes should support.

"This was very Navajo-centric," Hale says. "How do you get buy-in for this process when the other communities [tribes] haven't quite mapped out all of their interests?"

While some of the tribes with ties to San Juan County, such as the Zuni, had begun detailed mapping of cultural resources, others had yet to initiate similar processes. Indeed, some feared that identifying cultural resources might put sensitive sites at risk of looting or overvisitation and that the net benefit to the tribes could well be negative.

Hale knew that elders and spiritual leaders had significant influence in the political arena and in some tribes were considered as or even more powerful and influential than the politicians themselves.

Most sovereign Indian nations have elected tribal leaders who conduct official government business, pass legislation, and oversee departments that provide essential services to constituents. Traditional cultural and spiritual leaders operate outside of the official tribal government structure. Their roles in religious societies and their knowledge of songs, prayers, and ceremonies make them among the most respected members of their tribes. A tribe's elected leadership will often consult with spiritual leaders before making significant decisions; sometimes spiritual leaders will even play a role in selecting political leaders.

"If you find the right leaders within the tribes that are not necessarily political but cultural leaders, it changes the dynamic completely," Hale says.

She focused her energy first on connecting with those cultural leaders whom she had met through her reporting and policy work and making the case for supporting UDB's efforts as a means of protecting sacred landscapes and giving tribes a voice in how those lands would be stewarded. Then she turned her attention to the politicians.

"There's a process," Hale says. "You go to lunch, have coffee with the legislator, educate them about what you're doing and why."

With help from leaders within each of the five tribes, she succeeded in convincing tribal governments to join the nascent coalition and work toward creating a proposal for permanent protection of land still used by tribes across the Colorado Plateau for ceremonies, hunting, and gathering of wood, medicinal plants, and piñon nuts. But there was still uncertainty as to how best to prepare and target the proposal and then advocate successfully for its adoption in Washington. The tribes needed guidance. Hale knew whom to ask.

"Enter Charles Wilkinson."

The University of Colorado law professor who worked for the Native American Rights Fund in its early years and currently serves on the board of the Grand Canyon Trust is universally respected and sought after by tribes seeking an advocate for protecting or regaining land and water rights and for advancing tribal sovereignty.

"Tribes all over the U.S. want Charles to work for them," Hale says. "The tribes here asked him, and Charles accepted. That's when [our] ideas became something more."

Wilkinson helped to shape the coalition's proposal into a compelling case for President Obama to use his powers under the 1906 Antiquities Act to protect the tribes' sacred land. Invocation of the Antiquities Act would avert the need to approach a fractious Congress unlikely to act favorably toward the tribes' requests.

The truly revolutionary part of the proposal was Wilkinson's vision for co-management, in which the tribes would work with the agencies tasked with managing the land—the Bureau of Land Management, the Forest Service, and the National Park Service—to set policy regarding stewardship, resource allocation, educational programs, and visitor experience. The coalition's approach thus represented a significant departure from UDB's initial efforts to secure protection through Representative Rob Bishop's (R-UT) Public Lands Initiative (PLI) legislation.

"[UDB was] mostly betting on the [PLI] legislation . . . and were . . . convinced that they could build that support within San Juan County. Which they did, but which we saw was undermined completely" by what UDB viewed as an intentional effort by San Juan County elected officials to exclude them from participation in the deliberations of the county's lands council and hence from influencing the county's recommendations to Bishop's PLI legislation.

When it came time to assemble the leadership for the coalition, Hale contacted her former colleague Eric Descheenie, who was then working in a new capacity as special assistant to Navajo Nation president Russell Begaye.

"[Eric and I] understood what the different obstacles were going to be," Hale says. "Eric is a fantastic facilitator. He's able to get in a room and pull out what . . . people are thinking. I knew, too, [the Navajo Nation leadership] was going to step up in some way and that the staff are really integral to that."

Descheenie facilitated the July 2015 meeting that resulted in the formalized partnership among the five tribes as the Bears Ears Inter-Tribal Coalition, bringing together tribes with sometimes fraught intertribal histories and arriving at a consensus on how best to achieve their ambitious goals.

"He was fantastic," Hale says of Descheenie's facilitation efforts at the meeting, a sentiment expressed by other coalition leaders present that day. "He was pivotal in that moment. It came together so well."

Looking westward from Fry Canyon

Descheenie and then Hopi vice chairman Alfred Lomahquahu served as the coalition's first cochairs, and Descheenie served as the spokesperson for the coalition's official presentation of its proposal at the White House Press Club in October 2015. He moved on from the coalition in the spring of 2016 and focused his energy on a successful campaign for the Arizona House of Representatives, where he now serves as a Democratic representative from Legislative District 7.

Once the coalition had formed and articulated its vision, the monument proposal gained momentum both locally and nationally. There was fierce opposition to the coalition's vision from Utah's congressional delegation, which was steadfastly opposed to any use of the Antiquities Act and instead supported Bishop's PLI. San Juan County's elected officials also came out strongly and unanimously against the monument proposal. A number of Anglo citizens and a subset of Navajos and Utes in San Juan County felt as if their voices and views had been diminished by attention given to the Bears Ears Coalition. In their eyes, the coalition appeared on the scene at the last minute and championed a cause that was endorsed and funded by wealthy "outsiders" in environmental organizations and supported largely by tribes that didn't live in the area. Their opposition, coupled with the occasional use of racist language directed at the coalition and UDB, only served to strengthen the partnership between the tribes.

"Hearing things like 'I don't know why you guys want to manage public lands. You can't even take care of your reservation. There's so much trash' come out in a public way really helped UDB and the tribes to . . . stay strong together as a unit," Hale says. "You could see the opposition coming out, and that forces people to work together."

The tribes also found strong allies in Congress and in the conservation community, many of whom had fought numerous battles over the years to protect the land within the boundaries of the proposed monument.

Hale says that telling the leadership of powerful conservation nonprofits that they could not lead the Bears Ears campaign initially proved difficult, particularly as some of the environmental nonprofits needed to be convinced to pivot from a years-long campaign to create the Greater Canyonlands National Monument to instead support the coalition's new proposal.

"It was hard to tell people that, because they'd been working on this for such a long time, and they have such ownership, and [yet] their board is

[now] telling them that they need to help" with leading the new monument campaign.

"I remember we had a meeting up in Bluff, and I was really insistent on how we set up the room. It was so important, because it creates an energy between how people relate to each other. We had the elders sit right behind the political leaders that were sitting up front because they're the centerpiece of the conversation. But we had cultural leaders behind them."

The symbolism—and the reflection of tribal reality—was critical.

"There was a level of accountability in even how they were spaced out. I had told my peers within the conservation community that you guys aren't allowed to sit [at the table with the tribes]. I [said], 'If you're going to be here, you have to be helpful.'"

The impending departure of President Obama and the looming possibility of an incoming president who could dash the coalition's hopes and dismantle Obama's conservation legacy imbued the coalition's work with urgency.

Hale says this has been immensely helpful. "We have a deadline: January 20, 2017"—Obama's last day in office. "If this was [a campaign] that was ongoing, it wouldn't have the level of intensity and commitment.

"The Obama administration really [placing] a bigger focus on creating or protecting places for communities that have been historically underrepresented . . . changed everything too," Hale adds, "because it gave a platform for tribes . . . to step up."

Along with Interior Secretary Sally Jewell, Obama articulated clearly and frequently his support for Indian Country and created new initiatives to empower tribes in the areas of education, self-governance, and youth leadership development.

"I don't think a campaign like this is going to happen for a long time," Hale says. "It'd be hard for it to happen around any other place within the U.S. because there are just such dense cultural resources" in San Juan County— multiple groups estimate the number at well over one hundred thousand— that demonstrate the tribes' ancestral presence on the land.

Once the monument is declared—for Hale, it has always been a "when," not an "if"—she is uncertain what her role with the coalition will be.

"There's so many competing priorities as to what has to be done afterward," Hale says. "It has to be different people taking on different pieces. There's a lot of unknowns."

Badlands near Clay Hills Crossing (aerial image)

Hale hopes to devote energy to doing some of the same work for the coalition that she does with Grand Canyon Trust: working with grassroots communities to create projects and opportunities for entrepreneurs to develop locally driven economies and protect environmental resources. She was inspired by a woman at the public lands conference in Nevada she attended just before meeting with us.

"She was doing some really cool planning around businesses converging around a national monument, creating ownership around it," Hale says. "I think a lot of the businesses that [currently exist] within the protected region aren't Navajo businesses."

She hopes that tribal ventures can find the support they need to succeed and take maximum advantage of the economic opportunity presented by a monument designation—whether through organizations like the Trust, through foundation and private donor support, or, far less likely, through the support of communities within San Juan County, many of which oppose the monument. Like many people with whom we've spoken, she believes that bridging the cultural divides between pro- and antimonument factions, which in some cases stretch back over a century, poses the greatest challenge of all.

"There has to be a lot of healing between people and different relationships before that conversation can even be productive," Hale says.

Nevertheless, she maintains enthusiasm about the coalition's potential to effect positive, even revolutionary, change that strengthens Native communities and sets a new precedent for how tribes work with one another and with the federal government. No matter what the future brings for her, she intends to maintain her loyalty to the cause.

"What's happening now is not working for our communities," Hale says. "You hear people saying, 'I feel underappreciated. I don't feel like my interests are being represented. I don't feel like we're communicating enough.' It's the same issues within all these cohorts. But how do you bridge them together so that everyone is working well and hearing each other out? People don't think about how we can organize on the ground. [I'm] trying to bring together stakeholders."

It's so important to understand where everyone's coming from before you even begin to try and compromise. Clearly there's an ideological difference here. We won't be able to unpack the contents of [the Bears Ears proposal] until we get past this ideological problem. . . . Let's just understand where we're coming from. That can take a very long time. Achieving a national monument? Putting together a really unprecedented proposal? That's the easy part. The hard part is the humanistic part.

—Eric Descheenie, Arizona state representative, District 7, and former cochair of the Bears Ears Inter-Tribal Coalition, January 28, 2016

What does the [Obama] administration have to lose? Nobody wants to create a firestorm that would endanger the Antiquities Act. For some people, that is the fear. But how big is too big? Nobody really knows. It's uncharted territory. I think the main concern that the Obama administration has indicated is they want to be transparent about the process. They don't want to do a Grand Staircase.

—Matt Gross, communications director, Southern Utah Wilderness Alliance, July 28, 2015

What [Governor Herbert] said [in November 2015] was the idea that if through a legislative process a monument is included . . . he would be fine with that.

From the staff perspective, as we've talked about both Bears Ears and other areas, it has legitimately been considered whether some of these areas . . . should be protected legislatively as [a] national monument. I think all of us—the governor's office, congressional delegation—were open to that idea and continue to be so, as long as it's done through a transparent legislative process.

—Cody Stewart, staff director, House Natural Resources Committee, former director of Federal Affairs, and former policy and energy advisor to Utah governor Gary Herbert, October 13, 2016

Dark Canyon (aerial photo)

REGINA LOPEZ-WHITESKUNK
Responding to a Call to Lead,
Speaking for People and the Planet

The Homestead Steakhouse was supposed to be open. Yelp did not report a seasonal closure; neither did the Homestead's answering machine. But it is mid-January in Blanding, Utah, and despite the sandwich board outside the restaurant promising "Delicious Navajo Tacos," snow has been plowed into piles that abut the front door entrance. The locals think the Homestead might open again in March, but they're not quite sure. Were we merely trying to find lunch for ourselves, we would head to nearby Clark's Market and rustle up some sandwiches. But we are scheduled to meet with Regina Lopez-Whiteskunk, a member of the Ute Mountain Ute tribal council, and so we scramble to find an alternative meeting place.

We try to reach Whiteskunk by phone, but she is already on the road, somewhere along the ninety-five-mile-long stretch from tribal headquarters in Towaoc, Colorado, to Blanding, an expanse where reliable cell service is intermittent at best.

We finally settle on Yak's Center Street Café, a ma-and-pa diner where at 1:00 p.m. you can still smell the morning's servings of eggs and bacon. Following a few cell phone calls from the snowbound Homestead lot, we direct Whiteskunk to Yak's. When she arrives, with her shy teenage son at her side, Whiteskunk looks frazzled but somehow still regal. She moves through the restaurant with the effortless air of someone who is comfortable in her own skin. Like her fellow Bears Ears Inter-Tribal Coalition leaders, she commands attention.

She keeps her short brown hair cropped closely around her round face and wears thin-frame glasses and a fitted white jacket draped snugly over a teal blouse. Today she has chosen exquisitely crafted beadwork earrings

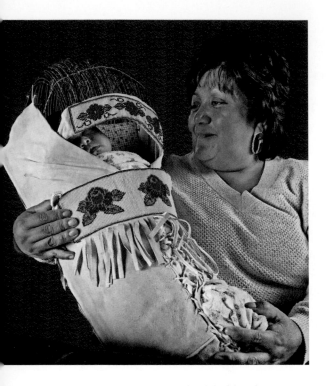

Regina Lopez-Whiteskunk holding her granddaughter (courtesy of Regina Lopez-Whiteskunk)

in a rainbow of colors and an equally striking circular pin on her jacket, all crafted by her niece.

"When I got into council, she said, 'You're going to be wearing jackets, so you'll need a pin!'" says Whiteskunk, laughing.

According to Whiteskunk, conversations about the cultural mapping work done by Utah Diné Bikéyah (UDB) began before she was elected to the tribal council in November 2014. A Native-led grassroots nonprofit organization, UDB had been working since 2010 to gather and map information about culturally and spiritually significant places in San Juan County to make a case for protection of land considered by Native peoples to be sacred and an essential part of their cultural heritage.

When she and her fellow council members were approached by UDB, they were initially wary of supporting the group's efforts.

"We were trying to figure out, how is that going to play out in terms of having different conversations with different federal agencies [and] at the state and local [levels]?" Whiteskunk says. "We didn't really feel comfortable saying, 'We're all in. Let's do this.'"

Over the next year, the Ute Mountain Ute Tribal Council explored the possibility of working with UDB to build on its proposal for a national conservation area (NCA). (See p. 388 for an explanation of national conservation area versus national monument.) In April 2015 a Ute Mountain Ute representative and leaders from Hopi, Zuni, Cochiti, and Hualapai pueblos met in Bluff, Utah, and concluded that, in addition to pursuing NCA

Whiteskunk with her grandmother (courtesy of Regina Lopez-Whiteskunk)

designation legislatively, they would explore the possibility of approaching President Obama jointly, as a coalition of sovereign nations, to seek protection of ancestral lands via executive declaration of a national monument. It wasn't until Whiteskunk attended a July 2015 meeting, during which the Bears Ears Inter-Tribal Coalition was formalized, that she realized the potential of tribes joining together to achieve shared goals, a potential that could extend far beyond protecting land around Bears Ears.

"We had a discussion about what sovereignty means to each of us and how we've seen that tribes always say and throw out the word *sovereignty*, but nobody actually exercises and utilizes it to the capacity that they could," Whiteskunk recalls. "In that moment . . . we said, 'What would sovereignty look like if we were to apply it to this?' There was this awakening of, we're going to do this! And if we're going to do this, we're going to do this wholeheartedly.

"What happened that day is what I call an awakening of true sovereign voices," she adds. "It was like a puzzle piece that fit from the very beginning. We asked the question, Who do we want to be, and are we ready to become a coalition and really exercise our sovereignty through this? And we were all in."

Whiteskunk recognizes the potential of the coalition tribes to use their combined sovereign powers to gain real bargaining power with the federal government. She credits members of the environmental community with providing guidance to the tribes as they learned to frame their arguments in the language of Washington politics.

"Everyone's brought a lot to the table," Whiteskunk says. "We know what we want to do, they've really helped us in terms of figuring out how to incorporate some of what we're thinking and feeling into the [political] process.

"We have some really important issues where we need to knock on doors in D.C. on a tribal level," Whiteskunk says. "I see us . . . getting frustrated because we can't maneuver that culture, because we don't really have an individual who can guide [us] through. But a number of [the groups supporting the coalition] . . . have helped give us the vehicle to get through that."

The coalition has placed the concept of healing at the heart of its proposal: healing of the land and healing of the wounds between tribes, between tribes and the federal government, and between tribes and local Anglos.

The five tribes leading the Bears Ears Inter-Tribal Coalition—Hopi, Navajo, Ute Indian Tribe of the Uintah and Ouray Reservation, Ute Mountain Ute, and Zuni—have had their differences over the years. Some have been relatively minor disputes; others have been truly painful battles that are part of the tribes' collective memory, from ongoing court battles over land to intertribal bloodshed in centuries past.

The history of the federal government's oppression of Native peoples is well documented, from appropriation of land, to violence, to attempts at forced assimilation through separation from blood relatives.

Whiteskunk believes that healing between tribes and many local citizens in San Juan County poses a great challenge and is also the most essential element in fostering a lasting peace with one another and establishing an environment within which Natives and locals can work collaboratively in stewarding the land.

"It's really tough because you have to be able to coexist, and historically, what's been fed is all the negativity, all the historical trauma. Nobody's ever

Regina Lopez-Whiteskunk at Ute Mountain Ute tribal headquarters, Towaoc, Colorado

taken the time to do that healing," Whiteskunk says.

"There's also healing [needed] between [us and] recreational groups," she adds. "We have been working for some time now, reaching out to some recreational groups" out of a need to acknowledge and then mitigate the damage done to the land by ATVs and other motorized vehicles, as well as by other types of recreation that have left a large footprint on the landscape.

In the summer and fall of 2016, the coalition forged alliances with a number of rock-climbing groups and outdoor recreation companies that advocated strongly for the Bears Ears National Monument in the media and among their membership and customer bases.

"We haven't reached out to the energy groups"—the extractive industry corporations and lobbying groups with existing activity or interest in the Bears Ears region—"and I think we are a little cautious about that," Whiteskunk says. "We know how focused they are on what their goal is, which is the bottom line. That's going to be a difficult one."

Like her fellow coalition leaders, Whiteskunk emphasizes the group's solutions-oriented approach. From her perspective, airing grievances, while essential to the healing process, is far from enough.

"We know everything that doesn't work!" she says. "Our challenge now is to make a very strong presentation of what possibilities will help us to heal some of those past declarations of national monuments."

She cites the designation of Canyon de Chelly National Monument, after which it is commonly believed that many Navajo families were pressured by the National Park Service to move off their land.

"Why didn't that work?" she asks. "How can we make it work? How can we recommend and put out options that help us to get to a better place?"

Whiteskunk believes that in the end the tribes chose to unite because they recognized their shared spiritual connection to the land. It is what has sustained them since time immemorial, and the land is where their stories begin.

"Everything is all rooted from our mother earth that provides [for us]," Whiteskunk says. "Our strong tie to the earth from a very young infancy helps us to pass along this comfort to our children. When [children are] born, and when their little umbilical [cord] falls off after a week or two, grandmothers will take that from the mother, and they'll put it in a little pouch. They'll bead it, they'll decorate it, and then for little girls we'll take the umbilical cord, and we'll go find an ant mound, and we'll bury their cords in the ant mound, because ants are very quick, they're hard workers, they never get lost. So these are all qualities that we pray that our daughters specifically possess as they grow up. We put their little cord in that mound so that they can grow with qualities from their youth into their adulthood and even into their older years.

"As we come through life, every day is a prayer that somebody has said for you, even before you were able or you were even thought of," she continues. "A lot of that ties us back to the earth, like burying that little part of [the umbilical cord] back in [the earth] and keeping that sacred."

When asked if there is a place within the proposed monument borders that has special meaning to her, Whiteskunk doesn't hesitate.

"Heading out to Bears Ears, if you're coming out of Blanding, you take the little turnoff at the service station, and you're going up, and then you're going down," Whiteskunk says, describing the turn westward at the junction of U.S. 191 North to Utah Highway 95 West, which eventually passes just south of Bears Ears.

"You go up a ways, and there's some water coming down there in a stream. When you're looking at Bears Ears even from afar you would never imagine those little places. . . . [My family is] part Shoshone, and so I participate in the Sun Dance, which is fasting, no food, no water for three days, sometimes four. So I've fasted, and for me it's real important to find those areas where water is and where it's very natural.

"There's a clean, clear, strong spirit of the water," Whiteskunk says. "Those areas are very, very important to me, and to be able to see water flowing is important because it draws me back to the days and times when I don't drink water. When I visit that place it always gives me a sense of how much a blessing it can be, no matter what it is. . . . I get to press that reset button and enjoy that moment and take shoes off and feel the ground beneath my feet and the rocks and know what the water feels like and smells like.

"I'm a traveler," Whiteskunk says. "I've always gone from here to there. I've lived in various locations, but I recall my grandmother always saying, 'Go and live life, but you always know where home is.' In a more spiritual sense, home will always pull you back when you need it the most. . . . Through our land and our ties to our area, we know what home is by virtue of how our grandparents and family took care of us. We've always been put in a certain place with great sacredness.

"I love the mountains," she adds. "When I fly to D.C., as soon as I come over that horizon, and I see the Rocky Mountains, I know I'm going to land. There's my mountains. I can take that cleansing breath and say, 'I'm home.'"

However strong those ties to home may be, many tribal members move away from the Ute Mountain Ute Reservations in Towaoc, Colorado, and White Mesa, Utah, typically to attend college or find jobs that they can't find closer to home.

"There's not always a lot of job opportunities on the reservation," Whiteskunk says. "Sometimes a lot of people end up in Blanding, having to find homes. Same thing with Cortez, [Colorado]. Sometimes they end up as far as Durango or Farmington, [New Mexico]. . . . Economically, that might be the best place for them to be close to home."

Another significant challenge the Ute Mountain Utes face is one that tribes across Indian Country are grappling with: how to preserve indigenous languages as elders pass on and young people are embedded within an English-centric digital media.

"It's really hard to communicate with our younger generations that your language is important and that it has a part in your cultural identity," Whiteskunk says. "I think sometimes our young people have disconnected from those thoughts and those ideas, and it's really hard to get them to be a little more active in some of the local events.

"I think there's only one way to teach a language and to revitalize it, and that's by needing to speak and respond in that language," she continues. "If you don't have that need, and that communication isn't necessary on a daily basis, then it doesn't really give [your language] its validity, and it doesn't give it the strength that it needs. I see this across the nation in a lot of Native American communities—everybody says they want to revitalize and teach their language, but when it comes [to] how many people speak it on a daily basis in their workplace, at home, at the grocery store, at the doctor's office, you don't hear it nearly as much as you used to."

Whiteskunk is nevertheless heartened by what she sees as a broad movement among indigenous youth to learn about and reclaim their heritage and traditional ways. Her hope is that tribal leaders can connect youth with elders to strengthen the cultural bonds while there's still time.

"In a lot of the tribal communities, the younger people are now the moving force," Whiteskunk says. "[The elders] are our encyclopedias. They are our knowledge books. They are our authority on traditional protocol, and that's who we need to connect the youth with."

She hopes that she can look to her tribe's young people to help lead the movement that arises from the coalition's work.

"Right now we have smaller groups of youth that are . . . organized in the community," Whiteskunk says. "I've been putting it out there: 'I may be calling upon you. I need your help.' So I think that by extending that 'I need you' that message will be answered."

Whiteskunk believes strongly, as do others in the coalition, that she was called to leadership by a higher power. She is also convinced that she has the opportunity and the capacity to expand her leadership beyond her tribe.

"If we put ourselves out there," Whiteskunk says, "we could really be advocates for a lot of people to help them to organize or elevate their voices."

She believes that the coalition has created a template and set a precedent that other tribes can adapt to their own organizing efforts—especially those tribes that are already engaged in endeavors to protect sacred sites from energy development and "industrial tourism."

"One of the things that I [have] communicated [is] that I'm a spokesperson not only for myself and my people but for those that aren't able to speak for themselves," Whiteskunk says. "And that's the land, the water, the air, and the animals. They're not able to speak for themselves or advocate.

"When we get to the next level of discussions I will be a leader of many more people: no color, no race," Whiteskunk says. "It will be something that needs to happen.

"And that's going to be a form of healing within me."

We must not ignore the painful history Native Americans have endured—a history of violence, marginalization, broken promises, and upended justice. There was a time when native languages and religions were banned as part of a forced assimilation policy that attacked the political, social, and cultural identities of Native Americans in the United States. Through generations of struggle, American Indians and Alaska Natives held fast to their traditions, and eventually the United States Government repudiated its destructive policies and began to turn the page on a troubled past.

—President Barack Obama, presidential proclamation, National Native American Heritage Month, October 31, 2013

We have been clear that this is a tribally led effort. We will help where we're asked to help and butt out when we're asked not to help. We'll offer whatever we can in terms of how other monuments have worked . . . or who are the contacts in Washington to work with. We can help in any of those ways. But really in terms of the boundaries [of the Bears Ears National Monument], that's a tribal discussion. The management language they want to see, that's going to be tribally led. It's really important, for the connection they have to the land is so powerful and so much more important than our interest in it. Therefore, we kind of need to follow their lead.

—Brian O'Donnell, former executive director, Conservation Lands Foundation, July 27, 2015

It's a powerful reminder to people that there are still Native Americans in this country. People think they all died out. This could be a model for how Native people organize.

—Matt Gross, media director, Southern Utah Wilderness Alliance, July 28, 2015

I am not for the monument. We have allotments out there [within the monument boundaries]. We own land out there. We have two cemeteries that are there. We had an elder request to be buried out there. She's ninety-three years old. So what do we tell her? No, the monument's more important? You can't be buried where you came from? We have a lot of history there. I just want everybody to think about what their traditions are and don't forget where you come from as Native Americans.

—Suzette Morris, Ute Mountain Ute resident of White Mesa, Utah, July 16, 2016

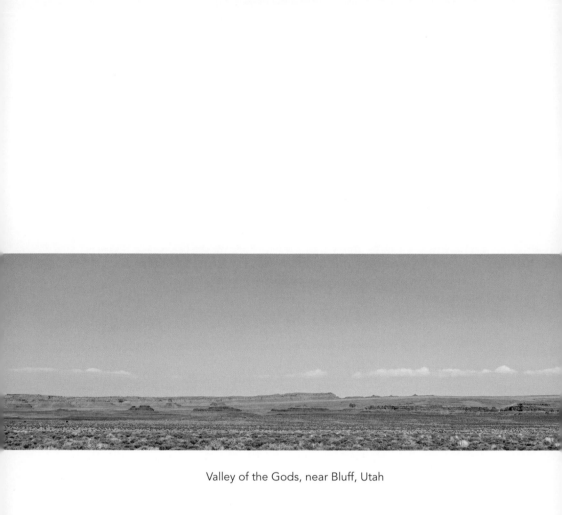

Valley of the Gods, near Bluff, Utah

CARLETON BOWEKATY
Protecting Zuni Sacred Sites, Championing Cultural Preservation

Zuni Pueblo feels at once strongly connected to northern New Mexico's urban centers and a world apart from the fast-paced, media-saturated society outside its small community.

Driving through coniferous hills, then descending into a sage and scrub valley bordered by layered multicolored mesas, we approach Zuni from the east. The evening air, brisk at 6,300 feet, is pungent with scents of sage and wood fires. After parking at Halona Plaza at the pueblo's center, we walk through narrow streets bordered by adobe brick homes. The smell of bread baking in wood-fired outdoor ovens permeates the air. Women converse in low voices, their barely perceptible chatter interrupted by occasional laughter. Dogs amble through the dusty streets, oblivious to visitors. Heading back to our car, we hear the sound of drumming and singing.

As dusk settles over the pueblo, the world outside the boundaries of its 720-square-mile enclave no longer seems to exist. Signs reading No Photographs in the Plaza speak to a fierce desire to protect culture from exploitation. But in reality, the pueblo lies only forty miles from the bustle of Gallup and Interstate 40 and a mere 2.5-hour drive from Albuquerque.

Like many tribal communities around the country—indeed, the world—Zuni has struggled with how to keep its language and traditional culture alive as the Internet and mass media become increasingly prevalent in young people's lives. The unfamiliarity of youth with the unique Zuni language creates a barrier to connecting with elders who are the keepers of traditional knowledge and who are passing on before passing down that wisdom to a new generation.

In part, the disconnect of Zuni youth from traditional culture is dictated by circumstance and opportunity, or lack thereof. Zuni is a small community—just over 7,500 people—and job opportunities outside the education and

Zuni councilman Carleton Bowekaty outside Zuni Pueblo

service industry fields are few. Many young adults leave to attend colleges and universities in Gallup, Albuquerque, and beyond. Their professional training often leads them to work in fields that have little relationship to traditional life in Zuni.

Despite the obstacles to connecting younger generations to a culture that has survived for thousands of years, some Zuni make a choice—or are called, as they see it—to return to their community and serve as teachers, political leaders, and spiritual advisors. One such man is Carleton Bowekaty, who returned to Zuni with his wife and two children after eight years in the military. Bowekaty has chosen to use the leadership skills honed during his tour as a U.S. Army counterintelligence officer to support his tribe, where he serves as a councilman and Zuni representative to the Bears Ears Inter-Tribal Coalition.

Bowekaty greets us warmly at the Zuni Governor's Office on a late April morning. We are tired after a week of crisscrossing the Colorado Plateau, rising at dawn to drive hundreds of miles to our next interview, all the while fighting the instinct to stop and linger in the landscape. But Bowekaty is gracious and forgiving of our bleary-eyedness, and his wide smile makes us feel at home.

He is tall and heavyset but not imposing. His dark-brown eyes are gentle, but they turn intense when he is speaking of issues that compel his passion. His crew-cut black hair is styled with mousse, and silver studs adorn his earlobes. His voice is soft, and while he laughs easily, his words convey a clear sense of purpose and a carefully constructed vision of how to achieve his goals.

Diligence, precision, and focus, all essential to thriving in a military environment, are traits Bowekaty exudes.

"[I learned], here's how you can protect your soldiers better, here's how you can make sure that the people that are helping you are actually helping you," Bowekaty says.

"On my last tour, I was the one mentoring and guiding and developing young soldiers," Bowekaty adds. "It was a progression that really made me confident in myself and my abilities and understand that sometimes you can have everything in place and sometimes something will work against you, and you just have to accept it."

Following his final deployment in 2009, Bowekaty and his wife, Janis, were faced with a choice: move to the East Coast, where Bowekaty would continue his military service, or leave the army and return home with their two children, Janessa and Ian.

"[We] would come [to Zuni] and visit, and I would really notice, my kids don't understand what goes on here in the community," Bowekaty says. "So we made the decision to come back, and I started working for the tribe about a week after my enlistment ended. It worked out really well."

Bowekaty initially served as a member of the tribe's child support enforcement program. His job exposed him to the pressing needs of his community and awakened in him a strong desire to serve his people.

In late 2014 Bowekaty decided to run for a seat on the Zuni Tribal Council. He felt called to a leadership role, but it took encouragement from his wife to place his name on the ballot.

"I'd been talking with my wife about a lot of ways to improve the community," Bowekaty says, "and she's like, 'Well, are you going to do this or not, or are you just talking?'

"She knows what gets me going," Bowekaty laughs.

Before making a final commitment, he carefully weighed his motivations.

"Are you doing this because your wife threw down the gauntlet, or are you doing this because this is really what you feel like you need to do?" Bowekaty recalls asking himself. "At a certain point, it became obvious . . . that this was the path intended for me."

Bowekaty's campaign was successful, and he was sworn in as one of six Zuni councilmen in 2015. Within a few months he became aware of Utah Diné Bikéyah's (UDB) efforts to protect 1.9 million acres in San Juan County as either a national conservation area or a national monument. In April 2015 he joined other tribal leaders at the gathering where UDB cofounder and board member Mark Maryboy welcomed them home.

"That's when we [at Zuni] decided we definitely want to have some input on this," Bowekaty says. He felt a strong ancestral connection to the land as he flew over the area of the proposed monument and then hiked into the canyons of Cedar Mesa and the sandstone of Comb Ridge.

"The landscape is very similar," Bowekaty says. "And once you get down on the ground and actually visit some of the sites, there's clear Ancestral Puebloan ties to the area. You have cliff dwellings, you have rock art that is very similar to what you will find in great kivas and in some of the areas around here. We identified different plants that we use in our ceremonies."

As with the other tribes that have connections to the area, Bowekaty says that Zuni people have an undeniable spiritual and cultural tie to the land, as manifest in prayers and in the migration stories that relate the journey of Ancestral Puebloans between 1250 and 1300 CE from the Four Corners region to their current pueblo settlements in New Mexico and Arizona.

"What really . . . connects us [to the Bears Ears area] are the prayers and the stories that go along with a lot of those prayers," Bowekaty says.

"It's really important to view the migration not just as a physical migration but as a growth in our people," Bowekaty continues. "In order to make us better in this world, we had to do a physical and then spiritual migration in order to balance out what we feel is our place in this world.

"You start making those connections back to that history. We know we've been here. We know we have family here. We know we have ancestors here. In a way, it identifies our path in life."

Protecting the connection—both physical and spiritual—to ancestral lands became a mission for Bowekaty. He, along with Hopi Vice Chairman Alfred Lomahquahu and leaders from the Navajo, Ute Mountain Ute, and Ute Indian Tribe of the Uintah and Ouray Reservation worked with UDB and conservation nonprofits to facilitate a July 2015 meeting on the Ute Mountain Ute Reservation in Towaoc, Colorado. Although the tribes all recognized the importance of their ties to the lands surrounding Bears Ears, it required much discussion, prayer, and passionate advocacy by Mark Maryboy and UDB before they reached consensus.

By the end of the meeting, the Bears Ears Inter-Tribal Coalition had formed and its leaders had committed themselves to protecting ancestral lands by seeking a national monument declaration. Of perhaps even greater significance was the tribes' collective agreement that they would approach

Ancestral Puebloan petroglyphs

the federal government as a partnership of sovereign nations and request that they have "active engagement in future management of the area."[1]

If adopted, the coalition's plan would represent a first: tribal leaders working as equals with representatives of the federal government. Bowekaty says the tribes envision a comanagement commission akin to a board of directors: members of tribal governments with appropriate background and skills would work with their federal counterparts to determine overall policy for the monument.

He sees parallels between what the coalition is proposing and the relationship the Zuni tribe enjoys with the New Mexico state government. New Mexico is the only state in the United States that has an Indian Affairs department. Zuni elected officials, along with members of other recognized Pueblos in New Mexico, work directly on a nation-to-state basis in developing policies and budgets, a direct parallel to the comanagement plan that the tribes advanced for Bears Ears.

Bowekaty believes that the management structure advocated by the Bears Ears Inter-Tribal Coalition could represent a profound shift in the relationship between tribes and the federal government, a change that may at first make some federal officials uncomfortable. However, he has faith that, over time, the tribal and U.S. governments can come to agreement on a working process that can serve as a template for other tribes and indigenous communities.

During 2015 and 2016 coalition members made numerous trips to Washington, first to formally present their proposal for the Bears Ears National Monument to the Obama administration and then to meet with the federal agencies with which they proposed to comanage the monument: the Bureau of Land Management, the National Park Service, and the Forest Service.

"[The federal agencies] are very supportive of this," Bowekaty says. "It's just a matter of making sure that [when] the legal foundation for this . . . is challenged when it does become law that we're firm. We have the solution, and we just need to help them realize that our solution is the best option."

Bowekaty leavens his idealism with a pragmatism that reflects his skill at identifying problems and crafting solutions.

"If it doesn't become a monument," Bowekaty says, "we'll find different ways to make sure that [the land is] protected. If it's challenged legally, that's fine. We're committed. You're not going to find [anyone] as committed as the tribes are, because it's important to us."

---

1. http://bearsearscoalition.org/about-the-coalition.

"When we're successful, I think we could outline some of the steps we took and . . . identify what the challenges were and how we answered those challenges," Bowekaty says. "Provide that model so it can be used in other areas, whether it's another tribe in the United States or another group that wants to use that model," such as groups in Central and South America to which Zuni and members of other tribes are tied culturally and historically.

"If we have those relationships in place, we could . . . collaborate with them and let them see that our approach is successful," Bowekaty says.

Perhaps the strongest challenge to the monument proposal came from supporters of Representative Rob Bishop's Public Lands Initiative (PLI), both residents of San Juan County and their elected representatives on Capitol Hill. They objected to the coalition including tribes and pueblos from outside southeastern Utah and argued that the views of Utah residents living adjacent to the public land comprising the monument should take precedence.

"We didn't draw the [state] lines," Bowekaty says. "It was forced on us, and we're just working with that. I think the biggest [problem we had with] the Public Lands Initiative was that while, yes, it's in Utah, geographically we've always had a tie to this place."

A large number of the more than one hundred thousand archaeological sites and cultural resources within the boundaries of the Bears Ears proposal are, in fact, linked to Hopi, Zuni, and other Pueblos outside of Utah. To the tribes, the monument supporters, and the archaeological community, these sites within the Bears Ears boundaries bear witness to the fact that ancestors of today's Pueblo people ranged widely over Bears Ears and the Colorado Plateau centuries before Anglos settled the area. That history provides powerful support to the proposal's assertion that today's Pueblos maintain a connection to the land and are deeply invested in its future. The Navajo and Ute people share this view.

"I feel that our role is to protect and preserve," Bowekaty says. "It's in the [Zuni] constitution; that's what we need to do."

Bowekaty views the challenge of bringing on board the Interior Department's bureaucratic agencies, steeped in tradition and slow to change, as a surmountable one. What concerns him more is "the disconnect between what tribes feel and how Utah people feel about this situation.

"I think the biggest heartburn with [Utahns]," Bowekaty says, "is the way the Grand Staircase[–Escalante National Monument] was established"—that is, behind closed doors in Washington, with no consultation with the area's residents. "That's what we're fighting almost every single step of the way."

How can such a stark divide be bridged? It's a question that has vexed local and national leaders for generations, particularly because there is not always a desire by the disputing parties to change the toxic yet comfortably familiar dynamic of conflict. Bowekaty hopes that education—about Native cultures and their presence on the landscape and about the potential of a national monument to stimulate economic gains in San Juan County—can play a role in building a future grounded in mutual respect.

"We're looking at . . . closing those gaps," Bowekaty says. "How does education help the local people of Utah realize that this will benefit them?"

Toward that end, Bowekaty points to the coalition's proposal to establish at the monument's headquarters a center that would serve as an education and research facility aimed at exploring connections between western and Native cultures. Bowekaty sees enormous potential for the center to educate visitors—local, national, and international—about the people who have called the Colorado Plateau home over millennia. He also envisions the center serving as a place where Native youth can learn about their own people—their language, their history, their dances, and their prayers.

"We can visit these places and show where we came from so that we can teach our younger generations, this is where your forefathers came from," Bowekaty says. "This is where your family has traveled. This is the heritage that you need to have."

He says that the tribal leaders recognize the extraordinary opportunity they have to shape federal policy to meet their shared desire to conserve and steward land they consider sacred. They do not intend to squander their chance to protect their heritage, share their cultures with the wider world, and preserve their cultures and the earth itself for future generations.

"We're not going anywhere," Bowekaty says. "We're not going to back out. We're not going to hedge. We're not going to roll over. We're going to stick by this, and we'll do what's necessary to make sure that it's realized and that we actually do have a place at the table.

"It's a part of our cultural identity," Bowekaty adds. "If we don't fight for it, then who will?"

(Former President Barack Obama established Bears Ears National Monument in December 2016. A year later, his successor, President Donald J. Trump, reduced the monument's boundaries by 85 percent, spurring numerous legal challenges.)

This order establishes a national policy to ensure that the Federal Government ment engages in a true and lasting government-to-government relationship with federally recognized tribes in a more coordinated and effective manner, including by better carrying out its trust responsibilities. This policy is established as a means of promoting and sustaining prosperous and resilient tribal communities. Greater engagement and meaningful consultation with tribes is of paramount importance in developing any policies affecting tribal nations.

—President Barack Obama establishing the White House
Council on Native American Affairs, June 26, 2013

I really want Obama to make this a national monument, to be brave, to sign the Antiquities Act. I am a hard-core wilderness person. In between my college years during the summer I worked for the Forest Service . . . restoring trails up by Dunton, Colorado, up in the wilderness [near] Navajo Lake. This past summer in July I took my kids up there. That trail seemed shorter when I was young. . . . I told my kids I used to run up these hills. They weren't this steep.

I love wilderness. I love what it stands for. Generations and generations to come. My great-great-grandkids. Their great-great-grandkids. I'd like them to see Bears Ears the way it was since Day One.

—Davis Filfred, member of the Bears Ears Inter-Tribal Coalition
and delegate to the Navajo Nation Council, October 4, 2016

Ancestral Puebloan petroglyphs, Colorado Plateau

DON SIMONIS

Preserving Archaeological Resources,
Educating the Public to Respect the Past

Working behind bulletproof glass and training to respond to violent acts are now realities for Bureau of Land Management employees at the epicenter of the war over land use that is raging across the rural West. Despite what appears to be a dire new norm for public land managers, Don Simonis somehow manages to seem at ease.

Laconic and understated, Simonis sports a faded T-shirt, shorts, and river sandals, a desert-rat uniform well suited to the hot April evening when we first meet him in Bluff. His deep tan speaks to decades of work on archaeological digs in the desert. For the last seven years he has served as an archaeologist for the Bureau of Land Management's Monticello field office. A mischievous glimmer in his warm brown eyes suggests a wry sense of humor and general bemusement with the ways of the world.

His temperament has no doubt proven essential to withstanding the animosity of San Juan County residents, many of whom perceive the BLM as a despotic presence that punishes rural people for continuing to use the land as they have for generations. Simonis is cautious and reserved at our first meeting, choosing his words carefully. He is well acquainted with the wrath of those who may misinterpret an innocent remark and has no interest in kicking hornets' nests.

Like many people involved in the debate over San Juan County's public lands, Simonis vacillates between cautious optimism and despair over the cultural divides in the county. As an example, he cites the BLM's Project Archaeology program. The program introduces school-age children and their adult educators to the fundamentals of archaeology, sponsoring a series of projects and camps in southeastern Utah. Its focus is on teaching scientific and historical inquiry and the importance of protecting cultural resources.

BLM archaeologist Don Simonis in the field (courtesy of Don Simonis)

Simonis expresses excitement about the program and its potential to foster intercultural understanding. The BLM has sponsored several successful Project Archaeology programs and camps in and around Blanding, Bluff, and Moab that have been attended by local families. The program is expanding statewide, bolstered by additional funding from the BLM's Washington, D.C., office. But Simonis says the same antigovernment sentiment that drives many San Juan County residents to oppose any BLM activity has recently impacted Project Archaeology as well—and that the proposal for the Bears Ears National Monument is to blame.

"I thought this whole Project Archaeology thing was going well," Simonis says, sighing deeply. "But now I'm not so sure it is.

"If anything, what we're seeing is kind of a withdrawal into different sides [of the monument debate]," Simonis says. "Every year we . . . have [had] several hundred Boy Scouts come down to Blanding. This year, ten showed up, and no local ones. Nobody."

Simonis and his colleagues asked local archaeologist and Blanding native Winston Hurst for his thoughts on the sudden decline in participants.

"He said, 'Well, it's a protest,'" Simonis recalls. "Their leaders are telling the kids, 'We're not doing this.'"

Such reactions have precedent.

"We noticed this in 2014 after the [Recapture] ride," Simonis says, referring to the ATV ride led by San Juan County commissioner Phil Lyman, protesting the BLM's closure of a road into Recapture Canyon, just north of Blanding, to protect fragile archaeological resources. Lyman and his supporters cited their ancestral connection to the canyon—generations of Lymans and other prominent families used Recapture Canyon as a north–south route from the Abajo Mountains to the San Juan River—and argued that the BLM's actions epitomized disdain for the heritage of local Anglos by a distant and far too powerful federal government.

"It's discouraging to us," Simonis says.

He and other archaeologists and educators, including his wife, Marcia, long active in education and stewardship in the Cedar Mesa area, have tried to make inroads with local teachers. Fear and pressure to conform to dominant local beliefs and ideological stances have kept them from forging a successful partnership.

"Some of the teachers kind of get it, and they'd like to [work with us], but I feel like they're overpowered by the local powers that be, the community and the [Mormon] church . . . to back off and not get too friendly with the BLM," Simonis says.

This arm's-length attitude applies not only to the BLM but to Edge of the Cedars State Park and Museum in Blanding, which houses a large collection of antiquities and is adjacent to one of the most intact Ancestral Puebloan dwellings in southeastern Utah.

"[Many locals] equate Edge of the Cedars, even though they're a state park museum, with the BLM and the agencies," Simonis says, noting that the San Juan County offices of the U.S. Forest Service and the National Park Service are colocated at the museum.

A number of vocal residents are equally dubious of the Canyon Country Discovery Center in Monticello, a museum and educational center that uses experiential, place-based activities to introduce people of all ages to archaeology, astronomy, geology, and ecology from western and Native perspectives. The center is run by the Four Corners School of Outdoor Education, seen by some as populated by radical environmentalists who wish to demonize ranching, mining, and motorized recreation.

When organizations actively working to establish relationships with surrounding communities are rebuffed, Simonis says, it eventually leads to increased polarization, which is difficult, if not impossible, to surmount. The possibility of the president establishing a national monument in San Juan County only intensifies division into ideological camps.

When we speak with Simonis again in June 2016, he tells us that the BLM is preparing for a battle it hopes it doesn't have to fight.

"We've had active shooter training," Simonis says. "And we've had violence drills—as opposed to fire drills.

"I'm not going to sugarcoat it," he continues. "I think it's got potential to get a whole lot uglier. But I don't think it's a reason [for the BLM] to back off. I'm worried that the BLM's going to back off just because of the potential for violence, say, 'Hey, it's not worth having a national monument if people are going to get hurt.'"

There had once been hope that a compromise on public lands issues could be reached through legislation. Representative Rob Bishop's (R-UT) Public Lands Initiative (PLI) in principle strove to work with local stakeholders to develop long-term plans for land use that would then be incorporated into a bill and brought before Congress. But tensions among various groups in San Juan County had been building since shortly after the PLI was launched in 2013. By the time the draft bill was released in January 2016, some groups had abandoned the process, while others skewered the bill as a giveaway to the oil and gas industry.

In September 2016 BLM director Neil Kornze testified before a House Natural Resources Committee hearing and opposed the Utah Public Land Initiative Bill (H.R. 5780) as written. He argued that the bill introduced by Bishop, who also serves as the committee's chairman, failed to provide adequate protection for ancestral sites and areas of great scenic and recreational value.

The agency's recommendations of substantive changes to the bill heartened supporters within and outside of its employ but enraged many San Juan County residents who backed Bishop's PLI and rejected establishment of the Bears Ears National Monument. Opponents of the monument believe that unilateral designation by the president represents the epitome of federal overreach and would ultimately result in devastating the local economy and negatively impacting the culture of San Juan County.

Utah's governor, Gary Herbert, Bishop, former representative Jason Chaffetz, and Senators Mike Lee and Orrin Hatch, all Republicans, have expressed not only their vehement opposition to the monument but also their concern that such a designation would spark antifederal government violence akin to the January 2016 armed occupation of the Malheur National Wildlife Refuge in Burns, Oregon. Such public statements have been viewed by some observers as manipulative at best and dangerous at worst, a warning that serves as an implicit call to arms.

Regardless, Simonis supports declaration of the Bears Ears National Monument.

"I'll come out and say it, I'm in favor of a monument," Simonis says, clearly relieved to state his opinion publicly after playing it safe and remaining neutral for years. He views a monument as the best way to ensure funding both for protection of the area and for educational programs. Preservation is dependent on teaching people to visit archaeological sites with appropriate care and respect and on monitoring the sites, currently patrolled by two officers responsible for 1.8 million acres.

An even more compelling reason to support the Bears Ears Coalition's proposal, he says, is the tribes' vision of a comanagement commission. Such an arrangement has never been attempted, much less implemented. Simonis sees it as a tremendous and long-overdue opportunity, though not without its bureaucratic challenges.

"It seems like it would be difficult to get any agreement on anything with everybody involved," Simonis says. "[But] at a minimum . . . I would hope that the tribes really do get a voice and have some kind of power or sway . . . in decision making, much more so than they've had.

"[Federal] agencies and the tribes, we've got so much we can learn from each other," Simonis continues. "We both know a lot, and we both really want to protect the area and do something with it. We want to improve, I think, our relationships and coordination of everything we do. And what better way to do it than something like this?"

Nevertheless, there are significant bureaucratic barriers that must be overcome in order to devise an efficient and effective mechanism for comanagement. Moreover, there is the potential for violence at and vandalism of ancestral sites fueled by supporters of states' rights. The greatest challenge, Simonis believes, is one that has vexed federal agencies, conservationists, and individuals on all sides of the public lands debate: how to promote the natural beauty and unparalleled cultural resources of the area in a way that brings in tourism dollars and encourages careful stewardship while not overwhelming the fragile landscape with crowds of visitors.

"The sites are just getting loved to death," Simonis says. "We're trying not to have billions of people out there, but . . . it's such a hard line of sharing things and not totally locking [them] up. Where do you draw that line?

"If we wanted to, we could promote this . . . in every paper and magazine, by word of mouth, and on and on," he adds. "On the other hand, if we want to save anything and study it before it gets all trampled and taken, we can't do that. It's a real dilemma, and that's what national parks have dealt with forever. It's nothing new."

There has been widespread speculation that should a monument be created, its headquarters would be in Bluff, population 258 as of the 2010 census, presently home to a handful of restaurants, three motels, and a municipal water and sewer system that by some accounts may not be adequate even for current residents and businesses. Simonis, a Bluff resident himself, knows that the town is in no way prepared for the building frenzy that would almost certainly begin within a year or two following a monument designation.

"We don't have any kind of infrastructure put in, such as restrooms, and . . . any kind of restrictions" on where and how the Park Service and its contractors can locate and erect a monument headquarters and amenities for "massive amounts of people."

"That's all going to have to be developed . . . and approved in a plan," Simonis says.

It can take three to five years to write and implement a comprehensive plan for a national park or monument. Whether Bluff can improve its infrastructure in that time frame is an open question.

The challenges to creating a successfully managed monument are considerable. How can federal agencies and tribes work together to ensure that a monument provides economic benefit to local residents and a role for the tribes in comanagement? Will there be sufficient funding for the BLM, the Park Service, and the Forest Service to protect the area's cultural and natural resources?

Simonis freely admits that he doesn't have the answers. He wants to believe that monument supporters and opponents alike can appreciate the significance and promise of the designation and begin to work together to develop a plan that integrates the monument into the community and provides for a robust economic future.

"I hope people can see the big picture, look five hundred years down the road to . . . the value of . . . what we're talking about here."

Then his tone changes, and the fatalism returns.

"As far as the [San Juan County] community getting behind BLM and working together . . . it hasn't happened, and I don't see it happening for a while, which is not good," Simonis says. "We need to try to somehow work together and keep everybody happy. But I don't know how that's going to happen."

I went on field trips with my children. And I got on the bus, and there were people I'd never seen before. In Blanding we know everybody. If there's somebody new, we want to know, just find out who you are. So there were Four Corners [School of Outdoor Education] people. And they were extreme. And a kid picked up a rock, and they freak out, "You've got to put that rock right back where it was! That can't be moved!" And it's like, how do they know somebody else didn't drop it there? How do they know it's in its original state? We were on the mountain in early fall, and they wouldn't let anybody pick off a leaf. Well, they're going to fall anyway. It's beyond extreme. And they literally had children hug trees. All kinds of crazy things. So I opposed [the Canyon Country Discovery Center].

—Merri Shumway, member and former chair,
San Juan School District Board, January 28, 2016

If we're going to change things here in San Juan County, we have to start somewhere, and we need to start educating the local folks on why archaeology is important. They don't really understand it. To change that bad behavior [pothunting and grave robbing], we need to start working with the local population and get that mindset changed.

In the past few years we have been very successful with the local school. [One of] the . . . teachers, he wanted Don [Simonis] to be there so that people don't think of all of the BLM as being those storm troopers and these horrible mean people; to have that interface with the community that, hey, we're normal people too, just like you. We're not out to hurt you or necessarily distrust you. There is that effort to try and build relationships with the community.

We are planning on having four to six Native representatives—Navajo, Pueblo, Ute—[on Girl Scout trips to San Juan County]. Eventually we want to involve other youth, other groups. Specifically, we have been asked to do field trips on Cedar Mesa. We want to have indigenous groups with the girls explain what this land means to them. Witnessing that and being around Native folks, that's a very powerful message they can give you. It instills a respect for other cultures, which we certainly need right now. It just fosters good relationships and respect and maybe a different way of looking at things in a new way than what we do with our Anglo eyes.

—Marcia Simonis, board member and former statewide site
steward coordinator, Friends of Cedar Mesa, January 26, 2016

Archaeological site, Cedar Mesa

WINSTON HURST

Studying Ancestral Puebloan Civilizations, Bearing Witness to Intercultural Conflict

For a man widely considered to be a legend in the field of Four Corners archaeology, Winston Hurst is as understated as he is venerated. He has invited us into his home west of downtown Blanding to discuss recent developments in Southwest archaeological research and how the Mormon culture of his hometown informs locals' perception of his field. His spacious living room has an eclectic aesthetic: needlepoint art on the wall is juxtaposed with Native American baskets and pots that occupy entire shelves, reflecting Hurst's deep and enduring appreciation of the cultures of the area's indigenous peoples.

With graying hair reaching below his shoulders and a small stud in his left ear, wearing faded jeans and river sandals, Hurst hardly fits the stereotypical image of a clean-cut Mormon. Yet Hurst was born in Blanding into a Mormon family and steeped in a culture that once viewed collecting Ancestral Puebloan artifacts as a natural part of life, either to enhance Mormons' own collections of pots and artifacts or, in their view, as a way to protect those artifacts from destructive, profit-hungry looters. For decades, Hurst has walked the line between his identity as a local who himself dug for artifacts as a child and his identity as a scientist dedicated to preserving cultural resources out of a desire to better document, understand, and honor the past. His eyes, framed by wire-rimmed glasses, convey both uncommon intelligence and world-weary resignation, reflecting perhaps the toll of decades spent navigating two vastly different worlds.

Hurst prefers to keep our conversation focused on recent developments in his field, particularly those that challenge prior research and spur archaeologists to explore new ways of collecting and interpreting data.

Archaeologist Winston Hurst
(courtesy of Winston Hurst)

"We're on the cusp of being able to see things in a whole lot more detail than we've seen before," he notes. "What we need to refine this is a lot more very careful, intensive documentation of whole landscapes . . . and as tight as possible dates we can get on as many sites as possible. [This work will] open up some really interesting insights into the comings and goings of community landscapes and shifting populations."

Hurst sees DNA collection as one of the most significant recent innovations in the field. But the manner in which DNA is collected and reported is a delicate cultural matter.

"It has the potential to be huge, but . . . it runs afoul of Native politics, so it's controversial," Hurst says. "There are a lot of ways of getting to DNA that don't involve disturbing human remains, ironically. Certain archaeologists are proceeding along those lines fairly energetically. Over time I suspect that we'll see Native attitudes about DNA studies evolve as they become a little more relaxed about the fact that they finally have some say in what we do with their dead people. . . . I suspect they'll become very interested themselves in the questions that can be answered by [DNA testing] and do some of the studies themselves."

Our conversation turns unavoidably toward the tensions between life-long residents and outsiders who come to San Juan County from around the world aiming to understand the evolution of indigenous cultures on the Colorado Plateau.

As someone whose early childhood years were spent casually exploring Ancestral Puebloan ruins and collecting artifacts, Hurst understands well the

University of Colorado students excavating in Comb Wash, 2004 (courtesy of Winston Hurst)

reaction many citizens have toward visiting scholars who are critical of the ways locals tread upon land dense with antiquities.

"When you're dealing with rather conservative folk who are used to being carped at, harped at, and criticized by the whole damned world for years and years, they tend to get very defensive," Hurst says.

In the midst of this politically fraught environment, archaeology has become an unlikely ideological battleground.

"The greatest tragedy in archaeology in the American Southwest is that we've allowed a situation to develop in which archaeology has become synonymous with environmentalism, with protectionism, with government rules and sanctions, things that you can't do," Hurst says. "In the political and cultural polarization that we've seen in the past twenty years, archaeology has been pulled over in the popular perception to the left of the cultural divide. And it's made it hard for the more conservative folks to feel comfortable being interested in it, being open-minded about it. [Politics] is the greatest obstacle to instilling a greater ethic of respect and appreciation of [cultural resources]."

The anger Hurst sees festering in San Juan County is mirrored in the Sagebrush Rebellion's most recent protest: the month-long armed occupation of the Malheur National Wildlife Refuge in early 2016 that resulted in significant damage to the refuge headquarters, records, and the surrounding land, including an archaeological site important to the Burns Paiute tribe.[1] It also resulted in the death of one of the protestors. The militants in Malheur and their followers in Utah decry any federal protection of public lands, even to protect cultural resources.

"You get these knuckleheads who are out there destroying archaeological sites, and they're justifying it on the basis of politics," Hurst says. "The big bad federal government is overreaching and telling them they can't do this, so they go do it to show the big bad federal government they can do anything they damn want!"

Hurst believes that education is essential, first to ameliorate and then to change deeply ingrained attitudes.

"When we reach out and try to teach their kids or open their mind to this stuff, we have to be really careful," Hurst says. "If we come across too strong in any way, it takes very little for them to completely shut off if they . . . feel like they're being propagandized by the Left."

Based on his observations and experience, he thinks that the BLM or any other federal agency cannot lead educational efforts, despite the fact that the government has deeper pockets than any school or grassroots organization.

"A few select teachers have come to us, and [Boy Scout] leaders have come to us, and [they have] said, 'We need to change the way we relate to this stuff. Can you help us?'" Hurst says. "Then it's organic. It's coming out of the community, it's the community thinking this stuff through. In the end that might take longer, and we might lose some stuff in the end, but it's going to be a hell of a lot stronger if it goes that way."

Hurst's greatest concern is that local attitudes won't evolve quickly enough to preserve the clues critical to understanding the history of past civilizations on the Colorado Plateau.

"I tend to be a pessimist at heart and a cynical, sad depressive about human nature," Hurst says. "Maybe I've studied human nature too long or not enough, I don't know. But I don't have a whole lot of hope that we're going to be able to really effectively save the archaeological record out here in the

---

1. Griffin, "New Indictment Alleges Damage."

Salt Creek Canyon (fall; aerial image)

form that it exists now, which is, sadly, pretty hammered already. It's going to be eliminated by attrition, one potsherd at a time, ten thousand boots pounding on sites, by people not teaching their kids, and as a far secondary side of that, looting is not going to go away."

While Hurst doesn't condone the actions or goals of Sagebrush Rebels, he does argue that key agencies of the federal government have made it far more difficult to gain the public understanding and respect needed to preserve antiquities. In his view, the BLM, the Forest Service, and FBI agents have treated Blanding residents with disrespect and substituted force for reason, education, and patience. He cites as an example efforts to enforce rules against pothunting and looting.

"In the late seventies and early eighties the government threw a bunch of money at [archaeological protection], put rangers out here on the ground, helicopters in the air, spying devices out there. . . . That culminated in the first great federal raid in 1986, which was an absolute damn disaster," Hurst says.

That raid, led by the FBI, was the outcome of a sting operation aimed at identifying individuals involved in artifact trafficking. Its aftereffects opened a massive wound in the Blanding community.

"At the time [the 1986 raid] went down, we were actually doing pretty well with hearts and minds in this community," Hurst says. "It scared the hell out of me, and . . . it took us a lot of slow, careful, quiet conversations [with community members] about it. And just about when we started to get it right, guess what?"

In 2009 FBI agents, accompanied by armed SWAT teams, conducted another series of raids in Blanding, the culmination of another multiyear sting operation in which sixteen people were arrested, including Dr. James Redd, a well-respected and well-loved physician in the community. Though the FBI dropped the charges against the majority of them, Redd and a Santa Fe man implicated in the multistate trafficking ring committed suicide in the days following their arrests.

The raids and their aftermath once again enraged and traumatized the town and frayed relations between locals and the federal government to the breaking point. The Blanding raids became national news, and as a result, the clash has shaped outsiders' clichéd view of southeastern Utah as a place populated by backward folk surrounded by postcard-worthy scenery.

"A lot of people in this community are very embarrassed by the way the press covers this community," Hurst says. "[Blanding] has such a nasty reputation in the popular American mind and in the subculture of media coverage. Whenever somebody does something stupid in Blanding, it makes the news. Whenever someone does something smart, nobody says a word. A lot of people in this town don't conform to that stereotype, but . . . the ones who do conform . . . tend to be loud, obnoxious, and bullying, so people aren't too eager to get out there and oppose them.

"But [politicians] are all more reasonable than they appear in the media," Hurst adds. "Get them away from the glare of the camera and put them nose-to-nose in quiet conversation [where] they know they're not going to get quoted anywhere and their base isn't going to react to it. The challenge is to keep it at the level of good people in conversation with each other with mutually respected points of view."

Hurst believes that, just as efforts at archaeological education have a greater chance of success if led by local people, the only way a sensible compromise on land-use issues can be enacted is by allowing local stakeholders to lead the process and forge a plan.

"If I could dictate the future and create the ideal situation, I would have the local communities and the local county commission and the local chambers of commerce and the pimps in the tourism industry . . . all recognize the fact that the family jewels are the land out here and the archaeological resources on it, and I would have them manage it," Hurst says.

Which is precisely why the prospect of executive declaration of the Bears Ears National Monument comanaged by representatives of multiple sovereign Native governments makes him more than a little uneasy.

"That Bears Ears thing scares the hell out of me," Hurst says. "A committee of comanag[ers] coming from entities that have not been friendly with each other for much of their history is probably not the most efficient way to manage something. I'm glad [the tribes] are engaged, I'm glad they're in the dialogue, but I'm a little cynical and skeptical about how that might work out and really nervous about the precedent it would set. I hope history proves me wrong on that.

"If [the federal government and the tribes] come up with some designation, I would certainly hope it'd come up from a deliberative, multivoice process," Hurst says—much like the process the PLI purported to be. "In a pluralistic society like ours, with a tremendous diversity of points of view, it can't be a win-or-lose situation. There's no such thing as a win-win situation. If something will cost all sides equally in the end and . . . pisses off everybody, that's the best solution there is. Because if you have something that only makes one group happy, you're going to turn everyone else into a bunch of damn revolutionaries.

"So we have to go with the dirty reality of democracy and compromise and frustration and imperfection," Hurst adds. "If there was some sense that you could come up with something and that'd be the end of the story, that we'd be stuck with it for the next hundred years, I think people would go for it, because they're so damned tired of dealing with this. But our experience is, it doesn't end with that. The door closes, the meeting's done, and immediately both sides are at it again."

(As of 2018, both sides were still at it. While a proclamation was issued by former president Barack Obama in December 2016 creating the Bears Ears National Monument, a year later President Donald J. Trump signed an executive order shrinking Obama's monument by 85 percent, leaving two noncontiguous units, Shash Jáa and Indian Creek, thus removing large landscape-scale protections. See map on p. 329. A lawsuit challenging Trump's order, filed by numerous conservation groups and the five tribes of the Bears Ears Inter-Tribal Coalition, is making its way through the courts.)

Winston grew up there . . . when [this area] wasn't discovered. He recognizes that it's going to change, but he doesn't want it to change, and he's just sort of in denial and bummed about it. He's not only one of the most knowledgeable archaeologists, but he's also a local who's lived in Blanding forever, and grew up in a Mormon family there, and has had the tensions of being a community member in Blanding while also advocating [for protection of archaeological resources]. When all those people were arrested for looting in these areas, he was in the crosshairs. He was one of the few people in Blanding that said they shouldn't be doing that, whereas everyone else is, "Oh, my grandfather used to dig up graves" [and] "It's a family tradition on weekends to go out there. Everybody's got a couple of pots in their backyard. What's wrong with that?" He can get ostracized at times, but then, when he's in that community, he's pushing to get them more conservation minded. When he's hanging out with conservationists . . . [he tells us], "You've got to remember the local people, and their lifestyles are going to change here, and you've got to respect that."

—Brian O'Donnell, former executive director, Conservation Lands Foundation, July 27, 2015

Since most kids now, and adults too, are into *CSI* and that kind of science, I somehow draw them in trying to explain how an archaeologist is the detective and the artifacts are the clues. If those artifacts are not there, we don't get the story, the clues are gone, we don't know the story of these people. Leaving those things alone, that's why it's important to do that.

—Marcia Simonis, board member and former state site steward coordinator, Friends of Cedar Mesa, January 26, 2016

I reflect upon several of the important questions anthropology has for human beings and human development. The big questions that should be concerning us are, what are the conditions around the physical development of human beings, what are the conditions or circumstances surrounding the development of the human mind, what are the circumstances around the development of agriculture, and what are the circumstances or problems associated with the process of urbanization, or becoming a city dweller? Two of those four questions can be [answered] best in other parts of the world. But the latter two, that of addressing farming and of addressing social complexity or urbanization, are best addressed right here, in the Southwest in general but, more specifically, here in Four Corners. This is the place to come on the planet to grapple with those two questions.

—Jonathan Till, archaeologist and curator of collections, Edge of the Cedars State Park, January 26, 2016

Book Cliffs at sunset

SHAUN CHAPOOSE
Fighting to Achieve Justice,
Finding Strength in Numbers

Another day, another drive, this time a 270-mile trek from Monticello to Fort Duchesne, Utah, a lonely town in the state's northeastern corner that is home to the headquarters of the Ute Indian Tribe of the Uintah and Ouray Reservation.

The first turn toward the tribal offices is obvious: we make a right at the Ute Tribal Plaza, a sizeable commercial center consisting of a truck stop, a supermarket, and the Kahpeeh Kah'ahn Coffee House. Once we're headed down the road, however, the signage stops, and Google Maps loses its bearings, firing off conflicting directions that take us in circles and ultimately lead us to a residential neighborhood, with no sign of government buildings or anything remotely official. We ask a woman climbing out of her truck where to find tribal headquarters; she tells us to take a right at the sign for the dentist's office and go up the hill. Easy enough, we think.

We find our way back to the main road and follow her directions, but once again, we find ourselves driving in circles, this time between several official-looking buildings, none of which is the one we seek. At last, a kind and infinitely patient woman sets us straight, and we arrive just in time for our meeting with the tribal chairman, Shaun Chapoose.

We wait for Chapoose in the lobby of tribal headquarters, a fluorescent-lit room festooned with Halloween decorations: papier-mâché witches, "Zombie Crossing" caution tape, and hand-carved jack-o'-lanterns. Suspended in a large corner near the front door is a massive windsock ghost, swaying and dancing frenetically. Framed photos of former Miss Ute pageant winners line the hallways. People mill about, talking quietly.

Chapoose emerges from the chambers thirty minutes after our scheduled appointment, spends a few moments sizing us up, then smiles and shakes our hands. He is tall and stocky, his silver-black hair pulled back

Shaun Chapoose, chairman of the Ute
Tribe of the Uintah and Ouray Reservation

into a ponytail, his face dominated by dark-brown eyes, which convey a mixture of shrewdness and ferocity. He wears a pair of small silver earrings, a blue button-down flannel shirt, and jeans. His shirt sleeves are rolled up to his elbows, revealing forearm-spanning flame tattoos. Chapoose has the dignity befitting one in his position and at the same time manages to project a cunning tough-guy persona ready to outsmart you in a game of chess or kick your ass into next week.

Some of these characteristics may reflect inherent personality traits, while others could well be rooted in the history of his people and their remarkable capacity for survival in the face of calamities suffered by their tribe.

Over the past 150 years, Utes have been fighters, fiercely defending their people and the land that is theirs by treaty. Today's Utes have not forgotten how their forebears were forced by the government to cede land both sacred and essential to their physical survival. Their present battles are with local and national politicians whom they believe are attempting to wrest land from them to access the rich trove of oil and gas that lies beneath the surface. Their latest fight is with Representative Rob Bishop (R-UT) over the Public Lands Initiative; their strongest allies, the leaders of the Bears Ears Inter-Tribal Coalition. We have traveled far north of San Juan County to hear from Chapoose why the fight is so important and how his tribe came to be one of the five founders of the coalition.

We follow him back to his office, which is in a state of organized chaos: stacks of paper over a foot high that surround his expansive wooden desk; shelves packed to capacity with thick binders; large maps of land parcels tacked to bulletin boards and rolled up behind the door; and, on a shelf near his desk, a small plaque that reads: "Welcome to my life: 50 shades of bullshit."

Chapoose may be surrounded by BS, but he is no bullshitter, or at least that's what he'd like us to believe. He speaks his mind and shares his views, no matter how harsh they may sound to a listener. He is unencumbered by insecurity or norms of decorum; he leans back in his chair as he looks us over, supremely confident and in control, and pops a large wad of tobacco chew in his mouth. Over the course of our conversation, he periodically pauses midthought to spit a small piece out into the air (no spittoon for him), caring not a whit about how we perceive him but, as always, testing us, seeing how far he can push the envelope before we express shock or discomfort.

His disarming bluntness is coupled with an utter lack of sentimentality. When asked about the stunning handmade quilt that covers the wall behind his desk, Chapoose downplays the fact that it was made for him by his elderly Sioux mother-in-law when he became the chair of the Business Committee, the tribe's most powerful government body, in early 2015. Instead, he grumbles about how his wife forced him to hang it.

"This ain't my house," Chapoose says. "This is my office. Why would I put my personal belongings here?"

While Chapoose advertises himself as a born fighter, he knows not to pick battles he cannot win.

"I have to appease her, because if I don't, she's worse than Bishop," he says, grinning.

His joke serves as an inflection point in his train of thought, and his eyes shift from reflecting his wicked humor to conveying a long-simmering anger over Representative Bishop's attempts to acquire the rich oil and gas reserves beneath the Utes' land in Duchesne County. Based on his experiences with Bishop, Chapoose has come to believe that the architect of the much-discussed Public Lands Initiative may have touted compromise to the press but that his ultimate goal in the three-year, eight-county PLI effort was to orchestrate a transfer of one hundred thousand acres of Ute tribal land to the state for oil and gas development.

"We knew what Bishop was doing," Chapoose says. "We kind of figured that he was trying to keep the discussion from his real intent."

Technically, the legislative language Bishop wrote for the PLI calls for the School and Institutional Trust Lands Administration (SITLA) to execute a land swap that would trade parcels of SITLA land in Carbon County to the south for a more mineral-rich tract of land in the Uintah Basin—land that the Utes believe belongs to the tribe.

SITLA parcels are one-mile-square sections interspersed, checkerboard-like, among public lands. These parcels, in Utah and in a number of western states, were set aside at the time statehood was granted in order to provide revenue to support schools and other state institutions.[1] Over the years, SITLA has garnered the majority of its revenue from mineral leasing.

"SITLA gets in, and they get dirty," Chapoose says. "Put their little children in front of the world—'this is about the children.'"

At the September 2016 House Natural Resources Committee hearing on the PLI, David Ure, SITLA's director, teared up during his testimony as he described his work to develop relationships with the Utes and stressed SITLA's commitment to bettering the lives of Ute schoolchildren. Given that context, Ure favors any mechanisms that maximize economic return from lands under SITLA's jurisdiction.

Chapoose was unmoved by Ure's emotional testimony.

"SITLA's been in the oil business from the beginning of time," Chapoose says, pausing to spit out flecks of his chewing tobacco. "I don't know who they're kidding. We all know that on our reservation, [we have some of the wealthiest] resources in the state of Utah. Which is kind of poetic humor, since Brigham Young didn't want this place because it was unfit for jackrabbits, right? It wasn't farmland. So here we sit on the pot of gold. We've got vast minerals."

Ute tribal leaders say they were never consulted about the proposed SITLA exchange. In a flurry of press releases and news stories in September 2016, they called the proposal in the PLI a "modern day land grab." They escalated their attacks in subsequent weeks, investing $100,000 in a tribal political action committee that launched a series of blistering online and televised ads assailing Bishop and attacking the PLI.

Chapoose and his fellow tribal leaders could have begun their anti-PLI campaign when a draft was released in mid-July, but they instead decided to bide their time, waiting until the final months of both the congressional session and the Obama presidency.

"You have to let them make the first mistake," Chapoose says. "If you fire off too quick, the rhetoric can change. If I got caught up in the schematic of the fight, I would have been the aggressor. You can lose momentum.

---

1. "What Are Trust Lands?"

"Bishop underestimated that," he says. "He thought we were just still sitting in our tepees, smoking peace pipes. What he didn't think I was going to do was launch a political campaign in the paper. They didn't think that I'd call it what I did: [a] land grab. That draws attention."

In case it wasn't abundantly clear already, Chapoose emphasizes that when it comes to defending his people and homeland from threats, he is no peacemaker.

"I'm the guy challenging the federal government," Chapoose says. "I'm the one who takes them to court. . . . I'm the one beating them up.

"We all have specific roles [as tribal members]," he adds. "There's people that are good at hunting. There's people that are good at medicine. There's people that are traditionalists. There's people that are good at fights. I'm skilled in that part. I'm skilled in conversation. I'm skilled in getting our point of view out in terms that people can understand. I'm well versed in federal law [and] legal issues, I know the playbook," which he mastered during his years working for the Environmental Protection Agency, the Bureau of Indian Affairs, and the Central Utah Water Project. "I know how to use [my knowledge] to my advantage. That's my role in this whole fight."

While Chapoose was battling the state and the feds in court and in the media, a years-long fight in the southeastern corner of the state was about to escalate.

In 2014, after more than a year of feeling slighted and effectively shut out of PLI discussions by both Bishop and the San Juan County commissioners, the Navajo-led group Utah Diné Bikéyah (UDB) decided to engage other Colorado Plateau tribal nations in its efforts to protect land that was considered sacred by all the tribes and that contained countless archaeological sites that bore witness to the presence of their ancestors.

Over the next months, leaders from the Hopi, Zuni, and Ute Mountain Ute tribes joined UDB and Navajo Nation representatives and began to assemble a coalition with the goal of petitioning President Obama to protect their ancestral lands by declaring a 1.9-million-acre swath of land in San Juan County a national monument. The tribes realized that the participation of Chapoose's tribe would significantly enhance the political clout of the coalition: the Ute Indian Tribe's twenty thousand members occupy one of the largest Native American reservations in the United States.

Eric Descheenie, representing the Navajo Nation, and Alfred Lomahquahu, then a Hopi vice chairman and Bears Ears Inter-Tribal Coalition cochair, traveled to Fort Duchesne to meet with Chapoose. Chapoose recalls discussing strategy for the meeting with his fellow Business Committee leaders.

"We had to think about it," Chapoose says. "Do we want to get caught up in this mess? Why do we want to go help them? So we thought about it . . . and finally I was like, 'Well, you know, it might be worth it. Let's see what they want.'"

In keeping with Chapoose's style, the meeting was no-BS from the start.

"[We all said,] 'Let's talk open, let's not talk politically correct,'" Chapoose recalls. "We're Natives. Let's talk like Natives. So we talked. And they painted a picture to us of what they were attempting to do. That's an honorable fight. It's fair. So I was like, 'Okay, we're willing. When the fight comes, give us a call.'

"If you notice, at a lot of [coalition] conversations, we're never there," Chapoose continues. "There's a reason we're not there. I told them, 'You know what you're getting yourself into with us. You go send your peacekeepers [to negotiate], you go play nice, but when the war comes, give me a call, and we'll show up for the war.'"

Chapoose says that he could have rebuffed the coalition leaders and focused all of his resources on defending his land from Bishop's attempts to use it for energy development.

"I said [to the coalition leaders], 'The bad thing about this fight is I'm going to suffer the worst,'" Chapoose recalls. "'None of you guys got nothin' in the fight.' If you think about this, they're fighting over something none of them own. PLI affects me. I'm the actual [land]owner.

"But once I gave 'em my word, that's forever," Chapoose says. "I told them I wouldn't step back, and I told them, . . . 'We'll go down that road with you. We won't stop.'"

Chapoose sees his tribe's contribution to a successful campaign to declare the Bears Ears National Monument, comanaged by the tribes, as a path toward gaining leverage in his own tribe's negotiations with federal government agencies.

Like other coalition leaders, Chapoose views comanagement as the most powerful way to assert tribal sovereignty and gain power in the tribes' relationships with the U.S. government.

"For a long time, [this nation has] been putting an Indian on the wall as an ornament," Chapoose says. "You use them, you benefit because of them, but they're never involved in the process. I may be a Ute, but I'm also an American citizen. I should have the same protections as an average citizen. At the same time, I have my right as a sovereign tribe, by treaty, by agreement.

"It was one of [those] moments as an Indian person," he says of the decision to join the coalition. "Hey, you know what, you guys [the federal government] had your run for a few hundred years. . . . Why don't you listen to someone who's been here before you? You might learn something if you listen a little. Let us bring to you the knowledge that you guys don't even know exists.

"The way I viewed it, it was a good way to test the water of sovereignty. It was a good test to see, are we part of this world, or are we still that noble red man out on the prairie and the mountains, ridin' his horse? It was a safe way to gauge that. It didn't cost me nothing"—and it gave him an additional point of leverage against Bishop.

When Interior Secretary Sally Jewell and leading officials from the BLM, the Forest Service, and the National Park Service visited southeastern Utah in July 2016, Chapoose was invited to meet with her at Bears Ears and to speak at a public hearing in Bluff on the PLI and national monument proposals. He describes the balancing act he tried to manage during Jewell's visit.

"I've got to be careful not to offend people," Chapoose says, "but at the same time I've got to remind them, 'Hey, you know, don't forget where you're at and who we are.'"

The public hearing held in Bluff following Jewell's meeting with the coalition was less of a "listening session" and more of a mass airing of grievances. People on all sides expressed, with varying degrees of emotion and coherence, their passion about the land and how it should be designated and managed. Nearly every elected leader and citizen speaker who spoke at the meeting directed their remarks at the secretary and federal officials, who sat on a stage elevated above the audience members, who were jam-packed into the auditorium seats. Chapoose took a different tack.

"I'll flip this a little on everybody," Chapoose recalls. "I'll put it back on everybody else. My speech," which he delivered with his back to the federal officials, "was . . . Well, what I would have said if I could speak normally was, 'Here you sit like a bunch of dumbasses in this hot, God-forsaken room like goddamn children, fighting over something that you really shouldn't be fighting over. Cooler heads should have prevailed. You should have sat in a room and hashed this shit out and not let it become this.'

Crowd gathers for public meeting with Interior Secretary Sally Jewell in Bluff, Utah, on July 16, 2016

"But I can't get away with saying that, so I have to sit there and think out this comment, and I've got two minutes," Chapoose says. "So I turned to the [federal officials] and said, 'I talked to you last night, so I'll address this to the [audience].' I made key statements" about the tribes' connection to the land and their right to determine how it should be managed. "And I meant them."

Chapoose says of the public hearing, "That wasn't the battleground. The battleground is where I'm at now, fighting over PLI."

As of the fall of 2016, Chapoose believed that Obama would declare a monument before the end of the year, but he also believed that the monument would be shrunk from the 1.9-million-acre vision of the coalition to a 1.4-million-acre swath of land, the boundaries of which may be almost identical to those that Bishop drew for the PLI's Bears Ears National Conservation Area.

"[Obama will] gut part of what they want," Chapoose says.

He views it as Politics 101: give the players—in this case, the tribes and Bishop—some of what they want in order to mollify them or help them save face, but don't give one side everything they want lest those on the other side paint themselves as victims and the government as the aggressor.

(In fact, Chapoose was either prescient or very well informed: Obama did designate Bears Ears National Monument in December 2016, and its boundaries were very similar to those of the PLI's national conservation area.)

Chapoose believes the coalition may temporarily splinter as tribes are reminded of their preexisting and ongoing conflicts with one another. "But people will get over [those conflicts], lick their wounds for a few days," he adds. "[Then] we'll say, we could do something. Let's start working. So you get two or three years of bad feelings . . . but in time, not all of [the land and archaeological sites] will be saved, but some will."

The tumult that followed President Obama's designation of Bears Ears National Monument tested the tribes' resolve to defend the monument from attempts to reduce or rescind it. There was no time for infighting or conflict; their efforts revolved around coordinating strategies for litigation and advocacy in a united effort to exercise sovereignty to the best of their abilities.

In a May 2017 press conference at the Press Club in Washington, D.C., Chapoose spoke to the tribes' unity, as well as to the need to fight if necessary.

"We're the first Americans," Chapoose said. In a nod to President Trump's "make America great again" campaign slogan, he added, "We want to help you become the great America you want to be. But [we can't] as long as we're left out of the conversation, as long as we're dismissed.

"Fights don't have to be fights, but for some reason, that's what [Trump administration officials] want," Chapoose said. "They're forcing me to fight. I don't think any tribal leader here has ill feelings toward them. This is the one moment in the history of the United States where [the federal government and the tribes] are gonna succeed together or we're gonna fight.

"We've been [fighting] for a long time," Chapoose said, gesturing toward his fellow tribal leaders. "If anything, we're geared to do it because of our history. If [Interior] Secretary [Ryan] Zinke's out there listening, it's time for you to step up to the plate. If they want to have a discussion with us, the Bears Ears Inter-Tribal Coalition is right here."

Chapoose takes a much less reverent view of cultural resources connecting Native peoples to their ancestors.

"It's history," Chapoose says. "You can't save it all. It's not possible. We lose it every day. But you'll save something. And it'll be like the Roman Empire: you'll have a coliseum and a perception of what it was, but you will never have all of the story. Time is what it is. History is what it's designed to be.

"A hundred years from now, Bears Ears might still be Bears Ears," he says. "It might not be what it is [now]. But it doesn't mean it's a tragedy. It is what it is. The fact that it got attention was a success. The fact that it got Indians to the table saying something, and somebody's listening."

Impermanence is a recurring theme in Chapoose's monologue.

Despite his aggressive defense of his land and his people, he makes it clear that he isn't in his leadership role for the glory or for public recognition.

"Most of us don't want to be here," Chapoose says. "But there comes a point where . . . your people call for you, they need you. Once you're here, though, you're waitin' to go. I'm waitin' to leave."

Chapoose comes from a well-respected family; his grandfather and other relatives were tribal leaders for many years. He has held office for only two years, but in that time, the Utes have achieved crucial victories in the courtroom and the press. He has no intention of overstaying his welcome.

"I'll do what I need to do as long as I think I can do it," Chapoose says. "But I'm not going to be like [my relatives]. The moment I cease to be effective, be what this tribe needs, I need to leave. I owe it to them to walk out.

"I might be remembered; I might not," Chapoose adds. "Who gives a crap? I really don't care."

What matters most, Chapoose says, is the land that has sustained his people for generations, the land where he learned to hunt, the mountains he knows "like the back of my hand." The land will always provide for them, if they are vigilant and protect it from those who would exploit it.

"We don't own this [land]," he says. "We never have. We're only here to use it: take from it what you need and leave it better than when you had it.

"I'm not [a] hero," he adds. "My time's limited. But I have an obligation to take what was passed on to me and pass it on to the next generation, to my family, to my children to make it better, like my father had an obligation to me to make it better than what he had."

As we leave, we ask Chapoose whether he would be open to a follow-up conversation. He pauses, then smiles.

"When we explain something, we only give you what we think you could understand," he says. "You might come see me in a year or two, and I'll tell you the second part."

When we go to Congressmen Bishop and Chaffetz, and we say, 'We are here as sovereign nations wanting to sit down with your sovereign, and you just completely disregard, ignore, or in some places insult our sovereign nations,' I think a lot of us take that deeply, because these governments are direct descendants of our ancestors and our treaties. I think that's why some of us are a little appalled that somehow Congressman Chaffetz completely sidesteps it.

When [Bishop's and Chaffetz's staffers] delivered the draft of the PLI, they sent a staff member to hand it to the [Ute Mountain Ute] councilman in White Mesa, Utah. If they wanted to do things appropriately, they should have sent a staff member to Colorado, to Towaoc, to the tribal chambers. That's another insult to the sovereign nation of the Ute Mountain Ute tribe. . . . They refuse to acknowledge tribal nations. They either refuse or they ignore the history, their own history especially, in respect to Indian people. It's disappointing, to say the least.

—Eric Descheenie, Arizona state representative,
District 7, and former cochair of the Bears Ears
Inter-Tribal Coalition, January 28, 2016

Layered hills, southwest of Bluff, Utah

A PATH FORWARD
Establishing Trust, Healing Wounds

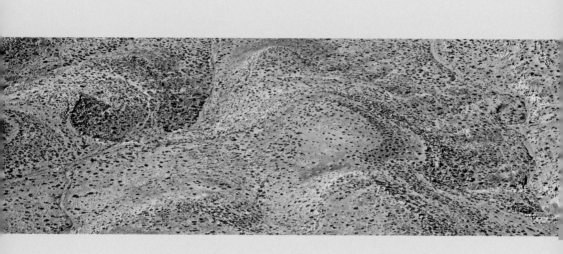

Mesa top above the San Juan River from Muley Point

KATE CANNON
Managing Utah's Public Lands, Strengthening Relationships with Local Communities

When we arrive at her Moab office on a sunny morning in late April 2016, Kate Cannon is on the phone wrangling with the press. Cannon, the superintendent of the National Park Service's Southeast Utah Group, which includes Arches and Canyonlands National Parks and Hovenweep and Natural Bridges National Monuments, is fielding a variety of calls, one about vandalism in Arches that occurred a few days earlier and another about an expansion of the park recently proposed by Representative Rob Bishop (R-UT) as part of his Public Lands Initiative.

Her voice chipper, her demeanor crisply professional, Cannon continues to answer the reporter's questions as she drags her landline phone across the office floor, stretching the cord that connects to the receiver. She stops in front of a map depicting the park's current boundaries and the potential land addition, patiently provides clear answers, exchanges pleasantries with the reporter, and ends the call with a slight sigh and a smile.

When we saw Cannon briefly a month prior, she was clad in classic park ranger garb: beige button-down shirt with an NPS badge stitched onto a sleeve and hunter-green slacks just formal enough for the boardroom yet casual enough for a ranger-guided hike on a park trail. Today she is sporting a geometric-patterned blouse, brown cardigan, dark slacks, and camel-colored flats, a look that is more business professional than trail leader. What hasn't changed is her quiet confidence and wry but sincere smile, which she deploys with care and control. She is petite, suntanned, and seemingly ageless.

At first glance, Cannon appears too pleasant and reserved to preside over an area that has been the subject of heated disputes for decades and that is located in a region where many residents deeply mistrust the agency she represents. But she has faced many challenges throughout her career that have served to prepare her for her current role.

Kate Cannon, superintendent of the Southeast Utah Group of Parks and Monuments

Cannon's devotion to these lands is rooted in her childhood.

"I grew up in Omaha, Nebraska, . . . and from my house I could walk out and up the street and dive off into what was a large expanse of woodland on the rolling hills above the Missouri River," Cannon shares. "I just would wander around and explore and look at critters and that kind of thing. I started watching birds, and [my dad] gave me a pair of binoculars, which gave a whole new kind of way to look at the world around me. So there was that. I was one of eight kids, and we did a station wagon trip that . . . at some point [brought us to a] national park where I saw park rangers, and I said, 'Oh, yeah, people work here. Maybe I could do that.'"

After receiving a degree in resource management from the University of Nebraska, Cannon realized her childhood ambition to combine her interest in nature with public service.

"I was a seasonal park ranger [in interior Alaska]," Cannon says. In 1978 "I got a job in a place called Eagle on the Yukon," which had just been designated by President Jimmy Carter as Yukon Rivers National Monument, now known as Yukon-Charley Rivers National Preserve.

"I knew that it was controversial," Cannon says.

As in San Juan County and much of southern Utah, many locals had made a good living in the mines, "and they did not welcome Yukon Rivers National Monument around them.

"That was a fascinating, very educational experience for me," Cannon says. "And I loved it . . . the challenge of working it out."

Her embrace of challenge and conflict resolution prepared her for her role at Grand Staircase–Escalante National Monument. Established in 1996, it was the first monument to be managed by the Bureau of Land Management, the most-reviled federal land agency in many parts of rural Utah. From the beginning of her tenure as monument manager, Cannon faced the anger of residents of Garfield and Kane Counties still furious about then president Clinton's surprise monument declaration the year before.

Their anger arose from far more than opposition to their perception of federal overreach. It was about jobs and lives. While the management plan for the monument allowed for continued grazing and limited oil and gas development by grandfathered leaseholders on the monument's lands, no future permits would be issued. In early 1997, shortly after the monument declaration, Andalex Resources Inc., abandoned its permit to build a coal-mining operation on the Kaiparowits Plateau, part of which lies within monument boundaries. Locals were enraged, believing that the monument declaration was responsible for Andalex's decision. Cannon says the decision and the monument declaration were not so intimately connected.

"The coal mining was lost not as a result of the monument designation," Cannon insists. "That was allowed to continue because it was a valid existing right, which can't be wiped out by a proclamation. That . . . operation died because . . . the quality of the coal was too poor to support the cost of extracting it. They [Andalex] actually asked to be bought out, and that wasn't because it was a monument. They had every right to develop that. [It] was because it wasn't economically a winning hand.[1]

"But that doesn't stop people from believing that [the monument was responsible]," Cannon says. "People need to have a culprit to blame for their state."

Residents of Garfield and Kane Counties, both of which have significant tracts of land within the monument boundaries, had already suffered a decades-long decline in the logging industry. The belief that the federal government was depriving them of yet another source of well-paying jobs further incensed them.

Despite a contentious environment in which acts of vandalism and threats against monument personnel were not uncommon, Cannon says that her memories of managing "the Grand Staircase," are positive.

"There were people who had lived there a long time and who were supportive of the idea," Cannon recalls. "In both Garfield and Kane Counties, the county commissions were very much involved in planning [for the monument]. And in some ways they worked very hard to solve long-standing problems through that planning process and were bold about it"—she pauses, smiling—"which unfortunately led to the ones in Kane County getting run out of town on a rail.

---

1. Spangler, "How Much Is Kaiparowits Coal Really Worth?"

"But it also brought things like . . . local visitors' centers and things like that. At that point the profitability of grazing, the profitability of mining, had been fading for a long time. There were occasional oil and gas drilling operations, which didn't pan out to be anything big. But the economy was not strong when mining [was ongoing]. . . . [T]he fact that it's not thriving is blamed on the monument. So people find a scapegoat."

These challenges inspired Cannon to reflect on her early years working for the Park Service in Alaska and "the value . . . of trying to meld those disparate points of view and different cultures. . . . That's the challenge, but if you can do it, if you can even move the ball a little further down the field, it bodes well for the future of public land management, as we have to be more and more collaborative across the West."

Following criticism by locals and members of Congress about decisions she made at Grand Staircase–Escalante, decisions they contend negatively impacted ranchers, Cannon was asked by the National Park Service in late 2001 to transfer and assume a post as deputy superintendent of Grand Canyon National Park. Five years later, she was selected to serve as superintendent of the Southeast Utah Group, a position she has held ever since.

Managing four parks and monuments would be difficult under any circumstances; it is even more so now that a well-funded national media campaign has resulted in the parks being inundated by crowds. Arches and Canyonlands are two of Utah's "Mighty Five" national parks (the others are Bryce Canyon, Zion, and Capitol Reef), and they are advertised heavily in promotional media sponsored by Utah's state tourism office, encouraging visitation to the state's most iconic places. San Juan County residents fear that declaration of another park or monument within the county will result in tourism that threatens to upend their way of life.

Despite concerns that many of Utah's most spectacular landscapes are getting "loved to death," most conservationists believe that designating national parks and monuments may be the best way to ensure that lands are protected from the destructive impacts of resource extraction.

Making decisions about how to manage crowds and their inevitable environmental impact is one of Cannon's significant challenges.

In her view, it is essential to involve communities in a structured planning process in order to create locally driven solutions, to decrease long-simmering tensions, and to make residents feel heard, whether the issue involves regulating access to parks or stimulating economic growth.

"Everybody can come to public meetings, they can talk, they can write their comments," Cannon says. "Those comments have weight, and we would have to, in a planning process, address them . . . publicly. You have to respond back. In BLM and in the Park Service and in any publicly accountable agency, that's how you do it.

"It's cumbersome," Cannon adds, "but it works."

She points to the BLM's Moab Master Leasing Plan as an example of an inclusive stakeholder-driven process that in her opinion was a success.

The final draft of the plan, released in July 2016, was crafted to serve as the BLM's blueprint for managing oil and gas development while simultaneously preserving wilderness areas on 785,000 acres of public land spanning an area from Moab to Monticello.

"The BLM invited groups to be cooperating agencies," Cannon says. "We [NPS] were invited, state government groups were invited, the counties involved were invited. Some of the nonprofit groups with an interest were invited, and I think there's a lot of strength in that, provided people will contribute and participate. That doesn't give them control over the decision, but it sure gives them every chance in the world to provide information and help with understanding the issues and to speak for what they would like to see the plan do.

"There's no perfect answer," she adds, "but as long as people are willing to—angry or not—honestly participate, that's where the power lies. That's where the ability to get your voice heard lies."

She cites the late Senator Robert Bennett (R-UT) as an example of a successful conciliator and praises his ability to bring together a diverse group of local stakeholders to create the 2009 Washington County Lands Bill, hailed as a model for balancing competing claims on public lands. It was the success of Bennett's efforts that foreshadowed Rob Bishop's initiation of the PLI process several years later.

"What he [Bennett] did was get things done," Cannon says. "And he did that by listening, by respectful discussion, by willingness to compromise, and he was able to do a lot of that, I think, just because he [was] admirable and people trusted him."

Echoing the voices of many Park Service employees spanning past decades, Cannon says the communities in San Juan County are "highly insular and want to retain that nature. That creates impediments that are really difficult to overcome.

"I think people who lived on the land and made their living off it—and their cultural history for hundreds of years was on the land—feel an ownership and a belonging there and guard against people coming in who want to change it or take it away," she adds. "The same could be said of the more recent pioneers who settled there, who made their homes there, and who value their own very strong culture and their community."

She sees the struggles and fears of communities adjacent to Grand Staircase–Escalante National Monument reflected in San Juan County's polarized views regarding the prospect of the Bears Ears National Monument. The desire to preserve and expand extractive industries is based on a belief that those industries not only are the best way to bring prosperity to residents' families but also are essential to their cultural identity.

"The pride of having made a living from working on the land, that's ingrained," Cannon says. "That's who we are.

"People have to make a living," she adds. "They used to make it by mining and grazing and things like that. Those aren't as available anymore. So then the question becomes, What do we have the aptitude, the knowledge, and the capital to do?"

What will it take to move San Juan County past the divisive rhetoric about the potential Bears Ears National Monument and the fear many people have that any layer of protection on their land will devastate their way of life?

"People have to believe it, embrace it," Cannon says. "If they're constantly being told that the reason you can't thrive is because of this evil, mean, wicked, bad, nasty [government], you're not . . . going to go out and do something bold. Some people might, and that will make the difference, but it does take time."

(The events following the designation of Bears Ears National Monument in December 2016 showed that many in San Juan County were not at all ready to embrace the reality of newly protected land. Monument opponents staged protests, launched campaigns to rescind Bears Ears, and motivated residents of Garfield and Kane Counties still seething from the designation of Grand Staircase–Escalante National Monument two decades earlier to advocate for rescission of that monument. Both efforts succeeded: in December 2017 President Donald J. Trump reduced Bears Ears by 85 percent and Grand Staircase–Escalante by nearly half, opening the Kaiparowits Plateau to potential coal mining and select areas in the Bears Ears region to uranium mining and oil and gas drilling.)

You can't let the BLM office down in Monticello write this management plan. They get a good guy down there, he gets run out of town. They did all sorts of bad stuff to the last guy. They get hung in effigy in a parade for the Fourth of July. Good people can't last. —Scott Groene, executive director, Southern Utah Wilderness Alliance, July 28, 2015

Those kind of relationships you cannot leave to chance. I got here in [19]91; [relationships between the Park Service and San Juan County residents] did not exist. San Juan County hated us. I started going down there. I went to county commission meetings and that kind of thing; I got to know those guys.

When I was here we were doing pretty well, and we started something called the Canyon Country Partnership. We took [San Juan County officials] down the river through Cataract [Canyon] where we're all sitting in beach chairs having a brewski at the end of the day. It's hard to be a jackass when you're sitting in a lawn chair with the Colorado River flowing by, and you had just a hell of a great day, and you talk about all kinds of things. We had county commissioners with us, we had all the different agencies, state and federal, and they absolutely loved it. We did all kinds of things with different people. You've got to work at it. Because I think if you spend a lot of time talking and doing stuff together and being out in the resource—the key is being out there, because the resource talks to you. It makes it real clear what the right answers are. But you've got to get people out there. You've got to be committed to do it.

You need to get the right BLM district manager and area manager that want to sit down with the county commissioners down there and say, "OK. What do we need to do together to do this?" That is totally doable.

—Walt Dabney, former superintendent of Arches and Canyonlands National Parks, 1991–99, March 8, 2016

INTERLUDE
Reflection on a Successful Compromise

The Boulder–White Cloud Mountains in central Idaho soar above rocky wild-lands that harbor bighorn sheep, mountain goats, moose, black bear, pronghorn antelope, gray wolves, and mountain lions along with some of the oldest trees on earth. The decades-long effort to shape the future of BLM and Forest Service land around the Boulder–White Cloud Mountains provides a case study of the elements needed to effect compromise regarding the use of public lands.

The initial threat to the area arose just a few years after the passage of the Wilderness Act in 1964, when a large open-pit mine was proposed at the base of the mountains. After a multiyear fight, the area received a modest level of protection via designation as a national recreation area. However, the area continued to be used extensively by motorized vehicles—motorcycles, ATVs, and snowmobiles—which conservationists argued threatened both wildlife and the wilderness qualities of the area.

Proposals for much stronger protection under the Wilderness Act foundered until Idaho representative Mike Simpson took up the cause in the late 1990s. A conservative Republican, Simpson worked with a range of stakeholders—hunters, fishermen, motorized vehicle users, mountain bikers, hikers, and climbers—for more than fifteen years to find common ground. In 2010 he introduced a wilderness bill that largely reflected consensus views but ultimately failed. He reintroduced his bill in the House, but by 2013 it was apparent that it stood no chance of passage.[1]

At that point Idaho governor Cecil Andrus, a Democrat, wrote to President Obama urging him to use the Antiquities Act to declare the Boulder–White Clouds area a national monument. While monument designation

---

1. Barker, "How the Boulder–White Clouds Wilderness Was Preserved."

would provide fewer restrictions than wilderness designation, it nevertheless provided a measure of preservation.

Presidential declarations of national monuments are nearly as toxic in Idaho as in Utah, and as a result, Simpson urged that any monument declaration be delayed by six months to provide time for a compromise to develop. Spurred by the threat of a monument, representatives of motorized vehicle users accepted wilderness designation for a portion of the land in return for removing several thousand acres from the original wilderness bill and leaving open ATV and snowmobile trails on the nonwilderness acreage. The compromise was accepted with reluctance by the conservation community, which nevertheless could look with some pride at the protection of over 275,000 acres as wilderness. Idaho senator James Risch (R-ID), who had earlier objected to Simpson's bill, was now on board.

Simpson then drew on his relationships with Representative Rob Bishop (R-UT) and then Speaker John Boehner (R-OH) to move the bill forward. Eager to avoid a national monument—a designation he abhors on ideological grounds—Bishop, in his role as chair of the House Natural Resources Committee, ensured that the bill reached the House floor, where Boehner then accelerated its passage. With Risch's help, the bill passed the Senate and was signed by President Obama on August 7, 2015.[2]

The compromise was enabled by a combination of leadership by Simpson, stakeholder buy-in over a period of fifteen years, a willingness for opposition groups to meet face-to-face, personal relationships enabling members of both parties to move forward even in the face of huge ideological divides, and creative cooperation between the executive and legislative branches to achieve the desired result.

In San Juan County people held out hope that a similar success might be achieved, but this time the ideological divide proved too great to bridge. The Obama administration held off on declaring Bears Ears National Monument until Bishop's Public Lands Initiative failed. The Bears Ears proclamation reduced the monument proposed by the tribes by nearly a third, and the final boundaries were drawn to be very similar to those proposed in the PLI. Despite these efforts to take local concerns into account, neither Utah's Republican politicians nor many locals consider this to be a compromise in the spirit of Boulder–White Clouds.

---

2. "Big News."

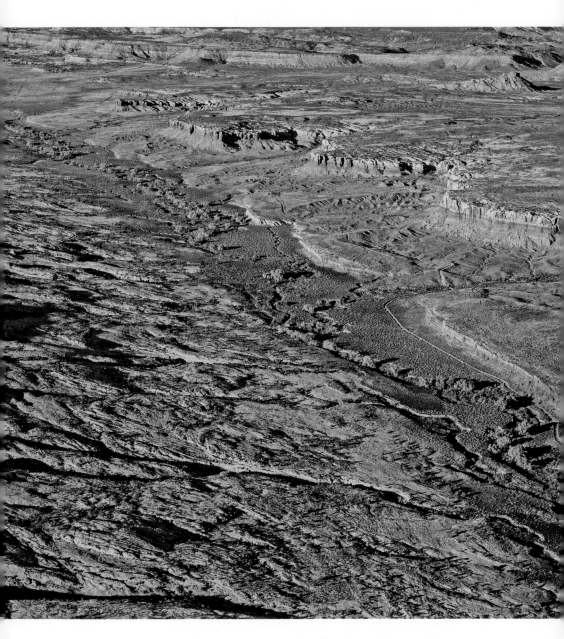

Comb Ridge (*left*); and mesas west of Bluff, Utah (*right*) (aerial photo)

ALFRED AND SAHMIE LOMAHQUAHU

Serving a Tribe and a Coalition, Connecting All People to Sacred Lands

At first glance, the Hogan Family Restaurant in Tuba City looks like a typical local diner—plastic laminated menus, weak coffee, the holy trinity of salt, pepper, and Sweet'N Low packets in caddies on the tables. What differentiates it from other eateries across America is its broad octagonal layout—modeled after a hogan, the traditional Navajo dwelling—and its clientele—nearly all Native American. The lunch offerings have a distinctly Navajo flair: mutton stew, green chiles, and Navajo tacos, a regional specialty comprised of a base of fry bread topped with chili, cheese, and lettuce.

In contrast to the bright January day outside, the diner's interior is dim, and the patrons are mostly silent. A television blares in the background, talking heads bloviating about the latest developments in the 2016 U.S. presidential race. It's an atmosphere in need of light (and perhaps a channel change).

When Alfred Lomahquahu and his wife, Sahmie, walk through the front door, the room instantly brightens. Alfred, who when we meet him is still the vice chairman of the Hopi tribe and cochair of the Bears Ears Inter-Tribal Coalition, has a gentleness and a humility that seem incongruous with his role as a politician who wields significant power in the government of a sovereign nation. (It is not until several months later that we become acquainted with his tougher side.) His perfectly fitted black bomber jacket and orderly appearance bespeak his years as a marine. He conveys a business-like demeanor, but at the same time his eyes dance with mischief. For every thoughtful reflection he shares, with each word he chooses deliberately, he interjects a wry joke accompanied by an infectious laugh that fills the room.

Alfred is a powerful man, but he readily acknowledges the strength and wisdom of the woman sitting beside him. Sahmie, an educator focused on

Alfred Lomahquahu, cochair, Bears Ears
Inter-Tribal Coalition (courtesy of Alfred
Lomahquahu)

offering opportunities for disadvantaged youth, is fierce and passionate. She speaks with force and eloquence about the movement to protect the tribes' shared sacred sites and the need to educate and empower the next generation of Native leaders. Like her husband, she disarms with unexpected humor. As we fumble for a culturally sensitive way to ask Alfred a question, Sahmie politely but persuasively tells us to come out with it already: "There's very little that offends him, so don't think too hard about saying it nicely. Be frank, be direct."

Alfred and Sahmie's love and admiration for one another are palpable. They express their feelings in words—Alfred values her insights on the coalition's work, Sahmie deeply admires his commitment to engaging youth in advocacy—and in their eyes as each regards the other with a mixture of delight and respect. Their bomber jackets match, as do a pair of flag pins, which speak to their pride in being both American and Hopi citizens.

Alfred did not seek to lead the Bears Ears Inter-Tribal Coalition. He feels, as do his fellow coalition leaders, that his path was somehow predetermined.

"We as individuals have our own experience, our own knowledge, and because of that we were put into these positions . . . by a higher power, and we are doing the work for that higher power," Lomahquahu says. "We always have to know it's there to support us."

Each meeting of the coalition begins with an invocation or prayer. Lomahquahu says that prayer has played a central role in the formation and coalescing of the group.

"Every decision we've made, we've done because we've prayed," he says. "And every decision we've made has been a good decision."

Spiritual leaders from each of the tribes and pueblos, many of whom are considered as or perhaps more influential than political leaders, have been praying for the success of this unprecedented partnership. It is his duty, Lomahquahu says, to heed those prayers.

"If we hesitate, if we're not moving, we're making those prayers wait," he explains. "We don't want to do that."

While spirituality informs much of the tribes' approach to daily life and even governance, the coalition leaders, with the help of numerous official and informal advisors, are intently focused on the practical: how they can work within existing legal and bureaucratic systems to create a completely new approach to managing a national monument.

"The Forest Service, Department of Agriculture, the Bureau of Land Management . . . they've been set in a way of thinking for generations," Lomahquahu says. "What we're trying to do is turn that around so that there's a different way of working with the tribes, a different mindset." He is deeply committed to a central tenet of the proposal for the Bears Ears National Monument: a comanagement plan that has representatives of each of the five founding tribes and pueblos working alongside federal agencies as equals to develop and implement a management plan for the monument.

"This initiative is breaking a lot of molds, and that's one of them," he says. "How do we break the mentality of federal government now?"

The Bears Ears Inter-Tribal Coalition is composed of five founding tribes—Hopi, Navajo, Ute Indian Tribe of the Uintah and Ouray Reservation, Ute Mountain Ute, and Zuni—with an additional twenty-one tribes having historical and cultural links to the area also expressing support for the Bears Ears conservation proposal. As important as it is for the coalition to speak with a unified voice, it is just as essential, both practically and symbolically, for each tribe to be seen, heard, and respected as an individual sovereign nation.

"We really needed to learn how to use [tribal sovereignty] as a tool effectively, because it has never happened before," Lomahquahu says. "We were always going to the state *asking*. But this time, one of our objectives was, we're going to go straight to the [federal] government with *solutions*, rather than asking them to help us, so that we're bringing something to the table."

Lomahquahu is adamant in his belief that the tribal representatives in the coalition be treated as representatives of sovereign governments and

Comb Ridge, near Bluff, Utah, at sunset

not just as another one of many individual stakeholders with interest in the Bears Ears area.

"I don't want to speak with [Interior Secretary Sally Jewell's] deputies . . . when we go to Washington," Lomahquahu says. "I want to speak to Sally Jewell. We want to be speaking to Obama. That's where we as tribal leaders should be. We have that government-to-government relationship.

"We just don't have the respect from the federal government," he adds. "And that's one of the things that we're also trying to change. If we ask for an audience with Sally Jewell, she should accommodate us, no matter what. Because she's there to work on behalf of the tribal nations."

The leaders of the Bears Ears Inter-Tribal Coalition knew robust public funding for the creation of a national monument management plan was unlikely. Therefore, they sought out and were awarded significant private funds from large foundations, conservation organizations, outdoor recreation companies, and other donors of means. Skeptics and outright opponents of the monument proposal have intimated that the tribes, benefiting from donations from outside groups, are mere puppets of environmental organizations that have long sought protection for the land contained within Bears Ears. However, the tribes are taking the lead, while environmental organizations and nongovernmental organizations (NGOs) such as the Grand Canyon Trust and the Conservation Lands Foundation are supplying support and expertise.

"One of the first things that happened when we started the coalition was, we told the NGOs, 'You're in the backseat now,'" Lomahquahu says. "'We want your resources, we want to work with you, but we're going to be the ones who are making the decisions.'"

This vision, if fully realized, could have a profound effect on tribes' relationships with both private sector supporters and the federal government. Over time, these relationships may fundamentally change tribal governance and economies.

"It's not just a template for a national monument; it's also a template for economic growth," Lomahquahu says. "Kids growing up, they're going to be going into BLM [jobs], government entities, and they're going to say, 'This is how I want to work.' This is an entire new way of life."

The tribes also see enormous potential in the expected influx of visitors to the area—visitors who bring their backpacks, bikes, climbing gear, river rafts, and money to spend at local businesses. But for Lomahquahu,

Sahmie and Alfred Lomahquahu
(courtesy of Sahmie Lomahquahu)

tourism represents more than an economic windfall. It is a valuable opportunity to provide visitors with a deeper understanding of the cultural history of the lands and the importance of caring stewardship.

"We want to make sure [educational resources are] there for those that go into Bears Ears," Lomahquahu says. "People coming in from cities, they don't always have that. So how do we use those funds to make sure [visitors] are educated?"

Both Alfred and Sahmie are strong advocates for youth and see in the Bears Ears effort a model for young people. They envision many Native youth emulating the model provided by the coalition and joining the movement for indigenous self-determination. But first, youth need to be engaged.

"How do we get them to understand how strong their voices are so that they can effect change and they can be this group of leaders in their own time?" Sahmie asks. "We're just here holding the chains until they're ready to take over."

For Alfred and Sahmie, the journey set in motion by the coalition's work has become intensely personal. The Bears Ears cause is leading them to a deeper understanding of who they are, where they come from, where they've been. It presents an opportunity to discover a new way of knowing their history, their ancestral lands, and one another.

"I really wanted to take her up to Utah last week [for the coalition meeting] because I wanted to show her Bears Ears [and] the northern part of Canyonlands," Lomahquahu says. "We'd been to the southern side, Cedar

Mesa, but I wanted to show her the whole thing, to give her an idea of what Bears Ears is all about.

"I wanted both of us to encircle the whole area," he continues. "In our travels as Hopi, if you want to be a part of something, you have to make a circle and close it, so that it's there and you've owned it. I wanted to give her a look at . . . what we're focused on, what we're fighting for."

"One of the greatest understandings that [the coalition] has come to is that they're doing this together," Sahmie says. "It speaks to the work that they're doing that other people are seeing it as historic."

"We as tribes didn't all get along, but we came together and formed this coalition because we all realized that we can't do it alone," Alfred says. "In the long run, we may not see our dreams realized in our generation, but we hope to see it in a later generation."

Lomahquahu is energetic and engaging when we meet him in late April 2016 at the Hopi Tribe's Arizona headquarters. He extends his hand and gives each of us a hearty handshake before asking us to follow him to his office. Once inside, we sit down in two chairs facing his large desk as he makes himself comfortable, straightening his dark-blue button-down shirt, leaning back in his swivel chair, and placing his feet on the desk, revealing black leather boots that complement his dark-blue Wrangler jeans. Today, his bomber jacket is not in evidence, but proof of his military service abounds, with photos, certificates, and flags commemorating his service adorning the walls.

Without prompting, he begins sharing stories of his military service, which saw him deployed to seven countries.

He joined the U.S. Marines less than a week after graduating from Sherman Indian High School in Riverside, California, in 1982. He traveled to Camp Pendleton in San Diego for basic training and later received instruction in heavy equipment engineering and demolition at the U.S. Army base in Fort Leavenworth, Missouri. His first deployment was to Okinawa, Japan, in 1983; from there he trained with marines from Thailand and Korea, building roads and supervising infrastructure projects in Africa, Lebanon, and Afghanistan.

Following his discharge in 1988, Lomahquahu landed in California, met and married a Navajo woman, and moved with her to Navajo Nation land in northeastern Arizona. He worked as a heavy equipment operator on the reservation, but when the company he worked for folded, he found himself adrift.

Alfred Lomahquahu as a young boy (courtesy of Sahmie Lomahquahu)

Alfred Lomahquahu as a young marine (courtesy of Sahmie Lomahquahu)

"I started carving kachina dolls just to see if I could do it," Lomahquahu says.

Kachina dolls, which depict spirits of Hopi deities, natural elements, or animals, are intricately carved out of wood and painted in a brilliant rainbow of colors. Each kachina is unique, as is its artist's interpretation.

"One of my brothers . . . gave me [an] unfinished piece and told me to work on it," Lomahquahu recalls. "So I finished it and I brought it in to McGee's [Gallery of Indian Art in Keams Canyon, Arizona], and I sold it. I said, 'Hey, I can do something!'"

He did that something for the next eighteen years, making a living from his art and earning numerous awards and accolades for his work. When Lomahquahu speaks of his achievements, he swaps his humility for a proud smile.

Lomahquahu pulls up an image on his phone and shows it to us. In it, he is beaming, holding one of his creations: a Hopi rainbow kachina. The doll, carved from a cottonwood root, is vividly colored, a celebration of peace and harmony among tribes. The craftsmanship is exquisite, testimony to Lomahquahu's considerable skill and artistic vision.

"Art, to me, is really important to the evolution of society," Lomahquahu says. "People want laws and this and that, but without art and music, your society isn't going to grow."

Art also helped Lomahquahu heal from the PTSD that haunted him after his military service and gave his life direction after his first marriage disintegrated.

"I was into a lot of things that weren't good," Lomahquahu says plainly, unafraid and perhaps eager to bring up a troubled past that saw him spend six months in a San Bernardino, California, jail. Prison "was really, really rough . . . bikers, gangsters, people that were coming off drugs.

"But it gave me the experience of [learning] where people come from, where people from other places are in their lives," he adds. "People that may be down and out. . . . I don't look down on them, because I was there, too."

It was carving kachinas, Lomahquahu says, that "brought me back to my Hopi roots. I'd been gone for almost thirty years, and I finally came back to the reservation. When I came back, I started working for [Northern Arizona University] as a cancer educator. I started going out to the communities, and nobody knew who I was, even the . . . younger generations from my own village! When I left they were just kids, so when I came back, they were adults, but they didn't know I was from their village. My sister was introducing me several times to other people, and they said, 'I didn't know you had a younger brother!'"

Lomahquahu had lost some of his fluency in Hopi during his lengthy absence and initially found it difficult to connect and communicate with elders and people of his generation. It wasn't until he returned to participating in traditional Hopi spiritual practices that he felt like he was truly home.

"I started going back to the kiva," he says, referencing the subterranean circular rooms where Pueblo peoples conduct religious ceremonies. "Going back to my spiritual, ceremonial side . . . really helped me as an individual to get grounded again. It mentally helped me be at ease with . . . all the things I did in the military."

Lomahquahu became a leader in kiva ceremonies. While Hopi custom precludes sharing spiritual information with non-Hopi outsiders, he conveys his role by analogy.

"We basically do the same thing [as] monks in other countries," Lomahquahu says. "Just harmonizing everything—the worlds, the sun, the moon, the galaxies—making sure everything is in order. Because once something deharmonizes, we're in a place called Koyaanisqatsi—chaos—and we're trying to keep that from happening."

Following his increasing involvement in the spiritual life of the community, he was called to politics and in 2013 was elected vice chairman of the Hopi tribe.

"I never thought in a million years that I would get into politics and be a leader," Lomahquahu says.

Over time, however, he has come to recognize that every step along his life's meandering, often-rocky path prepared him to lead his people in the kiva, on the tribal council, and most recently on the Bears Ears Inter-Tribal Coalition.

"Your experiences make up who you are and how you deal with situations and how you feel about, for instance, the land and Bears Ears," Lomahquahu says.

"The military side taught me how to evaluate, how to run things up the chain of command, and all that," he explains. "The kiva side taught me to be spiritual, always think of the people when I'm making a decision."

Lomahquahu believes that his spiritual role in the kivas translates directly to his service as cochair of the coalition, where his role is "to ensure that

Comb Ridge and Bluff Bench (aerial image)

everyone is working in harmony, that if there is discontent, it will be brought forward and dealt with accordingly so we can still be moving forward."

His experience has made him an effective leader within his own tribe and with other nations in the coalition.

"Yesterday I was in Window Rock"--the capital of the Navajo Nation—"and I don't feel out of place there because now I have a lot of friends there, too. And with Bears Ears . . . a lot of [Navajo] people, they look at Hopi a different way now, and by me being over there and working with them and coming to their house, I think they appreciate that. So it encourages me and the whole Bears Ears Coalition to work more in sync together."

He readily acknowledges the occasional interpersonal strife that arises in the coalition's work—"every organization is like that," he says—and the undercurrents of painful history among the tribes that can lead to tensions. But he chooses to focus on what unites them.

"We have to always remember our spiritual side, because that's where our strength lies, within us as different tribes, within us as different people," Lomahquahu says. "That's when the land accepts us as working for [it]."

Lomahquahu describes Hopi society as akin to a theocracy, where in many instances the spiritual leaders have more power than the elected political leaders. He takes this to heart and prioritizes his leadership duties according to cultural tradition.

"One of the things that I relayed to [the Hopi Tribal] Council when I was first elected was, the people elected me as their vice chairman and their leader, but . . . my religion, my ceremony, that comes before me sitting in this office," Lomahquahu says. "Certain times of year I'll take a sabbatical and just leave this office alone for a week or two and go do what I have to do. A lot of tribal people here, they understand that [my spiritual obligations are] my first priority."

The tribes have placed special emphasis on the many types of healing that permanent protection for the land can bring about: healing of long-standing wounds between Natives and the federal government; between Natives and non-Natives in the Southwest; among the five Native tribes that comprise the coalition; and between humans and the earth, which under the tribes' proposal would never again be threatened by new attempts to mine or d[rill] for oil and gas. Lomahquahu mentions another group that can find [heal]ing in the Bears Ears region: visitors who have become disconnect[ed from] nature.

"We need places like this," Lomahquahu says. "That's why tourists go out. And a lot of tourists don't understand it when they go to this place that has a lot of solitude. Somewhere along the line they may have lost something, the true essence of being human. But your inner human still has it; subconsciously, you still have it. So when they come out here, they feel a feeling that they've never had before. It's a good feeling. I think when they go back to the city they yearn to be back again.

"One of the things that I always think about is, we wear shoes now," he continues. "But back then, when our feet touched the earth, there was the connection there. So every now and then I'll go out there and take my shoes off and just put my toes in the sand. A lot of people, when they go to the beach they'll run their feet through the sand, and that's when that connection is coming back. It's an awesome feeling, and we can do that out here. If [visitors] learn about things like that, and we teach them to connect back to the earth for themselves, I think it will help them understand more about who they are and where they want to be and where they want to go."

Thank you to all of you for all the perspectives you brought to the table. I'd say that if there's one thing that happened just now, it's that everyone understands each other better. Thank you for being respectful. I know there are different points of view, and that's what we wanted to hear. When you do respectfully listen to each other, everybody moves a little bit. There are, I think, some concerns that need to be addressed. There are concerns that probably aren't fully accurate, and those are things that over time if we work with the Utah Governor's office, the Utah elected officials, and the Administration, we'll work through this. . . . We have not made up our minds about what way to go, that's why we're here. We're here to listen. I've heard from county commissioners, I've heard from [several] communities. I haven't heard from anybody who has said there aren't areas here that are worthy of protection. I think that is unanimous. The question is how? There are many voices here that say we want to be able to continue to use these lands in ways that we have. And that is not mutually exclusive with protection.

—Former interior secretary Sally Jewell, speaking at a public hearing on Bears Ears and the PLI in Bluff, Utah, July 16, 2016

CODA
December 2016–February 2018

Part 1: December 2016–June 2017

On December 28, 2016, President Barack Obama established Bears Ears National Monument, invoking his powers under the 1906 Antiquities Act to protect 1.35 million acres of land in San Juan County, Utah.

"From earth to sky, the region is unsurpassed in wonders," President Obama's proclamation stated, noting the importance of the region's dark skies, silence, and remoteness. "Protection of the Bears Ears area will preserve its cultural, prehistoric, and historic legacy and maintain its diverse array of natural and scientific resources, ensuring that the prehistoric, historic, and scientific values of this area remain for the benefit of all Americans."

Significantly, for the first time in history, Native Americans were given a powerful voice in managing a national monument. The proclamation calls for the establishment of the Bears Ears Commission, staffed by a representative of each of the tribes comprising the Bears Ears Inter-Tribal Coalition—the Hopi, Zuni, Navajo, Ute Mountain Ute, and Ute Tribe of the Uintah and Ouray. Commission members will work with their federal counterparts in the Bureau of Land Management and the U.S. Forest Service to set policy for preserving ancestral sites and artifacts and for providing access to monument lands for traditional cultural and spiritual uses. The proclamation's assertion that Native peoples' traditional ecological knowledge "is, itself, a resource to be protected and used in understanding and managing land" is a compelling acknowledgment of the role the coalition will play in developing culturally and ecologically sensitive guidelines for land use.

Many Americans, and indeed many people throughout the world, celebrated the declaration of Bears Ears National Monument as protecting with unique scenic, geological, biological, and cultural riches for

Signs *in favor* of and against the monument, Bluff, Utah, July 2016

to come and as a significant step toward righting historical wrongs perpetrated against indigenous peoples in the United States.

But as monument supporters exulted in their achievement, many citizens of San Juan County greeted President Obama's decision with a mix of anger and apprehension. Anger, because they believe that the public land comprising Bears Ears was improperly "locked up" by an overreaching federal government that failed to listen to local voices. Apprehension, because they feel that the designation will threaten their livelihoods by restricting or precluding ranching and mining on monument land, endanger the culture of their rural communities with a deluge of tourists, and limit their access to land they have cherished and stewarded for over a century.

Their fears have been reinforced by Utah's conservative politicians, who have spoken with the same polarizing partisan rhetoric that defined the 2016 presidential campaign, condemning President Obama's act as tyrannical, deeply offensive, even immoral.

Just hours after the White House announced the Bears Ears designation, the San Juan County commissioners released a joint statement saying the county "mourns after President Barack Obama gave in to pressure from extreme environmental groups, out-of-state tribal leaders, and outside interests." The commissioners and over two hundred county residents took part in a protest at the Monticello courthouse that afternoon.

In January 2017 San Juan County commissioner Bruce Adams testified at a hearing in Salt Lake City in which the Utah House of Representatives' Rules Committee voted six to two to pass a resolution asking President Trump to rescind the monument. The committee also passed a concurrent resolution asking Congress to dramatically reduce the acreage of the 1.9-million-acre Grand Staircase–Escalante National Monument in south-central Utah, designated by former president Bill Clinton in 1996 and reviled by many in rural Utah ever since.

In a phone conversation following the hearing, Adams told us he viewed Obama's decision as "a very spiteful way of getting back at Utah Republicans or people that had a disagreement with him for what he's done." Adams also took issue with the content of the proclamation.

"A monument is supposed to protect objects using the least amount of land possible," Adams said, paraphrasing the guidelines set forth in the Antiquities Act. "They are trying to protect silence, dark skies, solitude. T are not objects. Those are kind of abstract things."

Utah governor Gary Herbert said he was "deeply disturbed" by a decision that "ignores the will of the majority of Utahns." Former representative Jason Chaffetz (R-UT), who chaired the House Oversight Committee when the monument was declared, called the "midnight monument" a "slap in the face to the people of Utah, attempting to silence the voices of those who will bear the heavy burden it imposes."

And Representative Rob Bishop (R-UT), the architect of the Public Lands Initiative, which passed the House in September 2016 but never received a Senate hearing, vowed to do everything in his power not only to overturn the monument but also to repeal the Antiquities Act itself.

No matter how full-throated and highly publicized their complaints, however, Utah politicians alone could not undo Obama's action.

When the monument was declared, the tribes were the undeniable victors in a prolonged struggle to shape the future of a place beloved by people around the world and sacred to indigenous people across the Colorado Plateau. They had spent the months leading up to the designation crafting a plan, preparing for collaborative management of the monument with their federal agency counterparts.

But nothing in their plan could have prepared them for Donald J. Trump.

When Trump was elected the forty-fifth president of the United States on November 8, 2016, the political landscape underwent a seismic shift. Republicans gained control of both the presidency and Congress—a result not anticipated by either monument supporters or opponents. The unexpected election results triggered intensely emotional reactions both from voters who backed Trump and from those who supported Hillary Clinton, widening and deepening the already significant partisan divide.

During the January 2017 confirmation hearing for Ryan Zinke, Trump's appointee for interior secretary, Utah senator Mike Lee implored Zinke to heed the voices of locals who would be negatively impacted by former president Obama's decision on Bears Ears. Zinke pledged to make San Juan County his first stop as interior secretary, once again thrusting the county into the spotlight and casting it as the de facto epicenter of conflicts over public lands in the West. Orrin Hatch, Utah's senior senator and president pro tem of the Senate, met with President Trump during his first week in office to discuss Bears Ears and reported that Trump was "eager to work with" Congress on rescinding the monument.

April 26, 2017, Hatch's maneuvering paid off. President Trump issued executive order directing Zinke to conduct a review of all national monuments declared between 1996 and 2017—a time period bookended by the designation of Grand Staircase–Escalante and Bears Ears National Monuments. Zinke was given 120 days to issue recommendations on whether to keep, reduce, or shrink current monument boundaries. Bears Ears was an exception: Zinke was asked to provide a recommendation within 45 days. These unprecedented steps demonstrated the depth of the Utah delegation's political influence in the Trump administration. The truncated time line for Bears Ears made a decision to rescind or shrink the monument seem preordained.

Public comments poured in, imploring the interior secretary to keep Bears Ears, Grand Staircase–Escalante, and other monuments intact. During Zinke's visit to southern Utah, monument supporters attempted to meet with him, but the secretary chose to spend the large majority of his time with county elected officials and residents opposed to the monument.

On June 12, 2017, Zinke issued a preliminary recommendation regarding the Bears Ears National Monument, arguing that "rather than designating an area encompassing almost 1.5 million acres as a national monument, it would have been more appropriate to identify and separate the areas that have significant objects to be protected." He suggested that the areas deserving of monument designation be restricted to specific sites: "rock art, dwellings, ceremonial sites, granaries and other cultural resources."

President Obama's proclamation adopted a far more expansive definition of the "objects of historic and scientific interest" meriting protection, including not only specific visible manifestations of Native history but also the unparalleled beauty of the landscape, its geological and paleontological history, and a large and complex ecosystem supporting a wide variety of flora and fauna unique to the area. It moreover noted the importance of access to and protection of the lands within Bears Ears to tribes who continue to carry out religious ceremonies on sites spanning the entire Bears Ears landscape and who depend on the land to gather herbs and medicinal plants essential to physical and spiritual healing. All elements of the monument proclamation speak powerfully to the landscape *as a whole* rather than to isolated individual sites.

While presidents in the past have reduced the area of an already declared monument, there is some debate over whether a president can rescind an entire monument.

According to a November 2016 analysis from the Congressional Research Service, "It remains undetermined whether removal of a high enough proportion of a monument's acreage could be viewed as effectively amounting to

Moki Dugway, near Valley of the Gods

an abolishment of the monument."[1] Both proponents and opponents of the monument have their respective legal scholars who insist that the president either does or does not have the authority to rescind a monument.

When Zinke issued an initial recommendation to reduce the size of Bears Ears, he engendered gratitude from San Juan County's antimonument constituency and simultaneously catalyzed a widespread movement to defend the monument through grassroots advocacy and, if necessary, litigation. The tribes' victory seemed less secure and the path forward less certain.

The Tribes' Next Steps

The Bears Ears Inter-Tribal Coalition saw President Obama's decision to declare the monument and provide members of the coalition with a major voice in shaping its policies as a crucial step forward in the movement to heal painful history between tribes and the federal government. The tribal leaders, however, fully recognized both the opportunity presented by Obama's action and the political challenges confronting them moving forward.

Zuni councilman and Bears Ears Inter-Tribal Coalition cochair Carleton Bowekaty said the tribes were prepared to surmount what appear to be considerable obstacles to success.

"There's going to be a lot of roadblocks, there's going to be a lot of issues, but we have plenty of knowledge, [and] we have longevity in mind," Bowekaty said. "Our view is long range. We want to see this developed into the proper working model that can be used by other nations and other entities hoping to protect cultural knowledge."

Utah Diné Bikéyah's years-long effort to map culturally significant Native sites in the Bears Ears landscape laid the foundation for the coalition's monument proposal. UDB executive director Gavin Noyes and cofounder and board member Mark Maryboy said the tribes' celebrations of the monument declaration have been accompanied by the realization that defending the monument from threats of rescission will require resources.

"Most of our time is now spent trying to defend the monument and maintaining status quo," Maryboy said. "It's chaos with this new administration."

Tribes anticipated a move by the Trump administration to reduce or rescind the monument and began preparing to challenge the move in court.

---

1. Wyatt, "Antiquities Act."

Theirs would be the latest salvo in a fight over executive action that stretches back more than a century.

Challenges to the president's authority under the Antiquities Act date back to 1908, just two years after the act was signed into law, when President Theodore Roosevelt declared the Grand Canyon National Monument, spanning eight hundred thousand acres—the first step toward the Grand Canyon's eventual elevation to national park status.

Roosevelt's declaration was met by furious opposition from local ranchers and miners and resulted in a nearly immediate legal challenge to Roosevelt's efforts to protect what is now counted among the seven natural wonders of the world. The complainants argued that eight hundred thousand acres hardly fit the description of "the smallest area compatible with proper care and management of the objects to be protected."

In its 1920 decision in *Cameron v. United States*, the Supreme Court decided that the eight-hundred-thousand-acre landscape, taken as a whole, *did* in fact merit protection under the terms of the Antiquities Act and affirmed the authority of the president to declare national monuments of that scale.

A more recent challenge by the Mountain States Legal Foundation in 2002 maintained that six national monuments declared by President Bill Clinton "reach far beyond the purpose, scope and size of any national monuments contemplated by Congress under the [Antiquities] Act." Specifically, Mountain States argued that "Congress intended only that rare and discrete man-made objects, such as prehistoric ruins and ancient artifacts, were to be designated," precisely the argument put forth in Secretary Zinke's initial recommendation to the Trump administration.

In *Mountain States Legal Foundation v. Bush* (2002), the District of Columbia Circuit Court stated, "That argument fails as a matter of law in light of Supreme Court precedent interpreting the Act to authorize the President to designate the Grand Canyon and similar sites as national monuments." The court also dismissed Mountain States' contention that the powers delegated to the president under the Antiquities Act do not extend to his or her embracing environmental values or scenic beauty.

The current challenge to the Bears Ears designation thus mirrors the emotional and material concerns of monument opponents since passage of the Antiquities Act. Once the Trump administration issued its decisions with respect to the monuments under review, legal challenges followed. How the courts decide the fate of attempts by the Trump administration to rescind or reduce the size of Bears Ears and other monuments will play a major, perhaps decisive, role in determining how and for what purposes public lands throughout the United States can be used in the future.

The tribes were adamant in their commitment to moving forward as legal battles played out.

"In the event that the Bears Ears National Monument is rescinded, that [won't] rescind the coalition," Bowekaty said. "The coalition can still function, [and] each tribe or nation is designating a representative for [the federal agencies] to interact with on a government-to-government basis. The coalition can [serve] as . . . a commission for tribal consultation" so that the BLM, the Forest Service, and other federal agencies don't have to conduct separate consultations with each of the five coalition tribes. "We've been leading on the idea of collaborative management and will continue to develop and present the model, what we believe would work in our position as tribes."

Bowekaty said the tribes "recognize the fact that there's not one sole expert on cultural issues, and there's not one sole expert on conservation and land management issues. But [each tribal representative] would have the ability to draw on those resources and integrate the information needed between the tribal communities and cultural officers in order to make the best decisions on behalf of the tribes."

"We've done something that no other tribes have done before," said then Hopi vice chairman and coalition cochair Alfred Lomahquahu. "Now we have to talk the talk and walk the walk so we can use the monument as a way for other tribes to start working with the federal government. If we don't do that, it's not going to be able to happen for other tribes."

The coalition and its allies expect that, regardless of the eventual size of the monument, they won't be able to rely on robust funding from the Trump administration for management and staffing, particularly with a newly emboldened "antiparks" caucus led by Representative Rob Bishop (R-UT) and a more extractive industry-friendly interior secretary in Ryan Zinke. But Bowekaty has faith that private foundations will provide a vital infusion of financial support that will buoy the coalition's initial planning efforts.

"Initial appropriations for management of a national monument will be an issue, especially with an administration that has their own views of public lands and states' rights," Bowekaty said. "We'll continue to educate them on what we believe is a good monument that should receive appropriate

San Juan River from the Hole-in-the-Rock Trail

funding. At the same time . . . we will approach organizations and foundations for assistance."

"We can get outside funding sources that the government can't get," added Lomahquahu. "It's going to have to happen."

The tribes received a major boost when a number of foundations, including the Grand Canyon Trust, the David and Lucille Packard Foundation, the William and Flora Hewlett Foundation, and the Leonardo DiCaprio Foundation, established the $1.5 million Bears Ears Engagement Fund. A January 2017 press release announcing the fund described it as a way "to support robust tribal involvement in managing the monument and to also support community efforts to enhance resource conservation in the monument and to create economic opportunity."[2]

UDB also recently received a $400,000 grant from ArtPlace America. The grant will "support community dialogues around a future not dependent on extractive resource development, that is instead driven by local sustainable economic solutions and the strengths of the diverse Native American Tribes who live or share ancestry to San Juan County."[3]

Noyes said the ArtPlace grant "is [a] really great way to put something behind our talk of economic development," particularly as it relates to opportunities for economic growth tied to the monument. By placing arts and culture at the heart of its "Traditional Arts of Bears Ears" proposal, UDB seeks to celebrate Native contributions to the county's cultural heritage and to empower local artisans to build sustainable businesses that allow them both to support themselves and to provide a model for other county residents to seek opportunities beyond the oil fields.

Maryboy sees tremendous potential for traditional artisans to become more profitable. It's just a matter of providing the tools they need to succeed.

"I consider those Navajos that sell their wares every day to be a true entrepreneurial people," Maryboy said. "There are families throughout the Navajo Nation that sell their jewelry and what they make to tourists, but it's not organized. So I think with some sort of organizational support, a lot of those individuals can be economically independent. That would be a durable economic solution for the people rather than energy development that the county's pushing at this moment."

---

2. Wierzbicki, "Leonardo DiCaprio Foundation."

3. Utah Dine Bikeyah, "UDB Is 1st Utah Recipient of ArtPlace America Grant."

Jessica Stago manages the Native American Business Incubator Network (NABIN) at the Grand Canyon Trust. While she does not work closely with the Bears Ears Inter-Tribal Coalition, she recognizes the opportunity the new national monument presents for Native business owners and artisans who live in San Juan County—if local people are allowed to influence the trajectory of the tourism economy.

"It's for the benefit of all people, but the local community has to be the one to manage it," Stago said. "They know best the spirit of the land, they know what happens to the land when it rains, they know what happens when it doesn't rain. . . . Should we bring more people in, or should we not? Should we [endorse] this activity or limit this activity? They can gauge the economic benefit of those decisions."

Marjorie Dee spends her days developing initiatives to increase entrepreneurial opportunity for those living on the Navajo Nation's "Utah strip." In her position with the Navajo Nation's Northern Regional Business Development Office, Dee focuses on providing resources for small businesses to succeed. She sees the Bears Ears National Monument as a potential catalyst for economic development that creates a cluster of Native-owned businesses at the heart of a major tourism attraction.

"Economic development is not something that happens [with] just one store," Dee said. "If Bears Ears becomes a destination point for travelers nationally and globally, it will become [its own] town—a boomtown. You'll need to have a residential area, because if you're going to have people work there, they have to live there. [A] commercially zoned area would have hotels, restaurants, a strip [with] stores, where people would sell their wares."

Her ambitious vision also includes an airstrip where tourists could fly into the area and visit Bears Ears as one leg of a region-wide trip that includes nearby attractions such as Rainbow Bridge National Monument, Monument Valley Navajo Tribal Park, and Canyonlands National Park.

"The Bears Ears monument area could provide the key destination point," Dee said, "[but] it requires people that have some sense of how to do development."

The numerous challenges now facing the coalition should not detract from the magnitude of the tribes' accomplishments, nor do they diminish the strength of the community they have created among themselves.

"It's a family," Lomahquahu said. "You're going to have dissension here and there, but as a family you're always going to stick together."

That family includes what Lomahquahu refers to as a "higher power," part of the spiritual guidance in which the members of the coalition place their faith and to which they attribute their success.

"Somebody's guiding us and helping us, and when that's happening, then most likely it's going to succeed," Lomahquahu said. "The only way it's going to fail is if we start thinking that we're doing it on our own.

"It does give you a really neat feeling that you're part of something and you're doing it not because you want notoriety," Lomahquahu added. "You're doing it because you want to better something and hopefully that others can sustain it and down the road still be benefiting from that same project that you started on."

Compromise and Moving Forward

In the proclamation declaring Bears Ears National Monument, the Obama administration made several concessions to monument opponents and PLI proponents.

For one, the tribes' 1.9-million-acre proposal was pared down to 1.35 million acres—just slightly less than what was proposed for national conservation area designation by Representative Bishop in the Utah Public Lands Initiative. Moreover, the boundaries of Bears Ears National Monument were adjusted to adhere very closely to those proposed by Bishop and the San Juan County Lands Council. The final division between public lands set aside for the monument and those still available for future development was designed by the Obama administration to demonstrate that they had heard and responded to local concerns.

Among the areas from the Bears Ears Inter-Tribal Coalition's proposal that were excluded from the final monument boundaries were the Abajo Mountains, which are prized by communities in northern San Juan County as both culturally significant and a vital source of water for the towns of Blanding and Monticello; most of Recapture Canyon, which has both cultural import and potential for oil and gas drilling; and several large areas that have potential for uranium mining or oil and gas extraction.

Nevertheless, many residents of San Juan County fervently believe that their concerns regarding the potential effect of the monument on their economic future were in fact ignored by President Obama. Their resulting anger and fear reflect a deep longing among some locals for times when legacy

Comb Ridge from Butler Wash Road in the spring

industries—mining, ranching, oil and gas—were booming and brought prosperity to the area. Elected leaders continue to argue that ranching, mining,
and oil and gas drilling may yet offer the best path toward renewed prosperity. Given Trump's "America First" energy policy, Utah politicians' lobbying
efforts could be successful.

Those hopes notwithstanding, a 2015–2019 report on economic development strategy by the Southeastern Utah Economic Development District (on
whose board San Juan County commissioner Bruce Adams serves) notes that
today, the county's primary economic drivers are tourism and travel-related
services, areas that continue to grow as mining employment continues its
decline. Over the past decade, the amount of tax revenue generated from
hotel stays in the county has more than quadrupled, from $267,000 in 2006
to nearly $1 million in 2016.[4] The number of hotel rooms has increased by
30 percent, and three hundred new jobs in tourism-related businesses have
been added, according to Charlie DeLorme, the county's former economic
development director.

By contrast, economic return from extractive industries, subject as they
are to external market forces, have led to destructive boom-and-bust cycles
that in the past have crippled the county. Nevertheless, Adams and his fellow commissioners echo many of their constituents' powerful attachment to
ranching, mining, and oil and gas development.

The attachment to legacy industries and the culture of the 1950s and
1960s, when these industries were ascendant, is understandable and should
not be discounted. But that attachment also ignores some undeniable facts
and trends.

1. In San Juan County proper, the number of mining jobs declined significantly between 2015 and 2016, while the number of hospitality jobs increased significantly.
2. As stated in the Utah Economic Council's 2017 report to the governor,
   "Utah's natural resource extractive industries remain a drag on revenues."[5]
3. Data show national monuments have contributed to, not inhibited, economic growth in adjacent communities, including those neighboring Grand
   Staircase–Escalante National Monument.

---

4. Boyle, "Economic Development."
5. Utah Economic Council, "2017 Economic Report to the Governor."

4. Tourism is an $887-billion-a-year industry that supports over seven million American jobs.

5. In Utah tourism spending in 2015 provided an $8.1-billion boost to the state's economy.

Linda Gillmor, who directs the Governor's Office of Rural Development, stressed that the key to a prosperous future in San Juan County, as with all rural counties in Utah, is building a multi-industry economy that can withstand the volatility that has characterized extractive industries. She noted that there are ample resources for economic planning available to rural counties around the state, but she and her staff leave the decision making up to residents at the grassroots level.

"I would never negate the extraction industry or ranching, because those are part of the history of [San Juan County], just as Bears Ears is part of the history," Gillmor said. "We always encourage any economic development effort in a community to look at diversification. You don't want just one industry."

Responding specifically to pleas for local involvement in shaping the Bears Ears management plan, the language in the proclamation of the monument called for the creation of a local advisory committee comprised of key stakeholders, including state and local governments, tribes, private landowners, recreationists, and business owners.

Per a January 2017 charter issued by then interior secretary Sally Jewell, the advisory committee will consist of twelve stakeholders, "who will advise the BLM and U.S. Forest Service on developing a monument management plan and on key issues for managing the new national monument."[6] The BLM and Forest Service planned to hold the first series of public open houses on Bears Ears in February 2017, but the uncertainty surrounding the monument's fate has delayed formation of the advisory committee.

Ashley Korenblat owns Western Spirit Cycling, based in Moab, Utah, and is executive director of the nonprofit Public Land Solutions, which helps communities develop sustainable plans for recreation-driven economic development. She oversaw the crafting of a white paper, released in April 2017, that argues that San Juan County should be proactive in developing a locally driven economic development plan, one that takes advantage of the

---

6. Bureau of Land Management, "Next Steps for Bears Ears National Monument."

Signs welcoming tourists to Utah and San Juan County outside Monument Valley

opportunity presented by the designation of Bears Ears in a way that respects the local culture and existing industries.

"The recreation economy is coming to San Juan County," said Korenblat. "They can do all they want to try to stop it, but it's already happening. What they *do* have is the opportunity to shape it and control it and turn it into what they want it to become."

Involving locals who oppose the monument to participate in developing its management plan will be difficult. But Korenblat said that serving on the local advisory committee outlined in the monument proclamation could be a powerful vehicle for local control—something nearly all monument opponents say they want and fervently believe they were denied when the monument was declared.

"If they really don't want people there, they have an opportunity through the management plan of the monument to limit [visitation]," Korenblat said. "There's lots of ways that communities can take charge of public land without owning it."

Marjorie Dee of the Navajo Nation's Northern Regional Business Development Office also saw the possibilities of the tribe working with the local advisory committee to create a viable management plan.

"The [management model] is fresh, and the obstacles are not there that are really hard to address because of the bureaucratic system that's in place," Dee said. "I think this is a good opportunity for the federal government, the state, and the tribal representatives to be really collaborative."

She outlined her road map for ideal economic development in San Juan County.

"If the politicians would all agree to collaborate on economic development for the southeastern section of [Utah], it would be great," Dee said. "It has to be serious; there needs to be a plan of action in place. Before that, there needs to be a baseline determination of the economic profile, with statistics so everybody is on the same page as to exactly where we are . . . to determine what exactly the people want, what is really needed in [different] communities."

Then she shook her head in frustration and acknowledged the gap between her ideal and reality.

"You have these political parties involved that try to dismantle any type of collaboration," Dee said.

While residents of Blanding and Monticello in the northern part of San Juan County have largely resisted the Bears Ears Monument and any changes it might bring, one town in the county is beginning to consider the implications of the monument for its future.

Bluff: A Town in the Balance

Nestled against the banks of the San Juan River near the southern edge of San Juan County lies the small and unassuming town of Bluff. Home to 250 or so residents, Bluff is a haven for artists, archaeologists, desert rats, and river runners, the kind of place where residents come together to build and burn a pair of massive driftwood herons on the winter solstice. Bluff's largely non-Mormon population is more culturally and politically aligned with the surrounding communities on the Navajo Reservation than with the LDS-centric citizens of "the North." And its citizens jokingly call themselves

Entrance to Bluff, Utah, whose residents note that the area was first settled not by Mormons in 1880 but by Ancestral Puebloans in 650 A.D..

"Bluffoons," reflecting a self-deprecating humor that captures the town's eclectic character.

There is wide speculation that Bluff is likely to serve as home to the monument headquarters and the tribes' proposed Traditional Knowledge Institute, a center designed to provide visitors with the opportunity to explore the world through the eyes of both Western science and traditional knowledge.

Jennifer Davila grew up in Bluff and returned after college to help run Wild Rivers Expeditions with her father, Charlie DeLorme, the county's former economic development director. After the family sold the company, Davila saw an opportunity to start a boutique hotel in Bluff that catered to a relatively affluent crowd. In 2013 she and her husband opened La Posada Pintada, an eleven-room bed-and-breakfast that quickly became a favorite spot for European visitors. She was a strong supporter of the monument in part because she sees an opportunity for her community to capitalize on its potential.

"A lot of us in Bluff have been supportive of the monument from the beginning in hopes that we can 'get in on it,'" Davila said. "We're pretty pro 'put your [monument headquarters] right down here' because we want to be in on the ground floor and develop that monument into something we can all be proud of instead of something that we all end up hating."

Indeed, Bluff is slowly but surely evolving into a tourist-friendly community, with (limited) amenities for backcountry lovers and urban visitors alike. There are multiple higher-end restaurants—and one eatery with the county's sole liquor license—that stay open at least part of the year, a recently expanded luxury hotel, and Davila's B&B. Multiple tour operators provide ample opportunity for frontcountry and backcountry exploration, with options for the experienced backpacker or the novice "glamper." The pace is easygoing, and the setting is remote enough to appeal to committed adventurers interested in discovering places far off the beaten path. But after a year in which national media reported regularly on the controversy surrounding Bears Ears, Bluff has seen a dramatic uptick in curious travelers eager to explore the mind-bending landscapes at the center of so many news stories.

There is increasing concern that the community is not prepared for what's about to hit. Bluff resident and BLM archaeologist Don Simonis supported the monument but fears for the town and for "the resource"—the tens of thousands of cultural sites and the ecologically fragile landscape within the boundaries of Bears Ears.

Preparing a blue heron sculpture for the annual winter solstice ceremony in Bluff, Utah

"It could go astronomical," Simonis said of the potential for increased crowds. "It just depends how much you advertise something. You know, if you want a million people to show up, you'd better be prepared for it. And we aren't right now. In fact, we can't handle the fifty thousand that we have right now. It's a zoo out there."

At present, there are few basic visitor amenities provided by the BLM on or near Cedar Mesa, Comb Ridge, or other popular sites on agency land. Everything from restrooms to interpretive signage will need to be built, and it seems unlikely that the Trump administration will provide much, if any, support to agency employees for new or continuing projects.

That's where Bluff-based nonprofit Friends of Cedar Mesa's partnerships with the BLM may be able to bridge the gap. With its access to private funding and a cadre of volunteers, FCM can provide on-the-ground stewardship and visitor education resources that can begin to lay the foundation for enhanced visitor experiences. With its reward fund for reporting looters, it can provide some resource protection as well.

The Twin Rocks Trading Post & Café in Bluff, Utah

"The quintessential catch-22 here [is] the opponents [say], 'You can't make this a national monument. You don't have money to do what you have to do now!'" said FCM executive director Josh Ewing in early 2017. "But why don't we have money to do it now? Because you guys are the champions of undercutting funding for the BLM!

"Our role . . . is fund-raising to help fill some of those holes and be positive and have a landscape-focused view" of land management, Ewing said.

Steve Simpson was born and raised in San Juan County and has operated a highly successful business for decades. He and his family run the venerable Twin Rocks Café—often the only dining option in town once the busy tourist season winds down in mid-October.

"Everybody's starting to say, 'Whoa, we might really get rolled over,'" Simpson said. "[My family and I live] on a quiet side street. And we wonder, is it just going to be overwhelmed?"

Jim Hook, a longtime local, is the current owner of the Recapture Lodge, a Bluff institution and haven for adventurers for over fifty years. He and his wife, Luann, who have owned the lodge since the 1980s, support incorporation of the town (which would provide the political tools to plan Bluff's future) but are friends with old-timers who oppose it. He has seen multiple efforts at self-determination fail over the decades, owing to ferocious in-fighting among strong personalities, a lack of financial resources, and a fierce aversion to embracing change.

"The people who have moved to Bluff and invested here, 90-plus percent didn't come here because they wanted streetlights and sidewalks," Hook said. "They came because they wanted this open space, they wanted a small little town where nobody cared who you are or what you believed or anything like that. It scares me that the bulk of people [don't want] to talk about change."

Hook notes that geography has defined Bluff and, in his eyes, been its saving grace—to a degree.

"I think it's why Bluff hasn't exploded before," Hook said. "Moab is sitting in front of three or four national, big-time attractions," such as Arches National Park. "It's right there off [Interstate 70].

"You're not going to get a giant mass of businesses like Moab has, but I think there's a niche here," Hook added. "Focus on the niche, on what is good and what you can do, and be satisfied with having 90 percent of the traffic flow through there and not stop. It's a quiet place to go, and it's laid back, and you can do this and that, and there aren't the high pressures and lots of hype."

Steve Simpson agrees. The way to keep Bluff from becoming Moab, he says, is to devise and plan for a sustainable alternative. The reality of the monument may prove to be the impetus that brings the town together to envision and plan for its future.

"All of these issues—affordable housing, the planning, the zoning, the infrastructure—are all on the table now where they haven't been in the past," Simpson said. "We're definitely behind the planning curve . . . . [But] there's probably a three-to-five-year lag, maybe even longer, between the time [the monument's] designated and when we see the real impact. So maybe we have an opportunity if we really start to scramble to get things in order."

Beyond the threat to the landscape itself, a number of Bluff residents—including those who embrace and profit from tourism—are concerned about what their town could become if they don't play a proactive role in developing a plan that fits their culture and values.

"Bluff as a pocket in San Juan County, we have the opportunity to become this vibrant little center that's not overcommercialized but is what we want it to become . . . if we control our own destiny," Ewing said. "Otherwise you could totally see [chain] hotels" staking a claim to the town's available land and paving the way for rampant development.

Hook said the next few years will be critical for Bluff.

"Bluff still sits on that knife-edge of is it going to grow and become a town, or is it going to fail and just be . . . a wide spot in the road?" he said.

A Path Toward Healing

For all of the county's economic and cultural struggles, perhaps the most wrenching challenge its citizens face is how to heal the multigenerational wounds that were reopened during the national monument debate. Absent a good-faith effort by opposing parties to work together to build a promising future, San Juan County may remain the poorest and most racially divided county in the state.

The ideological stances, emotions, and past grievances we encountered during our two years of traveling and listening were all manifest when hundreds of citizens gathered in Bluff in July 2016 for a public hearing aimed at discussing the future of public lands in San Juan County. The battle lines had been drawn, revealing such stark and deep cultural divides that it seemed impossible to imagine a world in which opposing parties could come together.

Hillsides southwest of Bluff, Utah, during a rainstorm

Yet it was also clear that those holding widely different outlooks share a great deal in common: a deep love of the land, both for its physical beauty and for its spiritual significance, and a conviction that their voices had not been heard by the federal government, those outside of the county, or the media. There was a common cry for recognition—of culture, of connection to land and family—and for a role in shaping decisions about their future.

Reflecting on the hearing while walking on sandstone below Comb Ridge, we recalled statements by two people we interviewed, people who hold vastly different views on how public lands in San Juan County should be stewarded.

The first came a few months into our project, when an individual working with Native American tribes to protect the Bears Ears land they consider sacred told us that the tribes' main desire was not to declare victory in a bitter fight. Instead, he said, "They just want to be seen and heard."

Several months later, a politician who publicly opposed the national monument proposal and advocated for locally driven land-use planning shared his experiences as a missionary for the Church of Jesus Christ of Latter-day Saints. In discussing living among people in desperate poverty in the developing world, he said the most important thing he felt he did involved simply listening to their stories and hearing their views. As he described it, "It's an essential human thing, to be understood by somebody."

Are there respected community members who can step up and provide the leadership the county needs to help all factions feel seen and heard and understood? And then begin to move forward? Will its leaders embrace a future that includes a broad-based, diversified economy? Can pro- and anti-monument groups put aside their differences, recognize how much they do have in common, and find a way to work together to define the county's future?

In interviews we conducted in the six months following Obama's designation of Bears Ears National Monument, the responses we received from San Juan County residents, tribal leaders, and others invested in the Bears Ears battle were less than hopeful.

Twin Rocks Café owner Steve Simpson could not see any path forward until the county's leadership and citizens reconcile their "completely different visions for what the county is. Are we extractive? Are we tourism-based? Are we education-based?

"When I look at the extractive past and what I think of as the extractive future, it's not there," Simpson added. "You can get these really big economic explosions, and then they collapse. And when they collapse, it's really hard. They're never sustainable, because you're taking away that which provides the wealth."

Utah Diné Bikéyah executive director Gavin Noyes had yet to see evidence of either county or tribal officials embracing collaborative efforts.

"Nobody in San Juan County is talking to each other at all," Noyes said. "That is *the* challenge. People can go off and plan in a box with half the county, and then you're going to fail to solve the problem because you're not talking to the half of the county where all the challenges exist.

"There's four divides in the county," Noyes continued. "There's Native and non-Native. That splits north and south"—the northern part of the county is predominantly Anglo, while the southern half is majority Native. "Then there's Mormon and non-Mormon, and that's woven through, in both cultures. You've got splits in the Native community where they call Mormons apples—you know, red on the outside, white on the inside"—and non-Mormons who identify as traditionalists, including every member of UDB's board. "In the non-Native community you've got the Mormons and non-Mormons that don't really work together either."

Speaking to us in early 2017, *San Juan Record* publisher Bill Boyle believed that the uncertainty created by the upheaval in national politics has ground all discussion of the county's economic future to a halt until the status of the Bears Ears monument is resolved.

"Many local people anticipate that President Trump will roll back the designation," Boyle said. "Once they see that it will not be that easy, they may be willing to take the next step.

"I think that much of the immediate local perception is that any designation is counter to the 'people's will,'" he added. "Elected officials, from the top to the bottom of the state, lined up in unison to oppose [the monument], and it still happened."

Indeed, there was and still is an organized effort of monument opponents in the county. Stewards of San Juan, a group using the slogan "Trump this monument," organized protests and maintained a website whose URL until late 2017 was savebearsears.com. Now that URL redirects to sutherland institute.org/antiquities, a page hosted by the Salt Lake City–based conservative think tank Sutherland Institute. The institute, which has long supported monument opponents in San Juan County, is now advocating full repeal of the Antiquities Act. The site featured testimonials from county residents, both Anglo and Native, who feared the monument would devastate the local economy and limit access to places they used for hunting, ranching, and recreation and places they considered to be culturally significant. Some opponents contended that monument supporters were primarily out-of-state tribes or radical environmental organizations hell-bent on destroying local people's livelihoods. La Posada Pintada owner Jennifer Davila had little patience for that argument.

"A county commissioner can stand on the steps of the county courthouse and say, 'President Obama, you've just offended every resident of San Juan County,'" Davila said. "Well, maybe he's offended five hundred of you, but there's two or three thousand of us whom he did not offend. It's the blatant disregard for other people's thoughts and feelings that bothers me the most."

Yet Boyle saw signs of hope, with some local citizens reevaluating the potential impact of the monument. An article published in the January 18, 2017, issue of the *Record* details a Blanding City Council meeting in which Mayor Calvin Balch urged the council members to set aside their own strong feelings and instead draft a press release that more accurately reflects the views of the city as a whole.

In response to calls to "take a stand" and speak out against the monument and its perceived negative economic impacts on county residents, Balch noted that there were many Blanding residents who did not oppose the monument.

"We have a responsibility to represent all of the people—100 percent," he said.

Five months later, little had changed. At a June 27 city council meeting, Balch again called for the town to move forward and "jump on the bandwagon and embrace the monument." Once again, his fellow council members and residents in attendance opposed his stance and concurred with the sentiments of San Juan County commissioner Phil Lyman.

"These people pushing for the monument are not our friends," Lyman said. "They do not have good things in mind for Blanding."

"There are many people who recognize the need to move forward, but there has been quite an outcry from the community that the city council doesn't understand or care about the impacts of the monument designation," Boyle said. "The story of the decline in traditional use of the land in

Escalante with the resulting decline in school enrollment and community impacts [after the designation of the Grand Staircase–Escalante National Monument in 1996] resonates among many people in Blanding. They hear that Escalante was taken over by outsiders and fear that the same may happen in San Juan County. Many believe that this is an existential battle."

The negativity and social pressure exerted by power brokers in the county make the bridge building that Friends of Cedar Mesa executive director Josh Ewing started before the monument designation especially challenging. Yet he continued to work with Blanding resident Kay Shumway on restoring his family's cabin near Recapture Canyon, despite their differing views on land-use issues and the monument in particular.

"Working together bridges gaps," Ewing said, adding, "If you've got to agree with your friends on everything, you won't have any friends."

He held out hope for compromise, which he believes could be achieved through a good-faith effort by county citizens selected to participate on the monument advisory committee. But, Ewing wondered, "[will] the local Sagebrush Rebel part of the community boycott the management plan process? It would be a real loss if that process ends up [having] only a few of us participating.

"You can have really smart people working on these issues, but if the politics [dominates], it doesn't matter how smart or reasonable the person is," Ewing said. "If you've got that level of ideology, that practical level of compromise doesn't do anything."

Bruce Adams lamented the fact that his constituents are more polarized than ever.

"This whole monument discussion has created much more division in the county than we had prior to the monument discussion and all of the efforts that went into it," Adams said. He and his fellow commissioners will not move forward until there is a definitive resolution to the monument battle in Washington.

Utah state senator and minority caucus manager Jim Dabakis, a Democrat and outspoken critic of the state's promotion of extractive industries as primary economic drivers, hopes that a few courageous souls will step up and forge multistakeholder agreements.

"That's where leadership comes in," Dabakis said when we spoke with him in the fall of 2016. "That's where county commissioners, that is where

Mesas near North Flats Road, northwest of Monticello, Utah

governors, that is where state legislators come in and honestly and fairly explain to the public what the options are. Not just rhetoric and . . . fear."

Current Bears Ears Inter-Tribal Coalition cochair Carleton Bowekaty said the tribes were committed to listening to San Juan County's citizens.

"We plan on including local voices in the management planning," Bowekaty said. "There's still some misinformation about the specifics of the monument proclamation," and "a lot of education needs to happen. The co-alition and the [Bears Ears] commission will work in conjunction to educate the community."

"It's really tough," said Regina Lopez-Whiteskunk, a former Ute Mountain Ute councilwoman and member of the Bears Ears Inter-Tribal Coalition. "Historically, what's been fed is all the negativity, all the historical trauma, and nobody's ever taken the time to do [the] healing."

Mark and Kenneth Maryboy, brothers who both served as San Juan County commissioners, have endured decades of bitter conflict and out-right attacks from their fellow commissioners and other county residents. Despite the scars they carry, or perhaps because of them, the Maryboys are committed to the process of healing.

In a January 22, 2017, op-ed for the *Salt Lake Tribune*, Kenneth Maryboy articulated the tribes' willingness to work with county citizens to forge a path forward.[7]

"Native American citizens in San Juan County are ready to craft a future together in the place we have always called home, and we must ensure the next chapter is about healing," Maryboy wrote. "The Bears Ears National Monument can be a great thing for all Americans, but only if we realize its potential together."

Even though he insists on persuading Congress and the Trump administration to rescind or reduce the monument, Bruce Adams also recognizes the importance of moving forward. But he, along with the tribes and many others involved in the Bears Ears debate, believes that "we need some time for everybody to heal."

"There's a lot of jockeying going on between the groups, and so hopefully in the short term we can see finality to this whole thing," Adams said. "Once that happens, I think people can take some time to fix their bloody nose. Whatever happens, happens. [Then] we can get on with life."

---

7. Maryboy, "Op-ed: Native Americans Ready."

Part 2: July 2017–February 2018

If Secretary Zinke's initial work to reevaluate the boundaries of national monuments, including Bears Ears, was cause for concern among tribes and conservationists, his August 2017 memorandum recommending the reduction of the Obama-created monument was cause for outright alarm. The numerous organizations that had supported the Bears Ears Inter-Tribal Coalition's efforts spent months galvanizing their constituents to donate to "monument defense" funds and submit comments to the Interior Department in favor of keeping Bears Ears intact.

By the time the department's public comment period closed, over 650,000 Americans had weighed in—and 98 percent of them supported maintaining or expanding the boundaries of all monuments included in Zinke's review. But as the next chapter of the Bears Ears battle began, the will of the American public at large was suppressed by the combined power of the executive branch and a select few politicians from the Beehive State.

On December 4, 2017, during a whirlwind trip to Salt Lake City, President Trump signed a proclamation shrinking Bears Ears National Monument from 1.35 million acres to 202,000 acres—an 85 percent reduction— and another reducing Grand Staircase–Escalante National Monument from 1.9 million acres to just over 1 million acres.

The order was perhaps the clearest example to date of the influence Orrin Hatch, Utah's senior senator, had with the White House. Hatch had been asking the president to rescind or shrink the two Utah monuments since the earliest days of Trump's presidency, and there is no doubt that his success in convincing the president to do so will forever be part of his legacy.

Trump's action thrilled many Utahns and others who saw former president Barack Obama's designation of the original Bears Ears monument as a "land grab" executed by out-of-touch elitists in Washington, D.C., who lacked any connection to the people most directly affected by the Bears Ears declaration: those living in San Juan County, Utah. But many others in Utah and throughout the nation, both Native and Anglo, were angered and offended by the new president's move to gut the monument and replace it with two far smaller entities: Shash Jáa, in the southeastern corner of the original Bears Ears National Monument; and Indian Creek, at its northern tip.

Three core issues dominated the conversation in the aftermath of the Bears Ears reduction: legality, sovereignty, and money.

Hours after Trump acted to reduce Bears Ears and Grand Staircase–Escalante, a coalition of environmental and outdoor recreation groups, along with the tribes comprising the Bears Ears Inter-Tribal Coalition—the Hopi, Navajo, Ute, Zuni, and Ute Mountain Ute—filed five separate lawsuits challenging the legality of the proclamation. The three lawsuits related to Bears Ears were consolidated into a single case; the same occurred with the two Grand Staircase suits.

The plaintiffs alleged that a president lacks the authority to undo a prior president's national monument designation; that power, they argue, rests with Congress alone, as enumerated in the 1976 Federal Land Policy and Management Act (FLPMA). The matter may well be litigated for years before the fate of Bears Ears is resolved.

Tribes protested what they saw as disrespectful treatment by the Trump administration. In their view, the administration cast aside years of work by the Bears Ears Inter-Tribal Coalition, drafting a national monument proposal that would provide indigenous peoples a significant voice in how the land would be managed. The designation of Bears Ears National Monument by President Obama had promised to provide Native tribes for the first time with a meaningful role in working with federal agencies to shape management of public lands, thereby recognizing tribes' rights as sovereign governments.

As both sides continued their battle in the media and prepared for a face-off in court, Utah's newest congressman, John Curtis, was hard at work crafting what he termed a "compromise bill."

Introduced in early January 2018, H.R. 4532, the Shash Jáa National Monument and Indian Creek National Monument Act, sought to codify President Trump's December 2017 proclamation shrinking Bears Ears National Monument. In addition to dividing what was left of the original monument into two much smaller monuments, Curtis's proposed legislation would also change the relationship between the tribes and the two smaller monuments.

Obama's proclamation called for the establishment of the Bears Ears Commission, comprised of one representative from each of the five tribes that petitioned the federal government for a national monument in 2015. The commission was charged with advancing policy recommendations and guidance to the employees of the U.S. Forest Service and Bureau of Land Management; the federal agencies would retain ultimate responsibility for managing the land within the monument.

By contrast, Curtis's bill calls for the president, in consultation with the Utah delegation, to appoint a group of local elected officials and tribal leaders to a management council. Curtis and Utah politicians have argued that this approach will give tribes "real" comanagement responsibilities, as opposed to the advisory role laid out in Obama's proclamation.

Predictably, the tribes assailed this proposal, citing the fact that the Curtis bill requires that the two tribal representatives on the proposed management council be selected from the two tribes whose members live adjacent to the monument in San Juan County, Utah: the Navajo and Ute Mountain Ute. It excludes representatives from the other three tribes with ancestral connections to the region. Moreover, the five tribes comprising the Bears Ears Coalition believe that Trump, Zinke, and the Utah delegation are likely to fill the two Native positions on the management council with individuals who share their antimonument views.

Curtis did not consult with any of the leaders of the five tribes comprising the Bears Ears Coalition regarding the structure and composition of the management commission, allegedly intended to provide a voice to Natives having strong cultural ties to the Bears Ears region. This led Navajo Nation president Russell Begaye to state that the monuments were tribal "in name only."

Meanwhile, in the Senate, New Mexico Senators Martin Heinrich and Tom Udall joined fifteen of their Democratic colleagues in crafting a legislative response to Trump's shrinking of Bears Ears and Grand Staircase–Escalante. Just as Representative Curtis's bill would codify the boundaries of Trump's new Utah monuments, the America's Natural Treasures of Immeasurable Qualities Unite, Inspire, and Together Improve the Economies of States Act (ANTIQUITIES Act for short), introduced in February 2018, would codify the boundaries of all monuments established since 1996.

Adding to the intrigue and further infuriating the tribes and Bears Ears supporters, the *Washington Post* reported that Energy Fuels Resources, a Colorado-based mining company that operates the White Mesa Uranium Mill just outside the original Bears Ears National Monument, lobbied the Department of the Interior to change the boundaries of Bears Ears to exclude land with potential for uranium mining. This shift was seen by monument supporters as a blatant effort to revive a faltering industry and a symbolic gesture aimed at underlining Trump's commitment to his "America First" energy policy. The lobbying proved fruitful: the redrawn monument boundaries in large measure reflect the request of industry.

The company vehemently denied the reports, launching its own PR offensive with a series of op-eds placed in newspapers across the West. The Bears Ears Inter-Tribal Coalition, conservation organizations, and other allies of the tribes decried Energy Fuels' actions. They also warned of a coming "land rush" on February 2, 2018, the date the nearly one million acres slashed from the original Bears Ears monument would be open to mining claims.

Despite much alarm by environmental groups and tribes, there was no "land rush" following the removal of national monument protections for the land. Yet Energy Fuels' successful lobbying efforts demonstrated that extractive industry companies were planning for a new era of American energy dominance—and that the threat to the Bears Ears landscape, while perhaps not imminent, was still real.

Soon after the mining restrictions were lifted in early February, the *New York Times* revealed even more evidence of industry's influence on reshaping Bears Ears. A trove of Interior Department documents obtained by the *Times* demonstrated beyond doubt that Utah elected officials, Interior Department staff, and extractive industry companies worked in concert to carve out huge swaths of land from the original Bears Ears National Monument. Land removed from the monument is thought to contain economically viable uranium and oil and gas reserves.

Correspondence between Interior staff and Utah senator Orrin Hatch's office contains clear requests from Hatch to remove specific parcels of land with energy potential from Bears Ears, including one just outside Bluff. As Friends of Cedar Mesa executive director Josh Ewing noted on Twitter, "Utah is targeting Bluff's watershed for drilling/fracking . . . with absolutely no consideration of our community and against our express wishes to have this cultural landscape permanently protected."

In the midst of complex and high-stakes battles over the future of public lands, attempting to heal deep wounds among factions in San Juan County seems an impossible task. The politically charged environment that has widened the gulf between the county's residents transformed what once was a promising atmosphere for compromise into a tragic failure to reach a meaningful consensus.

But an opportunity to find common ground exists outside of courtrooms and county commission meetings. It can be found in the canyons of Cedar Mesa, the spires and mesas of Valley of the Gods, the sculpted sandstone of White Canyon, and the meadows and forests surrounding Bears Ears.

Natives and Anglos in San Juan County, regardless of spiritual beliefs or worldview, have used the same words to explain to us their connection to place: "The land is who we are." The land is not just a place to live, explore, or make a living; it is *everything*. Land is sacred, linking ancestors, families, future generations, gods, and spirits, and it is a source of strength, renewal, and identity.

Improbably enough, despite painful histories of conflict, division, and social strife, Native and Mormon spirituality and cultural values have surprisingly deep similarities. Both Mormon theology and Native cosmology speak to the earth as an entity to be revered and protected for its spiritual power and material sustenance; both strive for stewardship as a cultural and moral imperative; and both caution against taking more from the land than is necessary for survival.

> This earth, all men, animals, fish, fowls, plants, all things—all lived first as spirit entities. . . . This earth and all that thereon is our concern.
>
> —Elder Bruce R. McConkie, Quorum of the Twelve Apostles,
> Church of Jesus Christ of Latter-day Saints, "Christ and the Creation"

> As beneficiaries of the divine Creation, what shall we do? We should care for the earth, be wise stewards over it, and preserve it for future generations.
>
> —Russell M. Nelson, Quorum of the Twelve Apostles, and
> president, Church of Jesus Christ of Latter-day Saints, "The Creation"

> We understood this place and cared for it, relating to the earth literally as our mother who provides for us and the plants and animals to which we are related. The Bears Ears landscape is alive in our view, and must be nourished and cared for if life is to be sustained.
>
> —Malcolm Lehi, member, Ute Mountain Ute Council,
> in Bears Ears Inter-Tribal Coalition, "Bears Ears"

In their shared reverence for Bears Ears country lies hope.

The path toward healing might best be found in the words of Utah Diné Bikéyah board member and spiritual advisor Jonah Yellowman, who speaks to the ties that bind the region's residents and all Americans, to whom the land in the Bears Ears National Monument belongs: "This is everybody's land. We're all God's children. This is all of us."

Lime Ridge mesas in winter

ACKNOWLEDGMENTS

One of the challenges and delights of this project was that its trajectory changed multiple times in the course of two years and took us in directions we never could have anticipated. Fortunately, we have enjoyed the guidance and support of many remarkable people in the Four Corners states and across the country who provided vital information, guidance, access, food, lodging, and knowledge of the Colorado Plateau's landscape and history.

We are grateful to Vaughn Hadenfeldt, Marcia Simonis, and Jonathan Till for providing essential background regarding the significance of archaeological sites on the Colorado Plateau and current archaeological research in the Four Corners region. Special thanks to Vaughn for guiding us to Ancestral Puebloan sites on Cedar Mesa and Comb Ridge, sharing invaluable knowledge and colorful stories, and treating a medical emergency one fateful October day.

Mary and Tara Benally, Eric Descheenie, Davis Filfred, and Cynthia Wilson generously shared with us their personal stories and professional work, which helped us gain a greater understanding of the politics and spiritual underpinnings of the Bears Ears Inter-Tribal Coalition and Utah Diné Bikéyah.

Thanks to Brian O'Donnell of Conservation Lands Foundation; Bill Hedden and Tim Peterson of the Grand Canyon Trust; Sue Bellagamba of the Nature Conservancy; Scott Groene and Matt Gross of the Southern Utah Wilderness Alliance; former Arches and Canyonlands superintendent Walt Dabney; and Ashley Korenblat of Public Land Solutions for sharing valuable perspectives and connecting us to sources and resources that deepened our understanding and appreciation of conservation efforts in southeastern Utah and in the recreation industry.

We thank our contacts in Washington, D.C., and Salt Lake City who demystified the complexities of the legislative process and provided invaluable historical and political background information on the Washington County Lands Bill and the Public Lands Initiative: Jim Dabakis, Utah state senator; Fred Ferguson, former chief of staff to former representative Jason Chaffetz (R-UT); Tyler Owens, staff member, Senate Appropriations Committee; Senator Robert Bennett (R-UT); Brad Shafer, former senior advisor to Senator Robert Bennett; Casey Snider, former staff member for Representative Rob Bishop; Cody Stewart, former director of federal affairs for Utah governor Gary Herbert; Tim Stewart, vice president, U.S. Oil and Gas Association, and former staffer to Senator Robert Bennett; and Senator Robert Bennett (1933–2016).

Cedale Armstrong, Scott Boyle, Chris Giangreco, Cynthia Higgins, Joe Peterson, and Anna Hart shed light on the opportunities and challenges in providing and sustaining quality educational opportunities to San Juan County residents.

We thank Shane and Merri Shumway for inviting us to join them and their extended family and friends on a memorable trip along the Hole-in-the-Rock Trail; LaRue Barton and Robert McPherson for enhancing our knowledge of Mormon history in San Juan County; George Handley for providing a scholarly perspective on Mormonism and land stewardship; and Von del Chamberlain for his suggestions regarding sources who could deepen our understanding of Mormon teachings.

Nick Sandberg helped us to understand the complexities of land-use policy in San Juan County. Lynn Jackson and Ray Peterson provided valuable perspectives on the Public Lands Initiative process in Grand and Emery Counties.

In addition to our interviewees, Octavius Seowtewa and Vaughn Awalgate of Zuni Pueblo gave us a greater understanding of Native cosmology and the roles of spiritual advisors and cultural preservation offices in documenting and protecting traditional indigenous knowledge, and they shared with us the spiritual beliefs that inform Native views regarding land stewardship. Curtis Quam was our patient and knowledgeable guide through the A:shiwi A:wan Museum and Cultural Center. Belinda Tsabetsaye provided insight into ongoing efforts to develop school curricula that incorporate the teaching of the Zuni language.

Marjorie Dee gave us an enlightening crash course in economic development on the "Utah strip" of the Navajo Nation. Jessica Stago shed light on efforts to foster Native entrepreneurship on the Navajo Reservation and beyond. Charlie DeLorme was an expert source for data and perspective on efforts to create a diversified economy in San Juan County. Pam Hanson also provided valuable insights on economic development initiatives in the county. Jared Berrett shared his experience as a small-scale outfitter and trip leader in San Juan County. Vicki Varela and Linda Gillmor explained the state of Utah's role in promoting recreation-based tourism and fostering entrepreneurship in rural parts of the state.

Thanks to a trio of "Bluffoons": Brandt Hart for sharing stories of his time as a Bureau of Land Management river ranger; Brant Murray for explaining with warmth and humor the process of planning for Bluff's future; and Joe Pachak for his candor and his artistry.

Ken Sleight shared insight into battles to preserve wilderness in red rock country from the 1960s onward as seen through eyes that by his lights have witnessed some victories but too many defeats.

Pilot Nate Rydman flew us across southeastern Utah with skill and perpetual good humor, allowing Steve to take the aerial images that appear in this book. Nate's knowledge of and love for the landscape are palpable, and we thank him for his invaluable contributions to this work. We thank Light-Hawk Conservation Flying for providing support of the overflights.

Stephanie Smith of the Grand Canyon Trust created the stunning maps that appear in this book. We are indebted to her for lending her GIS and design skills to this project.

Rich conversations with author Stephen Trimble led us to some of our first sources and texts, and he generously reviewed early-stage excerpts of our manuscript. We are grateful for his insight as we continued to develop our work. Toby McLeod helped us to better understand the international movement for indigenous self-determination and protection of sacred sites.

Recapture Lodge owners Jim and LuAnn Hook housed us many times over eighteen months and made our stays in Bluff lively and enjoyable. La Posada Pintada proprietor Jennifer Davila provided us with a warm welcome, fantastic freshly baked bread, generous use of La Posada's back patio, and stories of life as a longtime "Bluffoon." Steve and Jana Simpson at Bluff's Twin Rocks Café and Trading Post have been feeding locals and visitors from around the world for many years. We partook of many a Navajo taco and pancake stack during our meetings with sources and on rare quiet mornings between interviews. We thank them all for their hospitality and good cheer and candid discussions regarding the economy and politics of Bluff and San Juan County.

Mark Meloy was our first source and sounding board. His willingness to provide contacts and valuable context for the complex issues at the heart of our story proved essential to beginning and developing this book. At our first meeting he warned us that we'd "really kicked a hornet's nest"; we hope he will be pleased to learn that we were undeterred, and even encouraged, by his words.

We thank Joy Harjo for permitting us to use the poem that sets the emotional stage for the book and Patty Limerick not only for her thought-provoking foreword but for several stimulating conversations and an unforgettable dinner.

Simmons Buntin at Terrain.org believed in our project and provided us a space to present the first excerpt of *Voices from Bears Ears*, as well as an ongoing blog to report and reflect on our work as it evolved. We are grateful for his editorial guidance and for the opportunity to be featured in a beautiful and vital online publication.

We thank George F. Thompson for editorial and aesthetic guidance throughout the preparation of the manuscript and Kathryn Conrad and Allyson Carter of the University of Arizona Press for their support and encouragement.

We extend our profound gratitude to our "portraitees," whose generosity, wisdom, candor, and willingness to speak with us time and again made this work possible: Jonah Yellowman, Kay and Patsy Shumway, Mark Maryboy, Phil Lyman, Rob Bishop, Gavin Noyes, Rebecca Benally, Heidi Redd, Josh Ewing, Bruce Adams, Bill Boyle, Charles Wilkinson, Natasha Hale, Regina Lopez-Whiteskunk, Carleton Bowekaty, Don Simonis, Winston Hurst, Shaun Chapoose, Kate Cannon, and Alfred and Sahmie Lomahquahu.

Kathy and Dan Huntington are the unsung heroes of this book, tackling the unglamorous work of fact checking, formatting, organizing, and generally keeping us on task and on deadline. They are also family, and their love, wisdom, and steadfastness anchored us during this project's peaks and valleys.

The author wishes to thank her husband, Jamie Schlessinger, for his patience through numerous extended trips away from home and many long nights and weekends of writing and revising and for his words of encouragement throughout. She is grateful for their shared love of red rock country, which first brought them together and continues to be a source of strength, inspiration, and endless adventure.

We dedicate this book to Karen Strom, a woman of incredible strength and formidable intellect who had an unwavering commitment to social justice and a passion for pushing the boundaries of photographic art. She sparked the author's love of the outdoors and encouraged her to tell stories, first as a pastime, then as a profession. We honor her memory the best way we know how: by searching for the beauty and magic in the world.

MAPS

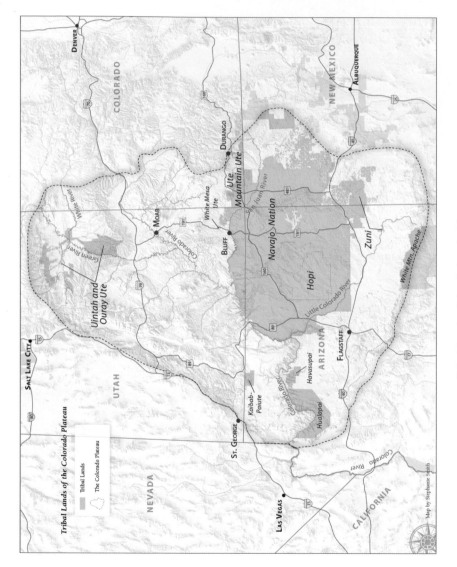

Tribal Lands of the Colorado Plateau

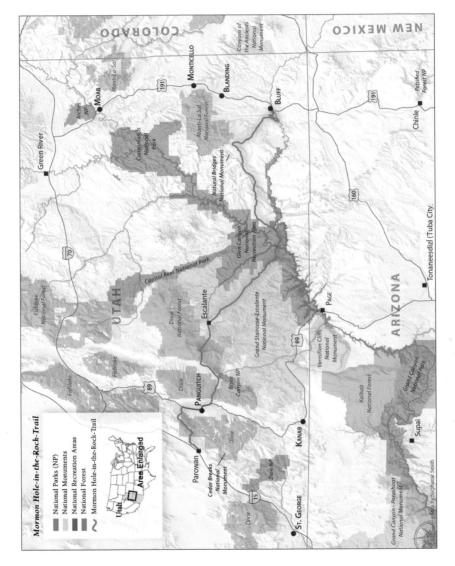

Hole-in-the-Rock Trail

Federal Lands on the Colorado Plateau

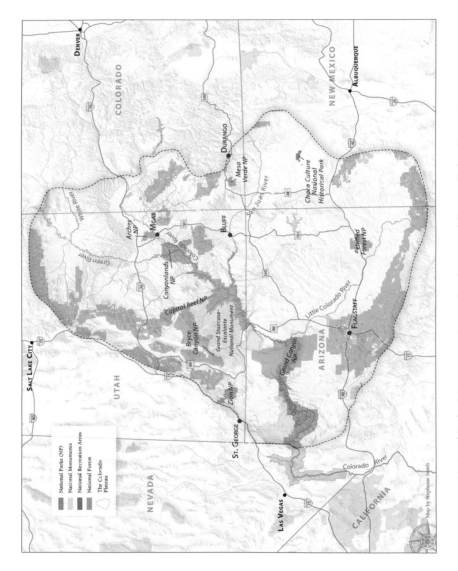

National Parks, Monuments, Recreation Areas, and Forests Before Bears Ears

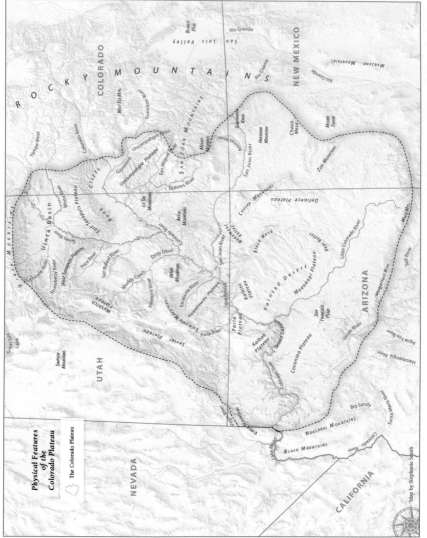

Physical Features of the Colorado Plateau

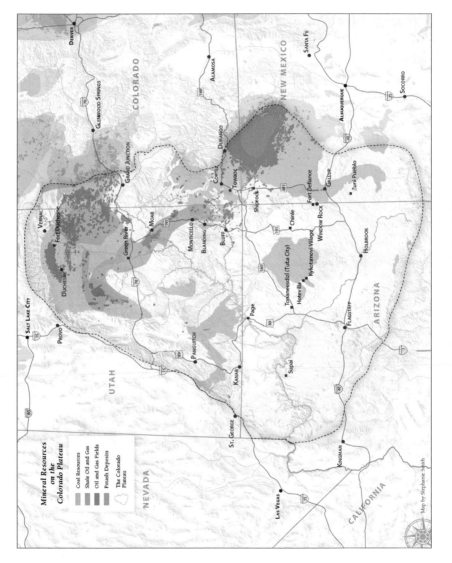

Mineral Resources on the Colorado Plateau

Within the map legend:

Mineral Resources on the Colorado Plateau

- Coal Resources
- Shale Oil and Gas
- Oil and Gas Fields
- Potash Deposits
- The Colorado Plateau

Map by Stephanie Smith

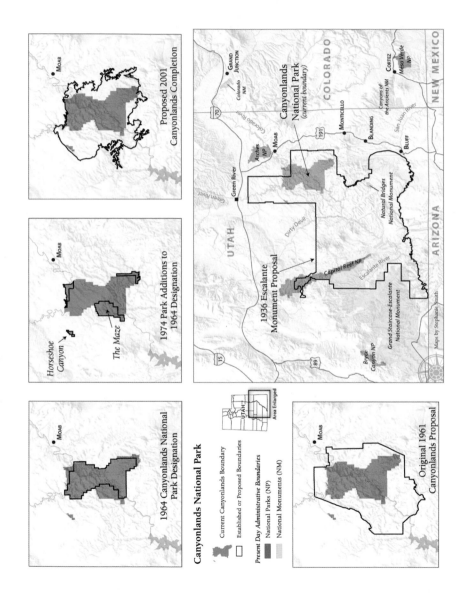

Canyonlands National Park

Proposed 2001
Canyonlands Completion

1974 Park Additions to
1964 Designation

Horseshoe
Canyon

The Maze

1964 Canyonlands National
Park Designation

Canyonlands National Park

⌐ Current Canyonlands Boundary
☐ Established or Proposed Boundaries

Present Day Administrative Boundaries
▮ National Parks (NP)
▮ National Monuments (NM)

UTAH

Area Enlarged

Original 1961
Canyonlands Proposal

MOAB

GRAND
JUNCTION

Colorado
NM

70

COLORADO

CORTEZ

Meso Verde
NP

NEW MEXICO

Canyonlands
National Park
(current boundary)

Arches
NP

MOAB

191

MONTICELLO

BLANDING

Canyons of
the Ancients NM

San Juan River

BLUFF

Green River

Colorado River

Dirty Devil

Natural Bridges
National Monument

ARIZONA

1936 Escalante
Monument Proposal

Capitol Reef NP

Escalante River

Green River

Grand Staircase-Escalante
National Monument

Bryce
Canyon NP

15

89

Maps by Stephanie Smith

History of Canyonlands National Park

326

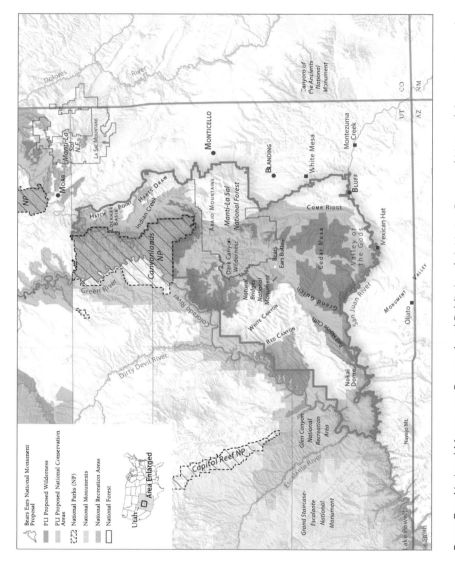

Bears Ears National Monument Proposal and Public Lands Initiative Proposed National Conservation and Wilderness Areas

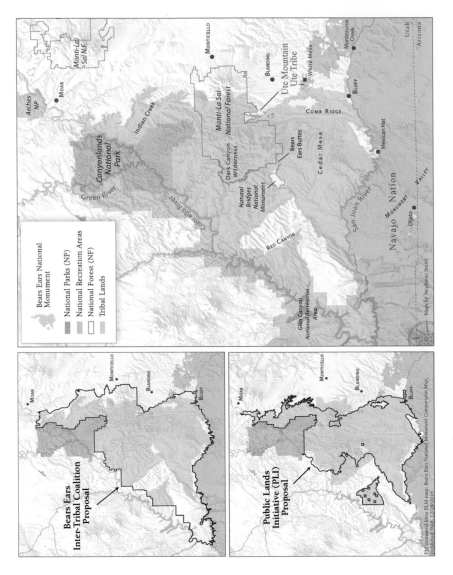

Boundaries of Bears Ears National Monument Declared by President Obama in December 2016 Compared to the Original Proposal by the Bears Ears Inter-Tribal Coalition and the Utah Public Lands Initiative

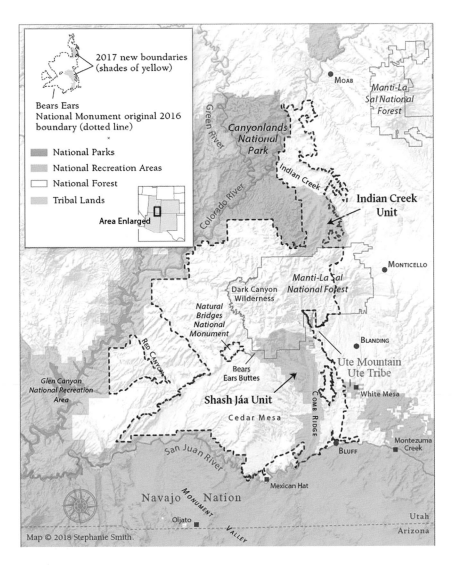

Boundaries of Bears Ears National Monument Declared by President Obama in 2016 Compared to the Boundaries After President Trump Reduced the Area by 85 Percent in 2017

INDIVIDUALS PROFILED

Jonah Yellowman is a Navajo traditional healer and board member of Utah Diné Bikéyah, an organization that "works toward healing of people and the Earth by supporting indigenous communities in protecting their culturally significant, ancestral lands." He has played an essential role as a spiritual advisor to the Bears Ears Inter-Tribal Coalition, a collaboration among five Colorado Plateau tribes—the Hopi, Navajo, Ute Mountain Ute, Ute Indian Tribe of the Uintah and Ouray Reservation, and Zuni—whose leaders crafted and presented to the Obama administration a proposal for a 1.9-million-acre national monument in San Juan County.

Kay and Patsy Shumway are longtime residents of Blanding with roots in San Juan County extending back six generations. Following an academic career as a botanist with a PhD in plant genetics, Kay returned to Blanding to help launch and grow Utah State University Eastern, Blanding campus. Patsy is a retired schoolteacher who spent her formative years herding sheep with her family and working

alongside one of the foremost cattlemen in San Juan County. The Shumways are members of Friends of Cedar Mesa, a nonprofit dedicated to protecting and preserving the landscapes and archaeological sites in San Juan County.

Mark Maryboy is a renowned politician and activist. He was the first Native elected official in Utah's history and served for twenty years on the San Juan County Commission and in the Navajo Nation government. As a cofounder and board member of Utah Diné Bikéyah, he played a pivotal role in conducting interviews of tribal elders and compiling a comprehensive map of cultural resources in southeastern Utah of importance to Navajos. This work laid the foundation for the formation of the Bears Ears Inter-Tribal Coalition and the national monument proposal its leaders submitted to the Obama administration.

Phil Lyman is a San Juan County commissioner and proud descendant of the first Anglos to settle the county. As part of Representative Rob Bishop's (R-UT) Public Lands Initiative, he organized the San Juan County Public Lands Council in response to Bishop's call for stakeholder-driven input that would inform the PLI legislation. Lyman strongly believes that decisions regarding the future of public lands in southeastern Utah should be the province of state and local governments. He gained national notoriety for a 2014 ATV protest ride through Recapture Canyon challenging the closure of roads on Bureau of Land Management land.

Representative Rob Bishop (R-UT) was elected to Congress in 2002, where he currently chairs the House Committee on Natural Resources. Prior to his election, he spent twenty-eight years as a high-school teacher and served for sixteen years in the Utah state legislature. In 2013 Bishop initiated the Utah Public Lands Initiative, which he describes as "a locally driven effort to bring resolution and certainty to the most challenging land disputes in Utah." Bishop is known for his opposition to use of the Antiquities Act, used by presidents to unilaterally establish national monuments, and for his belief that states, rather than the federal government, should manage public lands.

Gavin Noyes is the executive director of Utah Diné Bikéyah. Noyes worked closely with Mark Maryboy and others in assembling a database of cultural resources in southeastern Utah that became a template for the Bears Ears Inter-Tribal Coalition's national monument proposal. For more than a decade he has worked with tribes in Utah to protect their ancestral lands and assert their rights as sovereign nations. He continues to pursue economic development strategies that are inclusive of all the county's residents and are based on good-faith compromise.

Rebecca Benally is a San Juan County commissioner, representing the southern part of the county, including the Utah portion of the Navajo Nation. She has been an outspoken opponent of establishing the Bears Ears National Monument, believing that a monument would restrict energy development and mining, two sources of income for many tribal members in eastern Utah. She sees advocating for practical projects on the Navajo Nation—paving roads, enhancing schools, and expanding school bus service—as a major part of her job as an elected official.

Heidi Redd has been a cattle rancher since 1965, when she and her husband purchased the Indian Creek Cattle Company in San Juan County, near the border of Canyonlands National Park's Needles District. Redd's interest in long-term scientific study of ranchlands in the west led her to sell her ranch to the Nature Conservancy in 1997. The arrangement precludes development and retains the land as a working cattle ranch. Redd served as a member of San Juan County Commissioner Phil Lyman's Public Lands Council and sought to create a compromise that would balance wilderness preservation and economic development.

Josh Ewing is executive director of Friends of Cedar Mesa. Ewing served on Phil Lyman's San Juan County Public Lands Council and is a strong advocate for protecting endangered archaeological sites on Cedar Mesa and surrounding areas. He works closely with the Bureau of Land Management to prevent looting and to educate the public about how to respect ancestral sites.

Bruce Adams is a San Juan County commissioner, former science teacher, and manager of his family's ranch. He traces his ancestry to the first Anglo settlers in San Juan County. He, along with *San Juan Record* publisher Bill Boyle, has been an advocate for the Canyon Country Discovery Center, an educational center providing experiential learning programs in archaeology, earth science, and other place-based outdoor education. In addition, both he and Boyle supported the development of a wind farm west of Monticello. He has been an outspoken opponent of the Bears Ears National Monument and views himself as an advocate for locals in San Juan County who he believes have been ignored or disrespected by the federal government.

Bill Boyle is the publisher of the *San Juan Record*, San Juan County's sole newspaper. Boyle's roots in the county go back four generations; his great-grandfather was the first mayor of Monticello. Alongside San Juan County Commissioner Bruce Adams, Boyle has been active in supporting the Canyon Country Discovery Center and in developing a wind farm west of Monticello. He hopes to broaden the economic base of the county beyond dependence on extractive industries and ranching.

Charles Wilkinson is the Moses Lasky Professor of Law (emeritus) at the University of Colorado, Boulder, and a longtime advocate for Native American rights. Wilkinson helped lay the groundwork for President Clinton's 1996 designation of the Grand Staircase–Escalante National Monument in southern Utah. He worked closely with the Bears Ears Inter-Tribal Coalition in their efforts to have the Obama administration declare the Bears Ears National Monument, and he continues to serve as a pro bono legal advisor to the coalition.

Natasha Hale manages the Grand Canyon Trust's Native America Program, where she works with tribal members to create culturally appropriate economic development programs. She has played a major role in coordinating the leaders of the tribes comprising the Bears Ears Inter-Tribal Coalition.

Regina Lopez-Whiteskunk is a former Ute Mountain Ute councilwoman and former co-chair of the Bears Ears Inter-Tribal Coalition. Whiteskunk served as a highly visible spokesperson for the coalition as it built support for the Bears Ears National Monument. She sees the potential of the coalition tribes to use their combined sovereign powers as an important step in seeking greater recognition for tribal priorities.

Carleton Bowekaty serves as a Zuni councilman and as cochair of the Bears Ears Inter-Tribal Coalition. In addition to serving the Pueblo of Zuni as an elected leader, Bowekaty works toward the protection of sacred and cultural sites throughout the southwestern United States as part of his work with the Zuni tribal government and with the coalition. He has a strong interest in the preservation of Zuni language and culture.

Don Simonis is an archaeologist who most recently worked with the Monticello office of the Bureau of Land Management. In addition to his research, Simonis works with colleagues and volunteers from Friends of Cedar Mesa to protect Native archaeological sites from looting and vandalism. Simonis is helping to facilitate programs aimed at educating the public about the importance of protecting Native ancestral sites for both their scientific value and their cultural significance.

Winston Hurst is a renowned archaeologist who has been working for decades to catalog Native archaeological sites on the Colorado Plateau. Born and raised in San Juan County, he has deep roots in the Mormon community. He has been outspoken in efforts to protect Ancestral Puebloan sites from looting and desecration and to provide local residents with a deeper understanding of the importance of archaeological studies.

Shaun Chapoose held positions in the Environmental Protection Agency, the Bureau of Indian Affairs, and the Central Utah Water Project before assuming his current position as chair of the Ute Indian Tribe of the Uintah and Ouray Reservation's Business Committee. He serves as a tribal representative on the Bears Ears Inter-Tribal Coalition. Chapoose is a fierce protector of his tribe's water and mineral rights and an advocate for advancing tribal sovereignty.

Kate Cannon is the superintendent of the National Park Service's Southeast Utah Group, which includes Canyonlands and Arches National Parks and Natural Bridges and Hovenweep National Monuments. Cannon worked for the Bureau of Land Management as the first superintendent of the Grand Staircase–Escalante National Monument after its establishment in 1996, then spent five years as deputy superintendent of Grand Canyon National Park before moving to southeastern Utah.

Alfred Lomahquahu is the former vice chair of the Hopi tribe and former cochair of the Bears Ears Inter-Tribal Coalition. In addition to his tribal leadership, he has achieved national recognition for his kachina carvings. He believes that he and his fellow coalition members have been called to the mission of protecting ancestral lands.

Sahmie Lomahquahu is an educator focused on offering opportunities for disadvantaged Hopi youth. She is passionate about Indian education reform and has spent much of her career working in underperforming schools to improve student achievement. She is a strong believer in the potential of the Bears Ears Inter-Tribal Coalition to inspire youth to become leaders in the movement for indigenous self-determination.

Sandstone, near Bears Ears National Monument

AUTHOR'S REFLECTIONS

I still remember exactly where the creases crisscrossed the glossy cover of our battered Rand McNally *Road Atlas* and how the gallon-size Ziploc bag in which we kept our folded maps and national park brochures was bursting at the seams, the seal broken and curled outward, beyond repair.

I collected—and still have—the brochures, allotting them precious bookshelf space in my office, keeping them close for when wanderlust strikes. Simple and compact, packing the essence of a place into a single, accordion-folded sheet of paper, they boast the standard aesthetic of National Park Service literature: a black band across the top, white block lettering announcing the name of a legendary southwestern landscape—Zion, Bryce Canyon, Dinosaur, Natural Bridges, Canyonlands, Hovenweep, Capitol Reef, Arches—that my family and I explored when I was young. Below the first fold is an illustration of geologic forces that gave birth to the landscape. Rainbow layer cakes of rock, erupting volcanoes, sheets of ice, and walls of water tell the origin story of land so striking that it has become visual shorthand for the wild majesty of the American West. Vivid photos depict cougars, bears, hawks, bighorn sheep, elk, and other wild fauna that populate the parks. On the back of each brochure, a pine-green map with roads drawn in red and hiking trails marked with black dashes served as a guide to my family's summertime travels.

My grandparents first introduced me to the Southwest, taking me to Canyon de Chelly National Monument in northeastern Arizona at the age of four. It was summer in red rock country: temperatures in the triple digits, sun beating down on our backs and reflecting up from the red rock. I scampered down the sandstone trail, relishing the chance to explore a landscape so wholly different and vastly more exciting than the streets of my neighborhood back home. I insisted on removing my shoes in the sandy soil,

The author looking toward the Comb Ridge at sunset

imagining the warm soft sand of Florida beaches with which I was familiar. I promptly scalded the bottom of my feet and cried out in pain, then plunged my feet into nearby Chinle Creek and felt for the first time the primal need for water in the desert.

The creek's soothing cool water eased the pain, and I put my shoes back on and continued, undeterred by my injury and aided by a four-year-old's short attention span. We followed the trail across the canyon to White House Ruins. As I looked up at the cliff dwellings built into the sheer sandstone wall and at the pictographs on the rocks below, my grandparents described how the drawings were made by the ancient peoples—painted by hand with natural pigments—and they explained that the bighorn sheep and deer in the drawings were considered to be the peoples' brothers and sisters.

Every spring and summer my mother, my brother, and I would travel, exploring the national parks and monuments and lesser-known back roads across BLM lands throughout the Southwest. I looked for the pictographs, petroglyphs, and other etchings from the ancients as the landscapes became a familiar backdrop for the freedom and adventure of our road trips.

At age eleven I first visited San Juan County. Scrambling up the sandstone spine of Comb Ridge, marveling at the wind-and-water-sculpted buttes in Valley of the Gods, and taking in the vast surroundings from Muley Point with the mix of reverence and incredulity that overcomes many a traveler, I felt something I didn't understand. It wasn't quite love. It wasn't just wonder. It wasn't sheer awe. Rather, it was the feeling that I had just arrived at the place where I was meant to be. *I belonged.*

Over the next decade, my family returned often to southeastern Utah. We spent our days hiking, exploring the ruins and petroglyph panels of Cedar Mesa, driving countless dirt roads, and floating the San Juan River from Bluff to Mexican Hat. There were longer day trips to Capitol Reef National Park and the wild pastel moonscapes between Fruita and Hanksville, filled with hours-long explorations around Factory Butte and meals at Blondie's Eatery in Hanksville. Goosenecks of the San Juan, Dirty Devil River, Six Shooter Peaks, Newspaper Rock, Mule Canyon, Butler Wash, Mexican Hat, Moki Dugway, Recapture Lodge, and the Bears Ears all made their way into my lexicon.

The drives there were too long, our time too short. At the end of our trips, when we headed south on U.S. 163 for the last time, I would feel my heart ache. I craned my neck to watch as the Comb Ridge disappeared from view.

I slumped into my seat, leaning forlornly against the window as we drove home, wondering when I could return to the country I had come to love.

Back home in the suburban sprawl of southern California where my family had moved, I unfolded the crinkled maps, retracing trails with my finger. I delighted at the discovery of a few stubborn grains of red sand collected at the bottom of the battered map bag: a piece of the desert had followed me home. Such memories provided comfort in darker times, when my father's illness became crippling and cast a pall over our lives. I would find myself longing to drive the 650 miles to the Comb Ridge, where I would inhale the sage-scented air (and pluck a sprig to place behind my ear), thread my index finger through the plastic loop of my Nalgene water bottle, don my backpack, and strike out toward a canyon, any canyon.

At seventeen I began a month-long wilderness expedition in the Four Corners region, joining an eclectic group of teenagers from across the country. While rafting the San Juan River and backpacking in Dark Canyon, feeling vibrantly alive and connected to places that stirred my soul, I met and fell in love with my future husband. He, too, felt a strong pull to red rock country, and together we saw the land with fresh eyes. To this day, we feel strongest together when standing on sandstone, the foundation on which we built our partnership.

It would be more than a decade before I returned to the region that served as a source of adventure and sanctuary during my childhood and adolescence. Love, school, and work carried me to New England, the Pacific Northwest, and northern California. But southeastern Utah continued to call.

The power of this land releases me from chronic inhibitions and inspires contradictory impulses: the urge to sit in stillness atop a mesa and let the sun and silence wash over me collides with a desire to run fast and free, to laugh and shout joyously, high on the brilliant colors and otherworldly warps, curves, clefts, and folds of the landscape. The empty roads that spur off U.S. Highway 191 beckon me to chase the sun toward the horizon while losing any sense of time or speed. But just around a curve, the changing light on nearby bluffs slows me, compelling me to stop and watch while the landscape changes, revealing itself anew minute by minute. I feel the urge to share these wild places with everyone, but I also covet the solitude that is only possible in places where humans are scarce.

I am not immune to the desert's disarming and oft-oppressive whims. I have experienced the skin-cracked, parched daze of dehydration; the harsh bite of winter wind; the pain of blinding blowing sand in my eyes; and the hair-raising, pace-quickening rumble and crackle of a summer thunderstorm. Yet this land is made all the more alluring by an undercurrent of uncertainty. It coaxes me to slide under barbed-wire fences to find an unobstructed view of a mountain range, to round just one more bend, hike just one more mile, even as the sun sinks lower in the sky. My instincts for self-preservation are locked in a constant tug-of-war with my adventurous impulses. More than once, the urge to keep going has overriden my good judgment and threatened my safety. But just as I emerged unscathed from my foot-scalding introduction to the Southwest, I have repeatedly shaken off the fear of close calls and summoned an even greater desire to venture forth in search of the next natural wonder.

Red rock country has remained above all a place of renewal, a landscape that heals, and a nexus of family adventure and connection for me. Fitting, then, that what drew me back to southeastern Utah was a family gathering. This time, though, the focus was not on exploring a new trail but on mourning the loss of the woman who introduced me to this land and who became the inspiration for this book.

We rose at dawn and climbed silently into our cars, clasping coffee cups and bathing our faces in the steam that countered the biting cold. As we drove west toward the Comb Ridge, the sun's light touched the top of the mesas, and the red rock glowed as if on fire. Steve and I drove in silence, with so much to say and too few words able to capture the emptiness and the beauty of the moment. On another day, he and my grandmother Karen would have taken the drive together, pulling over from time to time to photograph a sweeping vista or to record the subtlest change of light on painted hills. But this time, we drove with but one purpose—and without Karen, his partner of fifty-six years.

We reached the bottom of the Moki Dugway and looked up at our path: a narrow gravel road carved into the edge of Cedar Mesa. I recalled my introduction to the Dugway two decades prior, straining against my seatbelt to see out the window of our family's minivan as we ascended twelve hundred feet to the top of the mesa, stunned when I spotted the rusty crumpled carcass of a truck that had gone over the edge. Now I scanned the cliffside for the truck. It was gone, but a trailer chassis had met a similar fate. I wondered how long it would stay there, haunting all the first-time drivers who crawled around the hairpin curves.

We turned left after reaching the top, driving for about five miles until we reached Muley Point, an isolated rock promontory perched above Valley of the Gods. Stepping out into the dust clouds kicked up by the cars, we collected ourselves: fathers, daughters, mothers, sons, sisters, brothers, aunts, uncles, all gathered to support Steve as he and we reflected on the life of his partner in a place that remained a touchstone in their wanderings.

We were tasked with choosing a spot that afforded a clear view of Navajo Mountain, a solitary laccolith some eighty miles to the southwest. Karen had been drawn to the mountain, and a decade ago she and Steve had begun a project to photograph it from the most distant viewpoints along the circumference of a circle centered on the mountain. And thus we all gathered in this spot to remember her life.

Walking out to the edge of the mesa, I looked down into the canyon, beyond the layers of sandstone carved by the San Juan River, to the barely visible ribbon of water cutting through the canyon floor. Looking toward the horizon, the monoliths of Monument Valley punctuated the horizon. As we all stood there in remembrance, I thought of *hózhó*, the Navajo word that roughly translates as peace, balance, beauty, and harmony. Standing at the edge of the earth, I felt the rawness of still-fresh grief. But I also found peace in the vastness of the country that inhabits and inspires me, and I gathered strength to heal the pain of loss and begin the journey forward.

———

The red rock country in southeastern Utah is written into the national imagination, the backdrop to western movies whose square-jawed heroes helped build and perpetuate the mythology of the American West, a vivid symbol of our country's culture of rugged individualism. But westerners experience and relate to this mythology in a much more personal way. For many of us, the mountains, deserts, canyons, long stretches of empty road, and infinite expanse of sky feel stitched into the fabric of who we are, imprinted on our souls.

Navajo Mountain in the distance as seen from Muley Point

My love—my need—for this place will never be as complex or as fundamental as that of the people who call red rock country home, but it has shaped and sustained me, too, in ways I can trace back to my early years and in ways I may never fully understand.

Spurred by our reconnection to this land at my grandmother's celebration of life, my grandfather and I were inspired to collaborate on a book. Our topic: the past, present, and future of public lands in San Juan County. I would write, and he would photograph.

PHOTOGRAPHER'S REFLECTIONS

The sandstone was cold on my back that early October morning. I lay there, opening myself to the Utah sky, imagining the infinite universe beyond, grasping for comfort in its vastness. I had come here to be with close friends and family, to reflect on how my late companion, muse, and closest friend of fifty-six years had touched our lives. She had passed suddenly from this world five months earlier, and in my post-dawn reverie, I recalled our last moments together as she lay unconscious, her body chilled, attached to machines that could not deny fate.

Why come to remember in *this* place, an isolated rock promontory on Cedar Mesa, fifteen hundred feet above the eroded sandstone mesas and pinnacles of Valley of the Gods? We were both academics, my wife and I, citizens of a world of scientists, moving with ease among collaborators in Japan, China, Europe, Latin America. Connected as we were with colleagues throughout the world and as well traveled as our professional lives demanded, there was no place, no land that we could call our true home. With one exception: the red rock country of southeastern Utah.

Neither of us were westerners, one born in New York City, the other in eastern Oklahoma. We made our first visits to the Colorado Plateau in our early forties, when we began to explore landscapes of the Navajo Nation. Drawn to both the country and its people, we decided to offer our services to teach a few classes at Navajo Community College (now Diné College) in Tsaile, Arizona, during the summers of 1981 and 1982. In following years, we developed and nurtured relationships not only with the land but with a web of Native writers, poets, sculptors, and painters. Our scientific careers led us eastward from Tucson to Amherst, Massachusetts, which was our base for fourteen years. But throughout those years, we were drawn to return to land we thought of as home: camping and hiking in southeastern

Stephen Strom photographing sandstone

and south-central Utah, capturing the landscape's chromatic and sculptural rhythms in photographs, and later joining those images with the work of Native poets Joy Harjo and Laura Tohe.

We invited our children and grandchildren to join us in exploring the slickrock, hogbacks, hoodoos, rivers, and canyon labyrinths of what was rapidly becoming "home." They came, and some learned to love the land as we did. One is the author of this book, who hiked to White House Ruins in Canyon de Chelly at the age of four and on a hot summer day in 1988 immersed her feet in the sands and waters of Chinle Creek, a baptism celebrating her joining the congregation of red rock worshippers.

Today, on Muley Point, she, a quarter-century older, stood near me as we gathered our thoughts in silence—the majesty of the land compels no less. And in that silence, she too, I imagined, felt the power of this place, the sun, the sky, the rock, the San Juan River nearby. This promontory and the Colorado Plateau on which it stands have borne witness to many changes: to the shift of tectonic plates that carried it on a journey spanning more than a billion years starting from near the equator to where it stands today, five thousand miles to the north; to the uplift, which raised it from sea level to more than a mile above the oceans; to the arrival of megafauna and then humans; to the rise of agricultural, then urban civilizations; to the coming of the Spanish and Mormons; to the gathering today to remember the life of a scientist, colleague, mother, grandmother, mentor, muse, and lover.

Soon the rest of our small party arrived. The sandstone warmed to the sun's rays, and the late morning light revealed a panorama spanning 270 degrees—from Valley of the Gods to Sleeping Ute Mountain, to Monument Valley, to the San Juan River and Navajo Mountain, to the Abajo Mountains—more than eighty miles in all directions. A gentle breeze arose as we drew together. I chose the words of Joy Harjo to break the silence:

I can hear the sizzle of newborn stars,
and know anything of meaning,
of the fierce magic emerging here.
I am witness to flexible eternity, the evolving past,
and I know we will live forever, as dust or breath in the face of stars,
in the shifting pattern of winds.

—Joy Harjo, *Secrets from the Center of the World*

After another hour or so of contemplation, remembrance, embraces, we sat down, with the landscape of the Colorado Plateau beyond, and enjoyed a meal on sandstone tables. Later, we dispersed, most compelled to explore the land before reconvening in the nearby town of Bluff. Finding myself alone provided the space and time to release the past and ponder the future. And slowly, thoughts that for months had been amorphous took form: loss could be transformed into work that could express the love I felt—for Karen, for my family, for my friends, for this place, venerating this land and its people.

I first thought to compile a collection of photographs taken over three decades and to produce a book of essays and images celebrating the region and its sublime grandeur. I imagined that such a book might be useful in supporting a then nascent effort to petition the president to protect a 1.9-million-acre swath of land within the watersheds of the Green, Colorado, and San Juan Rivers as the Greater Canyonlands National Monument.

And so, during the fall of 2014, I began to assemble, sort, and sequence images while reflecting how to effectively stimulate a constructive conversation about protecting Greater Canyonlands. The literature on land protection in the West is replete with panegyrics extolling the magnificence of its mountains, rivers, forests, canyons, and badlands. And in near-perfect symmetry, there are volumes of speeches and testimony denouncing land protection as inimical to economic prosperity and the freedom of individuals and businesses to shape the land as they see fit. Both sides see the fight for protection or use as a Manichaean struggle, a battle with no room for compromise or accommodation. As a result, decisions often reflect the momentary power and influence of one side or the other, rather than a continuing coming together of people around shared goals and understanding. In this universe of competing ideologies, land is either protected or not; wealth is extracted or not; people's lives are uplifted or not.

My first inclination was to choose the "side" closest to my heart and volunteer to put my work in service of the Greater Canyonlands campaign. But as winter approached my mood turned ever more contemplative, and I came to believe that my passions might best be channeled into an effort that explored land protection from far more nuanced perspectives. What did the people living closest to Greater Canyonlands think? How would their lives be affected? Have environmentalists and those who wish to develop the land carried out analyses to inform decisions that balance the need for protection with the economic, cultural, and spiritual needs of both local citizens and the broader populace? Is compromise possible? How might it be achieved?

While all these ideas had their appeal in principle, neither my forty years spent as a research astronomer nor my encore career as a photographer provided me with the tools or experience needed to both research and relate a story so complex and multidimensional. But I knew someone who might have the requisite skills: Rebecca Robinson. Though she was young, her oeuvre already included a number of long-form reporting pieces focused on topics of comparable complexity, ranging from efforts to reform California's prison system, the plight of homeless families and veterans, and a myriad of issues impacting low-income and marginalized communities in Vermont, Oregon, and California. That she was my granddaughter, baptized in the waters of Chinle Creek, offered collaboration that held the promise of being both emotionally and professionally compelling.

Following a few more weeks of rumination, I approached her, and by the end of January 2015 we set forth, not entirely without trepidation, outlining an ambitious project. Not long after beginning the first few of what were to become more than seventy interviews carried out over twenty-four months, we learned of the efforts of five tribes and their supporters to protect nearly two million acres of public land in southeastern Utah surrounding the iconic Bears Ears peaks. What began as a story relating a "simple" battle for Greater Canyonlands morphed into a far more complex narrative: a meeting of Native and Mormon cultures; a clash among local, state, and federal interests; a case study in the forces that roil rural America today.

As we spoke to tribal leaders, medicine men, county commissioners, congressional staff, environmentalists, businessmen, ranchers, representatives of the oil and gas industry, journalists, and citizens, three themes emerged: (1) the economic base of those living adjacent to Bears Ears is fragile, and the future is uncertain; (2) to Natives and Mormons alike the land is sacred and deeply linked to their culture; and (3) neither Natives nor Mormons believe that their voices are either heard or heeded by those in power. Together, they cry for recognition of culture and of connection to land and family and for a role in shaping decisions about their future.

Voices from Bears Ears: Seeking Common Ground on Sacred Land is dedicated to those voices and to the proposition that protecting land necessitates protecting both people and parcels. If the book inspires listening to and heeding the voices recorded here, it will have served well the thoughts first manifest following that October morning on Muley Point.

Technical Background

For the first twenty years in my explorations of the Colorado Plateau, the media available—a few 4 × 5 transparencies, several rolls of color film—required considerable agonizing: finding the right place to locate my tripod, carefully framing the image. With today's digital media, it is now possible to experiment: changing viewpoint and lighting, varying the ratio of complex to fundamental rhythmic modes in a scene.

The patterns that intrigue and attract me often emerge when sunlight is filtered through light-to-heavy cirrus. Shadows are muted, and subtle textures that might otherwise be lost in harsh desert light are given their rightful prominence in the image. At times, photographing a scene directly opposite solar illumination achieves some of the same effects.

Many of the early images in this book were made with a long focal length lens: 450 mm for a 4 × 5 view camera, 100–300 mm for a 35mm SLR. Use of long focal length lenses and small apertures (f/45 or f/64 with a view camera, f/22 or f/32 with an SLR) delivers an image with great depth of field (foreground and background in sharp focus) and creates the illusion of compressed space. Information on multiple planes appears projected onto a single plane. Hence, foreground plains and hills appear to be superposed on background mountains, creating thereby new rhythms in their juxtaposition.

More recently, I've taken to composing panoramic images that capture the vastness and scale of the landscape. In those cases, I often use shorter focal length (28–50 mm) lenses and stitch together a panorama digitally from multiple separate images.

A number of the images in the book were taken while flying in a Cessna 150 with pilot Nate Rydman of LightHawk Conservation Flying at the controls. The ISO settings and shutter speeds were adjusted to compensate for lighting, speed of the plane, and altitude above the ground. Typically, a shutter speed of 1/1500 seconds was used. Nate and LightHawk deserve enormous thanks for their generous support.

I capture my images in camera raw, with no in-camera adjustments for any adjustable parameter (e.g., white balance, image contrast). For processing, I use Adobe Lightroom and Photoshop. My adjustments are relatively modest, mostly cropping and adjusting brightness and contrast. If there is a highlight that needs to be toned down, I will make use of the digital equivalents of the dodging and burning I once did in the darkroom. The final images are usually printed on a matte paper so as not to interpose a glossy patina on an image conceived as subtle and muted in palette.

Raplee Ridge as seen from north of Mexican Hat, Utah

HISTORICAL TIME LINE

12,000–7000 BCE: Paleo-Indian peoples arrive

Small bands of hunter-gatherers arrive, possibly from Asia across the Bering land bridge, and disperse in North America.

7000–1500 BCE: Archaic peoples evolve

Nomadic hunter-gatherers begin to incorporate wild plants and, later, domesticated plants such as corn and squash into their diet. Distinct cultures, languages, and ceremonial practices arise among individual bands.

1500 BCE–750 CE: Basketmaker culture develops

Bands become more rooted to place as agriculture grows in importance as a primary source of sustenance. Permanent structures arise near farmland. Toward the end of this time frame, populations increase rapidly. Large public structures such as great kivas begin to appear, serving as focal points for public ceremonies.

750–1300 CE: (Ancestral) Puebloan cultures develop

Toward the beginning of the period, public structures become more common and move from belowground to aboveground. Later, a widespread cultural complex develops, with settlements spanning hundreds of miles and connected by roads. Multistory great houses appear, along with extensive trading arrangements spanning the continent. Toward the end of the period, large villages appear in what might be called a period of urbanization.

1250–1300: Puebloans migrate southward from Colorado Plateau

Puebloan peoples begin a mass migration from eastern Utah and western Colorado southward. Drought, breakdown of political structures, and the rise of new religious practices are thought to be among the forces driving out-migration.

1250–1350: Arrival of Utes

Precursors of today's Ute tribes migrate eastward to their present homes in Utah and Colorado from the Sierra Nevada. Some anthropologists place their arrival on the Colorado Plateau to as far back as 1000 CE.

1400–1525: Arrival of Navajos/Athapaskans

The ancestral Navajos, a hunter-gatherer tribe, migrate southward from eastern Alaska and northwestern Canada to the Colorado Plateau.

1540s: Coronado explores the region

Francisco Vásquez de Coronado leads an expedition comprising four hundred men northward from Mexico. In the course of his expedition, he "conquers" Zuni and other Pueblo settlements. Members of his expedition are the first Europeans to explore the Grand Canyon and the Colorado River.

1590s–1670s: Spanish conquer the Pueblos

Beginning in the 1540s, the Spanish begin extensive settlement of New Mexico. Soldiers and missionaries fan out over the region in an attempt to subdue and convert the Indians.

1680: Pueblo Revolt

Pueblo people kill four hundred Spaniards in Santa Fe and drive the remaining twenty thousand Spanish settlers out of New Mexico. The Spanish do not attempt another *entrada* until 1692, when Don Diego de Vargas leads the reconquest of Santa Fe de Nuevo México.

1776: Domínguez-Escalante expedition

Franciscan priests Francisco Atanasio Domínguez and Silvestre Vélez de Escalante spearhead the earliest European exploration of the Colorado Plateau. The goal of their expedition is to locate an efficient route from Santa Fe to the Spanish settlement in Monterey, California. Domínguez and Escalante make the first European maps of large areas of the Colorado Plateau; the Escalante River and the town of Escalante memorialize their contribution.

1700s–1850s: Fur trapping and sheepherding flourish

Fur trappers make a quick fortune and leave, while sheepherders remain in large numbers for more than a century, with Navajos adopting Spanish sheepherding techniques.

1824: Bureau of Indian Affairs is established

The Bureau of Indian Affairs is one of the oldest departments in the federal government, founded in 1824 by then secretary of war John C. Calhoun. Now residing within the Department of the Interior, the BIA provides services and support to nearly two million Native Americans from 567 recognized tribes. The mission of the agency is "to enhance the quality of life, to promote economic opportunity, and to carry out the responsibility to protect and improve the trust assets of American Indians, Indian tribes, and Alaska Natives."[1]

During the late nineteenth and early twentieth centuries, in response to the Dawes Act (see p. 368), the BIA played a central role in efforts to assimilate Native Americans into the dominant European American culture. It separated children from their parents, sending them to boarding schools, where they were forced to speak English and punished, often brutally, for speaking their language or engaging in any of their cultural or religious practices. In the mid-1970s the Indian Self-Determination and Education Assistance Act and the Indian Child Welfare Act directed the BIA to alter its long-held paternalistic stance and instead to support tribal efforts to achieve self-determination. Today, the agency's efforts are directed primarily at working

---

1. Bureau of Indian Affairs Mission Statement, https://www.bia.gov/bia.

to improve tribal governments and infrastructure and to support economic development efforts.

That said, owing to past contentions between the tribes and the BIA, some Native peoples continue to treat policies of the BIA with suspicion, with many fearing a return to a paternalistic past.

1840s–1890s: Rise of cattle ranching

Cattle ranching thrives in southeastern Utah, with favorable grazing in the mountains during the summer and at lower altitudes in the winter. The ability to ship cattle by rail provides access to lucrative markets. The lush public lands support Mormon ranchers and attract large herds from companies based in Texas and Colorado. Cattlemen and sheepherding tribal peoples fight over range and water, with Natives eventually losing both land and water rights. Toward the end of the century, large cattle companies emerge as an important part of the economic base of southeastern Utah. Access to public lands for grazing becomes an essential component of the economic model.

1847: Brigham Young and his followers arrive in the Salt Lake Basin

Men and women who join the Prophet Joseph Smith are driven westward by those who consider their religion blasphemous. Following the 1844 murder of Smith by an angry mob in Carthage, Illinois, the members of the Church of Jesus Christ of Latter-day Saints continue westward under the leadership of the Prophet Brigham Young, arriving at their Promised Land near present-day Salt Lake City in 1847. Young next calls followers to settle vast swaths of the Mountain West, extending from southern California to northern Idaho, hoping to create the Mormon state of Deseret.

1848: Treaty of Guadalupe Hidalgo

After the United States wins the Mexican-American War, the federal government and Mexico sign the Treaty of Guadalupe Hidalgo, in which the United States acquires the land that comprises modern-day California, Nevada, and Utah and parts of Arizona, Wyoming, Colorado, and New Mexico.

1854–58: Mormon "rebellion"

Brigham Young continues to govern his state of Deseret according to Mormon rules and teachings, which include the practice of polygamy. U.S. government officials view this "Mormon rebellion" against the country's laws as a danger to democracy. In 1857 President James Buchanan sends twenty-five hundred soldiers to Utah along with Alfred Cumming, whom Buchanan appoints to govern the territory. The LDS Church responds by declaring martial law in the territory and organizing a militia to defend Utah's Mormon residents from the U.S. Army. In June 1858, after a year of military occupation, a party of federal government "peace commissioners" pardons the church, thus ending the official conflict.

1859: Macomb-Newberry expedition

Captain John Macomb and botanist/geologist John Newberry explore the region between the San Juan River and the junction of the Green and Colorado Rivers. They are the first Anglo-Americans to explore the Canyonlands region.

1864–66: Long Walk of the Navajo

Raids on Navajo livestock by Anglos, Mexicans, and nearby Pueblo tribes lead to escalating skirmishes. In 1864 Col. Kit Carson is assigned by the U.S. Army to "solve" the "Indian problem." Aided by Ute allies who know the territory well, Carson's soldiers burn Navajo hogans to the ground, kill livestock, and destroy irrigated fields. Bands of Navajos in Arizona and New Mexico are rounded up and marched eastward to Fort Sumner, New Mexico, suffering considerable loss of life. They remain quartered at Fort Sumner until 1868. A band of Navajos under the leadership of warrior hero K'aayelli escape and hide out in the mountainous area near Bears Ears in southeastern Utah.

1868: Treaty of Bosque Redondo

In 1868 the United States and Navajos sign the Treaty of Bosque Redondo. The treaty allows the Navajos to return to a well-delineated reservation in western New Mexico and eastern Arizona. The Navajos agree to cease raiding, and the U.S. government agrees to provide seeds and other provisions.

Navajos agree to send their children to school, and in return, the government establishes schools and provides teachers. The terms of the treaty and its execution represent an early example of a series of efforts aimed at forcing assimilation of Navajos into the dominant culture.

1868: Confinement of Ute Mountain Ute tribe: Treaty of 1868

As migration westward increases following the Civil War, land once used by Native peoples for hunting is confiscated by Anglos. In 1868 the Ute Mountain Ute tribe signs a treaty, confining the tribe to a small reservation in the western part of the Colorado Territory. During the 1870s the size of their reservation is reduced still further as an influx of Anglos arrives to search for gold in the San Juan Mountains.

1869: Transcontinental railroad links Utah and the Colorado Plateau to the rest of the country

With the driving of the "golden spike" just north of Salt Lake City, the Union and Central Pacific Railroads join, and the United States becomes a continental nation. Settlement and commerce are facilitated as the Mountain West becomes far more accessible.

1869–71: John Wesley Powell expeditions

In 1869 naturalist John Wesley Powell begins a three-month scientific and mapping expedition, starting from Green River Station in the Wyoming territory, traveling down the Green and Colorado Rivers through Glen Canyon and the Grand Canyon, and ultimately reaching the Colorado's confluence with the Virgin River. In 1871 Powell retraces much of the route of his earlier expedition. Together, the Powell expeditions provide the first extensive description of the canyon country of the Colorado Plateau.

1878: Powell's *Report on the Lands of the Arid Region of the United States*

Based on his experience surveying the Colorado Plateau, Powell recognizes that the scarcity of water in the Southwest precludes the development model that worked successfully in the Great Plains. He develops a broad and imaginative conservation plan for the Mountain West that is thwarted by developers. Powell's is a prophetic voice that foreshadows the West's water wars, the dangers of dams, and overgrazing.

1879–80: Hole-in-the-Rock expedition

In 1879 the LDS Church calls a group of seventy southern Utah families to leave a settlement in Parowan, Utah, and to establish a new community on the banks of the San Juan River near present-day Bluff. The pioneers follow established wagon roads eastward to Escalante but then choose to follow what they thought would be a viable shortcut. Their path takes them through some of the most rugged territory on the Colorado Plateau and forces them to construct a road from fifteen hundred feet above the west side of a canyon carved by the Colorado River, down to the river itself, and then up the other side. Following completion of the road, they lower their wagons, livestock, and families through a narrow crevice that they dubbed the Hole-in-the-Rock. The pioneers eventually reach Bluff in 1880. Over the next decades, these Mormons spread out from Bluff to present-day Blanding and Monticello, later to be joined by others who flee their settlements in northern Mexico to escape the violence of the Mexican Revolution.

1880: Ceding of Northern Ute lands

In the late 1870s Indian agent Nathan Meeker attempts to convert the largely hunter-gatherer Northern Ute tribes to farming and Christianity. After Anglos plow a field that the Utes used for raising feed for horses, skirmishes ensue, and the army is called to "subdue" the Utes. The army attacks a Ute force, while a separate band of Utes attacks and kills Meeker and ten others. Following the "Meeker massacre" the army puts down Ute resistance. In 1880 a number of Ute bands are removed from western Colorado and resettled to far smaller tracts of land in eastern Utah, where it is no longer possible to continue their hunter-gatherer traditions.

1882: Hopi Reservation established

Hopi lands first come under U.S. control in 1848, with the end of the Mexican-American War. Following the 1868 treaty of Bosque Redondo, Navajos return to a large reservation that encircles Hopi villages. In 1882

President Chester Arthur establishes a Hopi Reservation by executive order. The reservation includes only a small fraction of the tribe's traditional lands and excludes the largely Hopi village of Moenkopi. Hopi lands "granted" in 1882 overlap Navajo land, and disputes ensue. In 1891 the Hopi are granted three hundred thousand acres of land for their exclusive use. The size of the Hopi Reservation is increased twofold in 1943, trapping a significant number of Navajos living within the newly defined Hopi Reservation. Land disputes between Hopi and Navajos continue until an agreement is reached in 1999.

1880s–early 1900s: Settling of San Juan County by Mormons

Blanding and Monticello are settled as Hole-in-the-Rock descendants and Mormon settlers from Mexico and elsewhere populate San Juan County.

1887: Passage of the Dawes Act

Named after its author, Henry Dawes of Massachusetts, the act authorizes the president to survey Indian lands and divide it into allotments. The act also declares a subset of Indian lands as "surplus" to be auctioned off to the highest bidders. Tribal governments and courts are dissolved. The ostensible purpose of the act is to accelerate "assimilation" of Natives. Its effect was to reduce Native-held land to less than a third of what it was prior to the act's passing; some reservations are decimated. It is not until 1934 that the provisions of the act are rescinded and the right to form tribal governments is reestablished.

1890s: Gold rush boom and bust

In 1891 rumors begin to circulate that gold nuggets are to be found in the San Juan River near Bluff. A gold rush ensues, as more than a thousand prospectors arrive to pan the river. While a few small grains of gold are found, the gold rush boom quickly becomes a bust, presaging multiple epochs of mineral booms and busts that extend well into the twentieth century.

1893–97: Wetherill expeditions

The archaeologist Richard Wetherill carries out two expeditions aimed at exploring Native archaeological sites in the Comb Ridge and Cedar Mesa areas, the first in 1893–94 and the second in 1897. In the course of these expeditions he uncovers the remains and artifacts of Basketmaker peoples and discovers, catalogs, and collects material from a number of Ancestral Puebloan sites. His work marks the beginning of extensive archaeological and anthropological studies in the area. Inscriptions from members of the expeditions can still be found on rock walls near ruins on Comb Ridge and in the canyons of Cedar Mesa.

1896: Utah statehood

Following five decades of clashes with the federal government and others who regard Mormonism as a blasphemous, false religion, LDS Church president Wilford Woodruff renounces polygamy and promises adherence to the marriage laws of the United States. In 1896 Utah, much reduced in size from Brigham Young's vision for the state of Deseret, is admitted as a state. As a condition of statehood, Utah accepts the presence of federally administered public lands within state boundaries and in return is given access to a checkerboard of sections (mile-square blocks) to be used by the state to fund schools. The Utah School and Institutional Trust Lands Administration (SITLA) manages these lands.

1906: Passage of the Antiquities Act

Looting of ancestral Native artifacts, often through grave robbing, becomes rampant toward the end of the nineteenth century as the desires of museums and collectors create a lucrative market in stolen antiquities. Native peoples consider disturbing and robbing graves to be a violation of their cultural heritage. In response, Congress passes the Antiquities Act in 1906, granting the president the authority to set aside public (i.e., federal) lands as national monuments "for the protection of objects of historic or scientific interest."[2]

1910–1920s: Mormon families from Mexico arrive in Blanding

Beginning in 1885, LDS families establish settlements in Chihuahua and Sonora, Mexico, where they are able to escape from U.S. prosecution and

---

2. An Act for the Preservation of American Antiquities (Public Law 59–209).

continue polygamous practices. Most Mormons leave these settlements during the second decade of the twentieth century as a result of the strong anti-American sentiment that arises during the Mexican Revolution. Many join the Hole-in-the-Rock pioneers in Blanding and Monticello.

1916: Passage of the National Park Service Organic Act

In August 1916 President Woodrow Wilson signs the Organic Act, creating the National Park Service to "promote and regulate the use of Federal areas known as national parks." A primary goal is to "conserve the scenery of natural and historic objects and the wild life therein and to provide for the enjoyment of the same in such a manner . . . as will leave them unimpaired for the enjoyment of future generations."[3] Passage of the Organic Act represents a landmark for a conservation movement that had begun to take root in the 1890s.

1918–1990s: Ebb and flow of ranching

Income from ranching and agriculture in eastern Utah rises and falls throughout the twentieth century in response to weather, the Great Depression, and federal regulations that restrict grazing on public lands. Once central to the economy of the area, ranching now serves as much as a cultural marker of rural identity as a basis for economic sustenance.

1934: Passage of the Taylor Grazing Act

The Taylor Grazing Act is intended to "stop injury to the public grazing lands by preventing overgrazing and soil deterioration; to provide for their orderly use, improvement and development; and to stabilize the livestock industry dependent on the public range."[4] The act dramatically reduces homesteading on public lands and establishes a federal system of grazing rights and fees. Following enactment, the number of ranchers and the volume of grazing livestock are significantly decreased. While the act achieves many of its goals, regulation of grazing on public lands produces growing resentment of

---

3. Organic Act (Public Law 64–235).
4. Taylor Grazing Act of 1934 (Public Law 73–482).

federal regulation and anger at what is perceived as an overreaching central government. In 1946 administration of the act is given to a newly formed agency, the Bureau of Land Management, which combines the Department of the Interior's General Land Office and the Grazing Service. The 2014 standoff between BLM officials and rancher Cliven Bundy in Bunkerville, Nevada, exemplifies the continuing conflicts over federal management of public lands.

1936–40: Attempts to create the Escalante Monument

In 1932 President Franklin Roosevelt appoints as his secretary of the interior Harold Ickes, a powerful advocate for conservation and a strong supporter of national parks. During the early years of the Depression, Utah's political leadership is eager to expand the economic base of the state and believe that declaration of a national park or monument may offer a way to attract tourist dollars and ameliorate the suffering in counties where the ranching and mining economies have collapsed.

In response, in 1936 Ickes puts forward a bold proposal for Escalante National Monument, named after the Spanish priest who was the first European to explore the Colorado Plateau. The area spanned by the proposed monument covers nearly seven thousand square miles surrounding what later would become Capitol Reef and Canyonlands National Parks, Natural Bridges National Monument, and the Glen Canyon National Recreation Area. Over the following four years, county, state, and federal officials wrangle over the roles of tourism, ranching, and mining and the roles of the federal government and local citizens in shaping the future of surrounding public lands. In the end, an idea for a monument that once enjoyed significant support on the state level succumbs to mutual suspicion. The coming of World War II brings an end to Ickes's vision.

1945–70: Uranium boom

The discovery of uranium in Moab and San Juan County fuels a boom that enables San Juan County to develop its infrastructure and fund a school system that is the envy of the state. Uranium mining reaches a peak during the height of the Cold War but rapidly fades as an economic driver in the 1960s. Despite the near inevitability of boom-and-bust cycles in extractive industries, many in eastern Utah continue to argue that public lands should be left open to mining and drilling.

1961–64: Attempts to establish Canyonlands National Park

The move to protect public lands gains renewed momentum with the appointment of Stewart Udall as secretary of the interior. A westerner and avid outdoorsman, Udall is a strong advocate for protecting open space and preserving untouched lands as wilderness. Spurred by Arches National Monument superintendent Bates Wilson and aided initially by Utah senator Frank Moss, Udall proposes the million-acre Canyonlands National Park, centered on the confluence of the Green and Colorado Rivers. Once again, conflicts arise between those who wish to preserve rights to grazing and mining and individuals who wish to preserve the land in its relatively primitive state. After three years of rancor coupled with the eventual bifurcation of the Utah congressional delegation along partisan lines, a bill creating a far smaller Canyonlands National Park is signed in 1964 by President Lyndon Johnson. In 1971 a small unit containing a dramatic pictograph panel, Horseshoe Canyon, is added to the park.

1964: Passage of the Wilderness Act

The Wilderness Act, signed into law in 1964, recognizes wilderness as "an area where the earth and its community of life are untrammeled by man, where man himself is a visitor who does not remain." The act further defines wilderness as "an area of undeveloped Federal land retaining its primeval character and influence without permanent improvements or human habitation, which is protected and managed so as to preserve its natural conditions."[5] Wilderness is the strictest form of land protection: no roads, vehicles, or permanent structures are permitted in wilderness areas; mining and logging are also prohibited.

1969: Passage of the National Environmental Policy Act

The 1969 oil spill off the coast of Santa Barbara, California, inspires passage of the National Environmental Policy Act, which promotes enhancement

5. Wilderness Act of 1964 (Public Land Law 88–577).

of the environment and establishes the Council on Environmental Quality. The act requires federal agencies to prepare environmental assessments and environmental impact statements to assess the effects on the environment of any proposed federal actions. It represents the culmination of a series of acts, the Clean Air and Clean Water Acts and the Wilderness Act, outcomes of an environmental movement spurred into renewed advocacy following publication of Rachel Carson's *Silent Spring* in 1962.

1976: Passage of the Federal Land Policy and Management Act (FLPMA)

The Federal Land Policy and Management Act shifts the BLM's mandate to include conservation and recreation in addition to resource management. It also requires the BLM to inventory all areas within its purview that might have wilderness characteristics. Following passage of the act, grazing and mineral extraction no longer receive automatic top priority in the BLM's evaluation of optimal use of public lands under its purview.

1976: Rise of the Sagebrush Rebellion

In response to the passage of FLPMA, many rural Utahns, most of them ranchers and proponents of resource extraction, rail against what they view as the federal government's usurpation of their land and livelihood. Their protests trigger a push for local control of public lands, known as the Sagebrush Rebellion, which sweeps through the West. Angry residents of the rural West lead a number of highly visible efforts over the ensuing decades aimed at reestablishing BLM focus on grazing and mining and ultimately at transferring federal lands to the state. Recent examples of Sagebrush Rebel activity include the 2014 Bundy standoff in Bunkerville, Nevada, and the 2016 armed occupation of the Malheur National Wildlife Refuge in Burns, Oregon.

1976: Utah Bicentennial Highway completed

Utah Highway 95, linking Blanding and Hanksville, Utah, represents the realization of one part of Stewart Udall's (secretary of the interior, 1961–69) dream of the "Golden Circle" highway. Udall's plan was to connect all of Utah's national parks by building a highway linking Capitol Reef, Bryce, Zion, Canyonlands, and Arches National Parks. Udall envisioned the highway as a means for tourists to conveniently visit the parks and a way for the state's communities to reap the economic benefits of increased tourism. Today, Highway 95 provides a major route to Lake Powell and the Glen Canyon National Recreation Area.

1979: Passage of the Archaeological Resources Protection Act

Following reports of continued looting and defacement of ancestral sites, Congress passes the Archaeological Resources Protection Act. ARPA defines what constitutes criminal removal of antiquities and substantially increases penalties for looters. It presages confrontations between law enforcement and local pothunters in San Juan County. Within a decade, prosecution of ARPA violations will vault the county into the national spotlight and catalyze even fiercer animosity toward the federal government than that unleashed by FLPMA.

1986: First FBI raid on pothunters in Blanding

From the turn of the twentieth century until the 1920s, the University of Utah compensated Blanding residents handsomely for each Native artifact they unearthed and donated to the school's museum collection. For decades, artifact collecting was a commonly accepted practice, and it remained a hobby for many locals even after the passage of ARPA. Some residents of Blanding, Utah, sought to profit from looting archaeological sites. Subsequent generations of pothunters grew ever bolder, using increasingly advanced tools to excavate archaeological sites and procure antiquities.

Newly empowered by the ARPA law, the FBI starts tracking artifacts traffickers across the Southwest. In May 1986 they raid homes and trading posts in San Juan County and Grants County, Colorado, and confiscate over three hundred stolen artifacts. No criminal charges are filed, but the trauma and indignity experienced by the residents of Blanding are searing.

1989: America's Red Rock Wilderness Act first introduced in the House of Representatives

During the late 1980s local and national environmental organizations, including Defenders of Wildlife, the Grand Canyon Trust, the Sierra Club, and the still-young Southern Utah Wilderness Alliance, join forces to form the Utah Wilderness Coalition. The coalition produces a four-hundred-page proposal for adding 5.7 million acres of public land currently administered by the BLM in southern Utah into the National Wilderness Preservation System. Representative Wayne Owens (D-UT) introduces the citizens' proposal as H.R. 1500—America's Red Rock Wilderness Act (ARRWA)—in the 101st Congress in 1989. The bill does not pass the House but has been introduced in every House session since, first by Owens and later by Maurice Hinchey (D-NY), Rush Holt (D-NJ), and Alan Lowenthal (D-CA). In 1996 Senator Richard Durbin (D-IL) introduces a Senate version, which in its current incarnation advocates for protection of over 9 million acres of public land in southern Utah and enjoys the support of twenty-three Senate cosponsors.

1995: Utah delegation introduces the Utah Public Lands Management Act

In response to the introduction of ARRWA, members of Utah's congressional delegation introduce a wilderness bill in 1995. Presented by Senator Orrin Hatch (R-UT) and Representative Jim Hansen (R-UT) as the Utah Public Lands Management Act, the bill is based on input received during a series of public hearings across the state. Conservationists object vigorously to the Hatch-Hansen bill, particularly to provisions that allow for future development on lands designated in their bill as wilderness and to "hard release" of land not designated as wilderness in the bill. Hard-released land can never be considered for wilderness status and would be open immediately to resource extraction. Moreover, the bill calls for designating 1.8 million acres of the state's public land as wilderness, compared to the 5.7 million acres proposed in the original ARRWA legislation. The bill eventually dies in committee.

1996: President Clinton establishes Grand Staircase–Escalante National Monument

The content and perceived anticonservationist intent of the Hatch-Hansen bill catalyzes both grassroots activists and members of President Bill Clinton's staff to explore options to protect Utah's public lands. White House staffer John Leshy is charged with forming a small working group to develop the concept for a large national monument matched to the spirit of Secretary Harold Ickes's 1936 vision of the Escalante National Monument. The group works in secret and drafts language to create the Grand Staircase–Escalante National Monument, spanning public lands from just east of Bryce Canyon to the westernmost border of Glen Canyon National Recreation Area. With only a few days' notice, President Clinton announces designation of the monument on September 18, 1996, using his authority under the 1906 Antiquities Act.

The monument designation instantly protects 1.7 million acres of federal land from drilling and mineral extraction and bans future grazing. Existing mineral leases are honored, and ranchers who own active grazing permits within the monument boundaries are allowed to continue using the land.

The Utah congressional delegation and locals feel blindsided and betrayed by what they perceive as a textbook "land grab" by the federal government that disregards the desires and needs of the local populace. In the eyes of many residents of Escalante, Boulder, and Kanab, Grand Staircase–Escalante robs them of access to vital sources of revenue and jobs. The impact of a national monument explicitly designed without local input and imposed by presidential proclamation has effects that will continue to reverberate strongly through current-day discussions of land-use decisions.

2009: Federal agents conduct a second round of raids in Blanding, Utah

Following a two-year undercover sting operation, agents of the FBI and the BLM conduct another raid in Blanding, targeting individuals still involved with acquiring and selling antiquities. Twenty-four residents are arrested; none serve a jail sentence. The aftermath of the raid heightens anger at the federal government because of perceived excessive force used on nonviolent citizens. In the aftermath, two of the accused and an FBI informant commit suicide. Antigovernment sentiment, already rampant in San Juan County, is compounded by the belief that the federal government now has the blood of local citizens on its hands.

2009: Washington County Lands Bill is signed into law

Congress passes the Washington County Growth and Conservation Act. In 2006 Senator Bob Bennett (R-UT) initiated an effort to craft a vision for public lands use in Washington County, home to Zion National Park and the rapidly growing city of St. George. Bennett, along with Representative Jim Matheson, encourages the county's leadership to develop a multidecade vision for the county. Together they forge Vision Dixie, a process that brings together a diverse group of local stakeholders and gives each a voice in recommending how best to use public lands. The Washington County Growth and Conservation Act (known locally as the Washington County Lands Bill) is included in an omnibus bill that is signed into law by President Barack Obama in 2009. The bill is hailed by many as a model for balancing conservation goals with the need to enable future economic growth in St. George.

2010: Senator Robert Bennett (R-UT) begins southern Utah land-use planning based on Washington County template

Senator Bennett hopes to replicate the Vision Dixie process in San Juan County, but soon after he and his staff initiate on-the-ground conversations and surveys in the area, Bennett fails to receive the endorsement of the state Republican caucus and soon after leaves the Senate at the end of his term in 2010. Tea Party favorite Mike Lee (R-UT) takes his place.

2010: Survey of Native American cultural resources begins

Members of the Navajo Nation, encouraged by Senator Bennett, begin to develop strategies for protecting ancestral lands in San Juan County. Their leader is Mark Maryboy, a long-serving member of the San Juan County Commission and a Navajo Nation delegate. Over the next three years, Maryboy, with the initial support of Round River Conservation Studies, interviews tribal elders, gleaning from them the location of sacred sites as well as plants and herbs that have sustained their people for generations. From these efforts, Maryboy and Round River staffer Gavin Noyes construct an inventory of sites in southeastern Utah that have past and continuing significance to Navajos. Their goal is to use these data to advocate for federal protection.

2011: *Diné Bikéyah* is published

In 2011 Maryboy, Noyes, and collaborators publish a book, *Diné Bikéyah*, that makes a case for protection of San Juan County's public lands as either a national conservation area or a national monument. In 2012 Maryboy and Noyes gain the endorsement of the Navajo Nation and form a nonprofit, Utah Diné Bikéyah (UDB), to advance their proposal. Bennett endorses the proposal. From 2012 onward Maryboy serves on the board of UDB, and Noyes serves as executive director.

2012: Coalition of environmental organizations proposes Greater Canyonlands National Monument

A group comprising over one hundred environmental groups and recreation organizations prepares a proposal to create the Greater Canyonlands National Monument. The boundaries of the proposed monument would come close to achieving the vision of the Escalante National Monument first advanced by Secretary of the Interior Harold Ickes in 1936. Utah representatives Rob Bishop (R-UT, chair of the House Energy and Natural Resources Committee) and Jason Chaffetz (R-UT, whose district includes San Juan County) immediately denounce the proposal. The Greater Canyonlands proposal is shelved in the summer of 2015 as environmental groups coalesce around a proposal for the Bears Ears National Monument.

2013: Representative Rob Bishop launches the Public Lands Initiative

Bishop initiates a process aimed at emulating the efforts of Senator Bennett and others that led to the passage of the Washington County Lands Bill. Bishop's Public Lands Initiative aspires to resolve the future of public lands contained within eight counties in eastern Utah. Each county seeks input from stakeholders representing numerous interest groups. The lands councils are tasked with creating a county plan to be vetted, reshaped as needed, and ultimately included in a Utah PLI bill, then submitted to Congress for approval.

January 2014: San Juan County Commission chair Phil Lyman forms the San Juan County Public Lands Council

Lyman selects individuals representing various stakeholder groups and the Navajo Nation and tasks them with developing a plan for the future of San

Juan County's public lands. The effort is praised by some locals and Utah's congressional delegation, but others, including UDB, accuse Lyman of selecting representatives who share his views while ignoring tribal voices.

May 2014: San Juan County commissioner Phil Lyman leads ATV protest ride

Lyman organizes an ATV protest ride into Recapture Canyon, just north of Blanding, to express opposition to the BLM's closure of a road into the canyon, a closure specifically aimed at protecting Native archaeological sites. The road was closed to motorized vehicles back in 2007, but as recently as December 2013 an application for a trail system through the canyon was open to public comment. Lyman is joined by members of the Bundy family and other antigovernment individuals and groups from around the West. His fellow county officials and Native groups ask him to cancel the ride or at minimum take steps to ensure that his actions stay within the legal norms of civil disobedience. Despite their entreaties, Lyman proceeds with the ride. Native groups and conservationists are outraged; Lyman's supporters and Sagebrush Rebels see him as a hero. Lyman's actions alienate UDB and members of other tribes with ties to the area.

July 2015: Bears Ears Inter-Tribal Coalition forms

Over time, UDB's board and staff begin to believe that Commissioner Lyman and Representatives Bishop and Chaffetz are not treating the group's proposal with the respect befitting its endorsement by the sovereign Navajo Nation. UDB members ultimately decide that they are unlikely to achieve adequate protection of ancestral sites and sacred lands through the PLI process. In order to achieve their goals, they initiate an alternate approach in 2014: using the combined political strength of sovereign tribal nations to negotiate directly with the federal government.

Over the next year, UDB staff and board members travel to reservations across the Southwest, making the case to tribal leaders for protection of land that they all consider sacred and to which they all have tangible connections.

The UDB staff and board invite representatives to a gathering in Bluff in April 2015. Following the meeting, the Navajo, Hopi, Zuni, Ute Mountain

Ute, and the Ute Tribe of Uintah and Ouray Reservation, supported by the All Pueblo Council of Governors in New Mexico, take the first steps to form the Bears Ears Inter-Tribal Coalition.

August 2015: San Juan County Public Lands Council presents recommendations to Representative Bishop

The lands council proposal is supported by some residents of San Juan County but is criticized by environmentalists in Utah and throughout the nation for favoring extractive industries, redefining "wilderness," and leaving key culturally significant areas unprotected. The Bears Ears Inter-Tribal Coalition finds the proposal insufficient.

October 2015: Bears Ears Inter-Tribal Coalition formally presents a proposal for Bears Ears National Monument to the Obama administration

Leaders of the coalition announce their proposal for the Bears Ears National Monument at the National Press Club in Washington, D.C. An essential component is a comanagement commission comprising representatives of the five tribes and designees from the Park Service, the Bureau of Land Management, and the Forest Service. The proposed commission would be charged with setting policy for managing the monument.

The coalition also submits the proposal to Representatives Bishop and Chaffetz and Senator Mike Lee, who in turn release a statement inviting the tribes to reengage with the Public Lands Initiative process.

December 31, 2015: Bears Ears Inter-Tribal Coalition formally withdraws from PLI process

The coalition charges that Congressmen Bishop and Chaffetz have "not taken seriously" the concerns of tribes and that during PLI discussions San Juan County officials exhibited overt discrimination against Native interests. The coalition announces its intent to abandon the PLI process and instead focus its efforts on pursuit of national monument designation through executive action by President Obama.

January 2016: Bishop and Chaffetz release the first draft of the PLI

Many residents in San Juan County, along with representatives of the oil and gas and extractive industries, applaud the draft PLI proposal. The PLI also receives measured support from the Western Energy Alliance, the Pew Trust, and the Nature Conservancy. Many environmental groups attack the proposal for what they perceive as its bias toward energy interests and for weakening protections in wilderness quality areas. Members of the Bears Ears Inter-Tribal Coalition reject the draft as "a slap in the face," as it fails to provide an adequate voice for the tribes in managing the land and in protecting antiquities. They also decry a parallel bill, the PLI Partner Act, simultaneously introduced, that would preclude the president's use of the Antiquities Act in the seven counties covered by the PLI. The divergent and apparently irreconcilable views of key interest groups lead many on all sides to believe that a national monument will be declared.

January 2016: Occupation of the Malheur National Wildlife Refuge

On January 2, 2016, Sagebrush Rebels, demanding the "return" of federal public land to the states, lead an armed takeover and occupation of the headquarters of the Malheur National Wildlife Refuge in southeastern Oregon. Under the guise of defending the Hammond family, Harney County, Oregon, ranchers who were convicted of arson for setting fires on public lands, Ammon and Ryan Bundy, lead the occupiers in a rebellion, arguing that the BLM and the U.S. Forest Service are constitutionally obliged to turn over federal land to the states. The Hammonds reject the Bundys' help, but nevertheless, the Bundy acolytes occupy the refuge until February 11, 2016, doing considerable damage to the headquarters, its contents, and surrounding federal lands. One of their members is killed during an attempted arrest. More than two dozen are charged with a variety of federal offenses.

July 2016: Bishop releases new draft of PLI

The revised version of the PLI bill, H.R. 5780, the Utah Public Lands Initiative Act, includes comments from the seven counties, as well as a broad range of individuals. The tribes, along with a large majority of environmental groups, continue to believe that the PLI provides inadequate protection for ancestral—and wilderness quality—lands.

July 2016: Secretary of the Interior Sally Jewell leads delegation to southeastern Utah

Secretary of the Interior Sally Jewell and the heads of the BLM, the National Park Service, the U.S. Forest Service, and the U.S. Department of Agriculture meet in Monticello with the San Juan County commissioners on July 14, 2016, and on July 16 hold a public meeting in Bluff attended by nearly fifteen hundred people. Officials from Utah and the tribes, along with a group of sixty randomly selected citizens, speak passionately about their love of the land and how best to preserve it, whether through a national monument or through the national conservation areas proposed by the Public Lands Initiative. Jewell's willingness to listen to differing visions for the future of public lands in San Juan County stands in radical contrast to the closed-door deliberations preceding the "stealth" declaration of the Grand Staircase–Escalante National Monument.

September 2016: PLI hearing in House Natural Resources Committee

H.R. 5780, the Utah Public Lands Initiative Act, introduced in July, is marked up by the House Natural Resources Committee and is forwarded to the House following a vote of twenty-one to thirteen in support of the amended bill.

December 28, 2016: Bears Ears National Monument established by President Barack Obama

President Barack Obama issues a proclamation designating Bears Ears National Monument, invoking his powers under the 1906 Antiquities Act to protect 1.35 million acres of land in San Juan County, Utah. The final boundaries of the monument hew closely to those outlined in Representative Rob Bishop's Public Lands Initiative. The proclamation calls for the establishment of the Bears Ears Commission, staffed by a representative of each tribe in the

Bears Ears Inter-Tribal Coalition, which will work with its federal counterparts in the Bureau of Land Management and the U.S. Forest Service to set policy for preserving ancestral sites and artifacts and for providing access to monument lands for traditional cultural and spiritual uses. Tribes and conservation groups celebrate the proclamation, while many citizens of San Juan County and the entirety of Utah's Republican political establishment are outraged.

January 2017: Utah state legislators pass antimonument resolutions

The Utah House of Representatives' Rules Committee votes six to two to pass a resolution asking President Trump to rescind the monument. The committee also passes a concurrent resolution asking Congress to dramatically reduce the acreage of the 1.9-million-acre Grand Staircase–Escalante National Monument. Largely symbolic, the resolutions are intended to express displeasure with the Obama administration's designation of Bears Ears and with President Clinton's establishment of Grand Staircase–Escalante in 1996.

April 2017: President Trump issues executive order on monuments review

President Trump issues an executive order directing Interior Secretary Ryan Zinke to conduct a review of all national monuments declared between 1996 and 2017—a time period bookended by the designation of Grand Staircase–Escalante and Bears Ears National Monuments. Zinke is given 120 days to issue a recommendation on whether to keep or reduce current monument boundaries but just 45 days to make a decision about Bears Ears.

June 2017: Interior Secretary Zinke makes initial recommendation to reduce acreage of Bears Ears National Monument

Secretary Zinke issues a preliminary recommendation regarding the Bears Ears National Monument, arguing that "rather than designating an area encompassing almost 1.5 million acres as a national monument, it would have been more appropriate to identify and separate the areas that have significant objects to be protected." He suggests that the areas deserving of monument designation be restricted to specific sites: "rock art, dwellings, ceremonial sites, granaries and other cultural resources."[6]

December 4, 2017: President Donald J. Trump signs proclamations reducing Bears Ears and Grand Staircase–Escalante National Monuments

Speaking from the Utah State Capitol in Salt Lake City, Trump officially shrinks Bears Ears National Monument by 85 percent, from 1.35 million acres to just over 200,000 acres. He simultaneously reduces the long-contentious Grand Staircase–Escalante National Monument from 1.9 million acres to just over 1 million acres. In keeping with monument opponents' talking points, Trump contends that past presidents had "severely abused" the Antiquities Act by instigating "massive federal land grabs" that limited the ability of local people to access and make a living off that land as they had for generations.

The official presidential proclamation also states that existing federal laws provided sufficient protections for the majority of land within the Bears Ears monument boundaries, thus rendering the monument declaration unnecessary. Finally, Trump establishes a pair of much smaller units, Shash Jáa and Indian Creek, on the remaining acreage from the original Bears Ears, along with a trio of distinct units on the remaining land in Grand Staircase–Escalante.

December 5, 2017: Pro–Bears Ears groups and tribes sue the Trump administration, challenging Trump's ability to shrink Bears Ears and Grand Staircase–Escalante National Monuments

A coalition of environmental and outdoor recreation groups, including Utah Diné Bikéyah, Friends of Cedar Mesa, Archaeology Southwest, and the outdoor retail giant Patagonia, join the tribes comprising the Bears Ears Inter-Tribal Coalition in filing five separate lawsuits challenging the legality

---

6. https://www.scribd.com/document/351066813/Interim-Report-EO-13792.

of Trump's proclamation. The lawsuits are consolidated into a single court challenge shortly thereafter.

The plaintiffs allege that a sitting president lacks the authority to undo a prior president's national monument designation; that power, they argue, rests with Congress alone, as enumerated in the 1976 Federal Land Policy and Management Act (FLPMA). Litigation may continue for years.

January 2018: Representative John Curtis (R-UT) introduces H.R. 4532, Shash Jáa National Monument and Indian Creek National Monument Act

Curtis's bill seeks to codify President Trump's proclamation shrinking Bears Ears National Monument. In addition to dividing what was left of the original monument into two much smaller monuments, the bill proposes to alter the structure of the groups tasked with developing policies for management of the lands within the monuments. Opponents of the original Bears Ears monument cheer Curtis's bill, citing its support of Trump's actions and a revised management structure that gives Native and non-Native locals more control than out-of-state tribes—and gives the Trump administration the ability to handpick the members of the management group.

Supporters of the original monument assail the bill, criticizing Curtis for not consulting with tribes before drafting the bill and for excluding tribes whose members currently do not live in southeastern Utah but whose ancestral connection to the land is unquestionable.

February 2018: Trump's new monument boundaries go into effect; land excluded from the new monuments is opened to new mining claims

Despite much alarm by environmental groups and tribes, there is no "land rush" following the removal of national monument protections for the land. Low uranium and vanadium prices made the prospect of major mining seem unlikely anytime in the near future. However, a December 2017 *Washington Post* investigation reveals that Energy Fuels Resources, which owns the White Mesa Uranium Mill, just outside the monument boundaries, lobbied the Trump administration to alter the Bears Ears boundaries to suit their future needs. This is a clear indication that extractive industry companies are planning for a new era of "America First" energy dominance—and the threat to the landscape, while not imminent, was much more than existential.

March 2018: A *New York Times* investigation reveals oil and gas companies influenced the redrawing of Bears Ears National Monument boundaries

A trove of Interior Department documents obtained by the *Times* via a Freedom of Information Act request following a successful lawsuit provides a window into how much sway extractive industry executives have in the Trump administration's decisions regarding Bears Ears. Correspondence between Interior staff and Utah senator Orrin Hatch's office reveals a concerted effort by Hatch to reopen lands closed to drilling and mining by the Obama monument proclamation in an effort to provide local people and the state a means of generating revenue.

PUBLIC LANDS GLOSSARY

Agencies of the federal government currently administer 640 million acres of land on behalf of all U.S. citizens. The primary agencies responsible for overseeing these lands are the Bureau of Land Management (BLM), the National Park Service (NPS), and the Fish and Wildlife Service (FWS), all housed in the Department of the Interior, and the U.S. Forest Service (USFS), housed within the U.S. Department of Agriculture (USDA).

The fraction of land that is federally owned is by far highest in the Mountain West, with federal holdings ranging from 36 percent of the total land area in Colorado to 81 percent in Nevada. In Utah 66 percent of the land is administered by agencies of the federal government.[1] The magnitude of these holdings is one of the major factors motivating calls for transferring some or all of these lands to the states and for sparking anger at the federal government retaining ownership of lands that might offer economic gain. Public land holdings have already decreased from a high of 1.8 billion acres and that the remaining 640 million acres contain large regions of immense beauty, isolation, and, in many cases, areas of great scientific or historical significance.

Over time, congressional or executive actions have resulted in various levels of protection for lands originally designated as BLM or USFS lands. These include:

National parks, designed "to conserve the scenery and natural and historic objects and wildlife therein and to provide for the enjoyment of the same in such manner and by such means as will leave them unimpaired for

---

1. Hicken, "From 0.3 to 81.1."

the enjoyment of future generations."[2] They are designated as parks by acts of Congress and managed by the National Park Service.

National monuments are declared to protect public lands most often via proclamation by the president of the United States under the executive powers granted him or her under the Antiquities Act of 1906 but occasionally by acts of Congress. (The Antiquities Act was enacted in response to rampant looting of Native artifacts and archaeological sites and empowered the president to set aside monuments to protect "historic landmarks, historic and prehistoric structures, and other objects of historic or scientific interest.")[3] Monuments are typically administered by the BLM, the USFS, or the NPS. The level of protection offered by a monument designation varies. In most monuments, livestock grazing is permitted, though often with significant restrictions. Mining activities are permitted so long as such activities do not cause significant degradation. No new mining claims can be issued once a monument is declared.

The Bears Ears National Monument declaration called for a unique arrangement in which management is shared between agencies of the federal government and members of a Bears Ears Commission. Supporters of the monument seek the protection of a landscape of unsurpassed beauty replete with hundreds of thousands of archaeological sites, which, left unprotected, would experience continued looting and desecration. Opponents see a monument declaration as a federal "land grab" declared by an overreaching chief executive, one that robbed them of cultural heritage and a robust economic future.

National conservation areas are designated by Congress to conserve, protect, and manage public lands for the benefit of current and future generations. Factors that enter into consideration when deciding to establish an NCA include cultural, ecological, historical, scientific, and recreational values.

The level of protection offered by NCAs varies. Typically, management plans are developed over a period of years via consultation with the public at large and key stakeholders. Livestock grazing and mining can usually continue, subject to the regulations spelled out in either the enabling legislation

---

2. Organic Act (Public Law 64–235).

3. An Act for the Preservation of American Antiquities (Public Law 59–209).

or the management plan. The BLM is the agency most frequently charged with managing NCAs.

The Utah Public Lands Initiative advocated for designation of two national conservation areas in the Bears Ears region. Many residents of San Juan County believe that NCAs managed with strong input from nearby residents and enterprises represent an appropriately local solution to stewarding what they regard as their lands. The Bears Ears Inter-Tribal Coalition and many in the environmental community were at one point open to NCA designation but came to believe that plans proposed by the Utah delegation provided insufficient protection of antiquities and lacked mechanisms for substantive tribal input.

Wilderness areas, designated by Congress in accordance with the Wilderness Act of 1964, are "area[s] where the earth and community of life are untrammeled by man, where man himself is a visitor who does not remain."[4] Wilderness areas provide the strongest protection of public lands: logging, mining, and motorized vehicles are not permitted, although in some areas, livestock grazing and mining are allowed if they antedate the declaration of the wilderness area. Some areas permit regulated hunting.

National recreation areas provide for federal management of large reservoirs, urban open spaces, or other areas that enable opportunities for outdoor recreation for large numbers of people. Lake Powell NRA in the red rock country of Utah and Arizona and the Golden Gate NRA in San Francisco are among the most well known and highly visited of the existing NRAs. Since 1963 Congress has sole authority for establishing NRAs. NRAs are managed by the National Park Service, the Bureau of Land Management, and the U.S. Forest Service.

State trust lands are parcels of land that were granted to Utah and other western states at the time each state was admitted to the Union in order to generate revenue to support state institutions such as public schools, colleges, universities, and hospitals. These lands are distinct from public lands managed for the citizens of the United States by the BLM, USFS, or the U.S. Park Service. A typical parcel of trust land is a "section" one square mile (640 acres) in size; sections are spread out in checkerboard fashion across the state. In Utah 3.4 million acres of state trust lands (about 6 percent of Utah's

---

4. Wilderness Act of 1964 (Public Land Law 88–577).

land area) are managed by the Utah School and Institutional Trust Lands Association (SITLA). Purchase or leasing of SITLA lands yields revenue from oil, gas, and mineral leases and royalties and from real estate development and sales.

Approximately 109,000 acres of SITLA land lie within the boundaries of the originally declared Bears Ears National Monument. The monument declaration specifically encourages swapping SITLA parcels interior to monument boundaries for parcels located within Forest Service or Bureau of Land Management lands elsewhere in the state. Following the 1996 declaration of Grand Staircase–Escalante National Monument, SITLA lands within the monument were exchanged for lands elsewhere in the state, adjusting the size of the monument to 1.9 million acres and netting $50 million to the state of Utah.

Mesas east of Goosenecks State Park

RESOURCES AND
SUGGESTED READINGS

An Act for the Preservation of American Antiquities (Public Law 59–209). https://www.nps.gov/history/local-law/FHPL_AntiAct.pdf.

Aitchison, Stewart. "A Natural History of Cedar Mesa." *Archaeology Southwest* 28, nos. 3–4 (Summer/Fall 2014): 8–11.

———. "The San Juan Mission." *Archaeology Southwest* 28, nos. 3–4 (Summer/Fall 2014): 43–44.

Alexander, Thomas G. "Stewardship and Enterprise: The LDS Church and the Wasatch Oasis Environment, 1847–1930." *Western Historical Quarterly* 25, no. 3 (Autumn 1994): 345.

Allen, Steve. *Utah's Canyon Country Place Names, Volume 1*. Durango, Colo.: Canyon Country Press, 2012.

———. *Utah's Canyon Country Place Names, Volume 2*. Durango, Colo.: Canyon Country Press, 2013.

Baccellieri, Emma. "For Campaign Cash, Many Lawmakers Use a Big Map; Rob Bishop Nears 93 Percent Out-of-State." OpenSecrets.org. July 8, 2016. https://www.opensecrets.org/news/2016/07/for-campaign-cash-many-lawmakers-use-a-big-map-rob-bishop-tops-the-out-of-state-list/.

Barker, Rocky. "How the Boulder–White Clouds Wilderness Was Preserved." *Idaho Statesman*, August 7, 2015. http://www.idahostatesman.com/news/local/environment/article41563677.html.

Bears Ears Inter-Tribal Coalition. "Proposal to President Barack Obama for the Creation of Bears Ears National Monument." Bearsearscoalition.org, October 2015.

———. "Bears Ears: A Native Perspective on America's Most Significant Unprotected Cultural Landscape." Bears Ears Coalition.org. September 1, 2017. http://www.bearsearscoalition.org/wp-content/uploads/2016/03/Bears-Ears-bro.sm_.pdf.

Bears Ears Inter-Tribal Coalition and Utah Dine Bikeyah, eds. *Bears Ears National Monument: A Cultural Vision for Public Lands Conservation*. Salt Lake City: Bears Ears Inter-Tribal Coalition and Utah Dine Bikeyah, 2016.

"Big News: Idaho's Boulder–White Clouds Protected as Wilderness!" The Wilderness Society. August 2015. http://wilderness.org/big-news-idahos-boulder-white-clouds-protected-wilderness.

Boyle, Bill. "Economic Development / Visitor Services in Upheaval after Termination of Director." *San Juan Record*, March 14, 2017. http://sjrnews.com/pages/full_story/push?article-Economic+Development+-+Visitor+Services+in+upheaval+after+termination+of+director%20&id=27381133&instance=home_news_1st_right.

Bureau of Indian Affairs Mission Statement. https://www.bia.gov/bia.

Bureau of Land Management. "Next Steps for Bears Ears National Monument." Washington, D.C.: U.S. Department of the Interior, January 2017.

Cappon, Lester J., ed. *The Adams-Jefferson Letters*. Vol. 1. Chapel Hill: Omohundro Institute and University of North Carolina Press, 1959.

"Chapter Thirty-Three: A Decade of Persecution, 1877–87." The Church of Jesus Christ of Latter-day Saints. https://www.lds.org/manual/church-history-in-the-fulness-of-times/chapter-thirty-three?lang=eng.

Childs, Craig. *Finders Keepers: A Tale of Archaeological Plunder and Obsession*. New York: Little, Brown and Company, 2010.

Church of Jesus Christ of Latter-day Saints. *The Doctrine and Covenants of the Book of Jesus Christ of Latter-day Saints*. Intellectual Reserve edition. Salt Lake City, Utah: Church of Jesus Christ of Latter-day Saints, 2013.

Coalition of Western States. http://cowstates.com/.

Cole, Sally. *Legacy on Stone: Rock Art of the Colorado Plateau and Four Corners Region*. Johnson Books, 1990.

Crampton, C. *Standing Up Country: The Canyon Lands of Utah and Arizona*. New York: Knopf, 1964.

Dunbar-Ortiz, Roxane. *An Indigenous Peoples' History of the United States*. Boston: Beacon Press, 2015.

"The Economic Importance of National Monuments to Communities." Headwaters Economics. August 2017. https://headwaterseconomics.org/wp-content/uploads/Escalante.pdf.

Enote, Jim, and Jennifer McLarren, eds. *A:shiwi A:wan Ulohnanne: The Zuni World*. Zuni, N.M.: A:shiwi A:wan Museum & Heritage Center, 2011.

Federal Land Policy and Management Act of 1976, 43 U.S.C. §§1701–1785 (1976). https://www.fs.usda.gov/Internet/FSE_DOCUMENTS/fseprd488457.pdf.

The Four Corners: A National Sacrifice Area? Dir. Christopher McLeod. Bullfrog Films, 1983.

Gessner, David. *All the Wild That Remains: Edward Abbey, Wallace Stegner, and the American West*. New York: W. W. Norton, 2015.

Gomez, Arthur R. *Quest for the Golden Circle: The Four Corners and the Metropolitan West, 1945–1970*. Albuquerque: University of New Mexico Press, 1994.

Goodman, Doug, and Daniel McCool, eds. *Contested Landscape: The Politics of Wilderness in Utah and the West*. Salt Lake City: University of Utah Press, 1999.

Griffin, Anna. "New Indictment Alleges Damage to Burns Paiute Site." Oregon Public Broadcasting, March 9, 2016. http://www.opb.org/news/series/burns-oregon-standoff-bundy-militia-news-updates/sean-anderson-charges-burns-paiute-archaeological-site/.

Grover, Hannah. "Bears Ears Region Is at Center of Land Debate." *Farmington Daily Times*, February 17, 2016. http://www.daily-times.com/story/life/outdoors/2016/02/17/bears-ears-region-center-land-debate/79696672/.

Gutjahr, Paul. *The Book of Mormon: A Biography*. Princeton, N.J.: Princeton University Press, 2012.

Handley, George B. "The Desert Blossoms as a Rose: Toward a Western Conservation Aesthetic." In *Stewardship and the Creation: LDS Perspectives on the Environment*, edited by George B. Handley, Terry B. Ball, and Steven L. Peck, 61–72. Provo, Utah: Religious Studies Center at Brigham Young University, 2006.

Handley, George B., Terry B. Ball, and Steven L. Peck, eds. *Stewardship and the Creation: LDS Perspectives on the Environment*. Provo, Utah: Religious Studies Center at Brigham Young University, 2006.

Harjo, Joy, and Stephen Strom. *Secrets from the Center of the World*. Tucson: University of Arizona Press, 1989.

Headwaters Economics. "The Importance of National Monuments to Local Communities." July 2014. https://headwaterseconomics.org/public-lands/protected-lands/national-monuments/.

Hibley, Preston. *Brigham Young: The Man and His Work*. 4th ed. Salt Lake City, Utah: Deseret Book Co., 1960.

Hicken, Jackie. "From 0.3 to 81.1: What Percentage of Each State Is Owned by the Federal Government?" *Deseret News*, March 7, 2014. http://www.deseretnews.com/top/2318/0/From-03-to-811-What-percentage-of-each-state-is-owned-by-the-federal-government.html.

H.R. 1268 (103rd): Indian Tribal Justice Act. Govtrack.us. March 9, 1993. https://www.govtrack.us/congress/bills/103/hr1268/text/ih.

Hurst, Winston B., and Jonathan D. Till. "Monumental Landscapes on Cedar Mesa." *Archaeology Southwest* 28, nos. 3–4 (Summer/Fall 2014): 31–34.

Hurst, Winston B., and James G. Willian. "Younger Traces: Other Cedar Mesa Archaeologies." *Archaeology Southwest* 28, nos. 3–4 (Summer/Fall 2014): 40–42.

In the Light of Reverence: Protecting America's Sacred Lands. Dir. Christopher McLeod. Bullfrog Films, 2002.

Indian Country Today Media Network. *Intergenerational Trauma: Understanding Natives' Inherited Pain*. Verona, N.Y.: Indian Country Today Media Network, 2017.

Johnson, Andrew. "Treaty Between the United States of America and the Navajo Tribe of Indians." New Mexico State University Regional Educational Technology

Assistance. http://reta.nmsu.edu/modules/longwalk/lesson/document/treaty .htm.

Josephy, Alvin. *The Indian Heritage of America*. Boston: Houghton Mifflin, 1968.

———. *Now That the Buffalo's Gone: A Study of Today's American Indians*. Norman: University of Oklahoma Press, 1982.

Kappler, Charles J. "Indian Affairs: Laws and Treaties." State of Oklahoma. December 1, 1902. http://digital.library.okstate.edu/kappler/V011/HTML_files/SES0180 .html.

Landry, Alysa. "Assimilation Tool or a Blessing? Inside the Mormon Indian Student Placement Program." *Indian Country Today*, January 7, 2016. https://indiancountry medianetwork.com/history/events/assimilation-tool-or-a-blessing-inside-the -mormon-indian-student-placement-program/.

Langlois, Krista. "How a Utah County Silenced Native American Voters—and How Navajos Are Fighting Back." *High Country News*, June 13, 2016. http://www.hcn .org/issues/48.10/how-a-utah-county-silenced-native-american-voters-and-how -navajos-are-fighting-back.

Lapahie, Harrison, Jr. "U.S. Treaty with the Navajos 1861." Lapahie.com. August 27, 2001. http://www.lapahie.com/Dine_Treaty_1861.cfm.

Lyman, Albert R. *History of Blanding, 1905–1955*. Blanding, Utah: Self-published, 1955.

Maffly, Brian. "Republicans OK $14M Land-Transfer Lawsuit, Say Utah Must Regain Sovereignty." *Salt Lake Tribune*, December 9, 2015. http://archive.sltrib.com/article .php?id=3287281&itype=CMSID.

Marshall, John. Opinion of the Court in *Worcester v. Georgia*. 31 U.S. 515. March 3, 1832. http://teachingamericanhistory.org/library/document/worcester-v-georgia/.

Maryboy, Kenneth. "Op-ed: Native Americans Ready to Work with Others to Make Bears Ears Monument Succeed." *Salt Lake Tribune*, January 21, 2017. http:// archive.sltrib.com/article.php?id=4835172&itype=CMSID.

McConkie, Elder Bruce R. "Christ and the Creation." The Church of Jesus Christ of the Latter Day Saints. June 1982. https://www.lds.org/ensign/1982/06/christ-and -the-creation?lang=eng&country=nz.

McFall, Michael. "After Navajo Nation Sues, Judge Orders San Juan County to Redraw Lines." *Salt Lake Tribune*, February 23, 2016. http://www.sltrib.com/home /3568518–155/after-navajo-nation-sues-judge-orders.

McNitt, Frank. *Richard Wetherill: Anasazi*. Albuquerque: University of New Mexico Press, 1966.

McPherson, Robert. *Comb Ridge and Its People: The Ethnohistory of a Rock*. Logan: Utah State University Press, 2009.

———. *A History of San Juan County: In the Palm of Time*. Salt Lake City: Utah State Historical Society, 1995.

Meloy, Ellen. *The Anthropology of Turquoise: Meditations on Landscape, Art and Spirit*. New York: Pantheon Books, 2002.

Momaday, N. Scott. *Man Made of Words: Essays, Stories, Passages*. New York: St. Martin's Griffin, 1997.

"Monuments Protected Under the Antiquities Act." National Parks Conservation Association. January 13, 2017. https://www.npca.org/resources/2658-monuments-protected-under-the-antiquities-act#sm.00017g898fmg2cruz2q1bgq7mzy04.

Nash, Elder Marcus B. "Righteous Dominion and Compassion for the Earth." Mormon Newsroom. April 12, 2013. http://www.mormonnewsroom.org/article/elder-nash-stegner-symposium#_ednref22.

Nelson, Russell M. "The Creation." The Church of Jesus Christ of the Latter Day Saints. April 2000. https://www.lds.org/general-conference/2000/04/the-creation?lang=eng.

Nibley, Hugh W. "Man's Dominion." The Church of Jesus Christ of Latter Day Saints. January 1981. https://www.lds.org/new-era/1981/01/mans-dominion?lang=eng.

Nies, Judith. *Unreal City: Las Vegas, Black Mesa and the Fate of the West*. New York: Nation Books, 2014.

Organic Act (Public Law 64–235). http://www.legisworks.org/congress/64/publaw-235.pdf.

Peck, Steven L. "An Ecologist's View of Latter-day Saint Culture and the Environment." In *Stewardship and the Creation: LDS Perspectives on the Environment*, edited by George B. Handley, Terry B. Ball, and Steven L. Peck, 165–75. Provo, Utah: Religious Studies Center at Brigham Young University, 2006.

The People. "The First Inhabitants—the Hopi." The People's Paths. N.d. http://www.thepeoplespaths.net/articles/HopiTribe/HopiTribe010803TheHopi.htm.

Pestano, Andrew V. "Utah Politician Blames 'Tree-Huggers' for Brian Head Fire." UPI.com. June 27, 2017. https://www.upi.com/Utah-politician-blames-tree-huggers-for-Brian-Head-Fire/3351498563470/.

Powell, John Wesley. *The Exploration of the Colorado River and Its Canyons*. New York: Penguin Classics, 2003. Originally published in 1875.

———. *Report on the Lands of the Arid Region of the United States with a More Detailed Account of the Land of Utah with Maps*. Washington, D.C.: U.S. Geographical and Geological Survey, 1879.

Roberts, Barbara. "Program 101: Elder Wisdom." Wisdom of the Elders. N.d. http://www.wisdomoftheelders.org/program-101-elder-wisdom/.

Roberts, David. *In Search of the Old Ones: Exploring the Anasazi World of the Southwest*. New York: Simon and Shuster, 1996.

———. *Sandstone Spine: Seeking the Anasazi on the First Traverse of the Comb Ridge*. Seattle: Mountaineers Books, 2006.

"San Juan County Resource Assessment." USDA Natural Resources Conservation Service. August 2005. https://www.nrcs.usda.gov/wps/portal/nrcs/detail/ut /technical/dma/nri/?cid=nrcs141p2_034124.

Siegler, Kirk. "With National Monuments Under Review, Bears Ears Is Focus of Fierce Debate." National Public Radio, May 5, 2017. http://www.npr.org/2017/05 /05/526860725/with-national-monuments-under-review-bears-ears-is-focus-of -fierce-debate.

Smart, William B., Gibbs M. Smith, and Terry Tempest Williams, eds. *New Genesis: A Mormon Reader on Land and Community.* Salt Lake City: Gibbs Smith, 1998.

Smith, Joseph F. "Editorial Thoughts: Kindness to Animals." *Juvenile Instructor,* February 1, 1912, 78–79. https://www.lds.org/ensign/1972/08/the-gospel-and-animals ?lang=eng.

Spangler, Jerry. "How Much Is Kaiparowits Coal Really Worth?" *Deseret News,* September 17, 1996. https://www.deseretnews.com/article/513781/HOW-MUCH-IS -KAIPAROWITS-COAL-REALLY-WORTH.html.

Staff of Representatives Rob Bishop, Jason Chaffetz, and Chris Stewart. "Utah Public Lands Initiative: Status Report for Stakeholders, Interested Parties, and the Public." Washington, D.C., November 19, 2013. https://collections.lib.utah.edu/ details?id=785661.

Steele, Rupert. Parliament of the World's Religions home page video. September 1, 2017. https://parliamentofreligions.org/file/goshute-shoshone-member-rupert -steele-gives-spiritual-keynote-indigenous-plenary.

Stegner, Wallace. *Beyond the Hundredth Meridian: John Wesley Powell and the Second Opening of the West.* New York: Houghton Mifflin, 1954.

———. *Mormon Country.* New York: Duell, Sloan and Pearce, 1942.

———. *The Sound of Mountain Water: The Changing American West.* New York: Penguin Random House, 1946.

———. "Wilderness Letter (1960)." *Wilderness Society / Living Wilderness Magazine,* December 1980.

Swearingen, Marshall, ed. *Sagebrush Rebellion: Evolution of a Movement.* Paonia, Colo.: High Country News, 2016.

Taylor Grazing Act of 1934 (Public Law 73–482). http://www.legisworks.org /congress/73/publaw-482.pdf.

Tohe, Laura. *Tseyi / Deep in the Rock: Reflections on Canyon de Chelly.* Tucson: University of Arizona Press, 2005.

"Tribal Sovereignty: History and the Law." Native American Caucus of the California Democratic Party. N.d. http://www.nativeamericancaucus.org/content/tribal -sovereignty-history-and-law.

Trimble, Stephen. *The People: Indians of the American Southwest.* Santa Fe: Center for American Research Press, 1993.

———, ed. *Red Rock Testimony: Three Generations of Writers Speak on Behalf of Utah's Public Lands.* Torrey, Utah: Torrey House Press, 2016.

Trimble, Stephen, and Terry Tempest Williams. *Testimony: Writers of the West Speak on Behalf of Utah Wilderness.* Minneapolis: Milkweed Editions, 1996.

"2011 Navajo Nation Visitor Survey." NavajoBusiness.com. February 2012. http://navajobusiness.com/pdf/Ads/NavajoNationFinalReport5-4-12.pdf.

Udall, Stewart. *The Forgotten Founders: Rethinking the History of the Old West.* Washington, D.C.: Island Press / Shearwater Books, 2002.

———. *The Quiet Crisis.* New York: Holt, Rinehart and Winston, 1963.

Utah Diné Bikéyah, ed. *Diné Bikéyah.* Salt Lake City: Utah Diné Bikéyah, 2011.

———. "UDB Is 1st Utah Recipient of ArtPlace America Grant." December 6, 2016. http://utahdinebikeyah.org/udb-is-1st-utah-recipient-of-artplace-america-grant/.

Utah Economic Council. *2017 Economic Report to the Governor.* Salt Lake City: University of Utah Kem C. Gardner Public Policy Institute, 2017.

Utah Public Lands Initiative Act, H.R. 5780, 114th Congress, 2016.

Utah Tribal Leaders Association Letters. BearsEarsCoalition.org. March 26, 2010. http://www.bearsearscoalition.org/wp-content/uploads/2015/10/Letters-referenced-in-timelline.pdf.

Utah Wilderness Coalition. *Wilderness at the Edge: A Citizen Proposal to Protect Utah's Canyons and Deserts.* Salt Lake City: Utah Wilderness Coalition, 1990.

Warner, Ted. J., ed. *The Dominguez-Escalante Journal.* Salt Lake City: University of Utah Press, 1995.

Waters, Frank. *Book of the Hopi.* New York: Penguin Books, 1977.

Watkins, T. H. *The Redrock Chronicles: Saving Wild Utah.* Santa Fe: Center for American Places; Baltimore, Md.: Johns Hopkins University Press, 2000.

"What Are Trust Lands?" Trust Lands Administration State of Utah. N.d. https://trustlands.utah.gov/our-agency/what-are-trust-lands/.

Wierzbicki, Angie. "Leonardo DiCaprio Foundation Donates to Bears Ears' Fund." *Nonprofit Quarterly*, January 17, 2017. https://nonprofitquarterly.org/2017/01/17/leonardo-dicaprio-foundation-donates-bears-ears-fund/.

Wilderness Act of 1964 (Public Land Law 88–577). https://www.gpo.gov/fdsys/pkg/STATUTE-78-Pg890.pdf.

Wilkinson, Charles. *Blood Struggle: The Rise of Modern Indian Nations.* New York: W. W. Norton, 2005.

———. *Fire on the Plateau: Conflict and Endurance in the American Southwest.* Washington, D.C.: Island Press / Shearwater Books, 1999.

Williams, Terry Tempest. *Red: Passion and Patience in the Desert.* New York: Vintage Books, 2001.

Winslow, Ben. "San Juan Co. Ordered to Redraw Boundaries in Gerrymandering Lawsuit." Fox13 Salt Lake City, July 22, 2017. http://fox13now.com/2017/07/21/san-juan-co-ordered-to-redraw-boundaries-in-gerrymandering-lawsuit/.

Wyatt, Alexandra M. "Antiquities Act: Scope of Authority for Modifications of National Monuments." Indiana University Maurer School of Law. November 14, 2016. http://www.law.indiana.edu/publicland/files/national_monuments _modifications_CRS.pdf.

Yazzie, Ethelou. *Navajo History: Volume 1.* Chinle, Ariz.: Rough Rock Demonstration School, 1982.

Young, Brigham. "Remarks." *Deseret News,* August 16, 1866.

Zwinger, Ann. *Wind in the Rock: The Canyonlands of Southeastern Utah.* Tucson: University of Arizona Press, 1978.

INDEX

Note: Page references in *italics* refer to illustrative matter.

ABOUT THE AUTHOR

Rebecca M. Robinson is a writer based in Portland, Oregon. She received her undergraduate degree from Bennington College in 2006 and since then has pursued a career in journalism. Her work has been widely published and broadcast in numerous print, online, and radio outlets, and she has received awards from the Society of Professional Journalists, the Alliance for Women in Media, and the Associated Press. She began her work on the manuscript for *Voices from Bears Ears* at the 2015 Fishtrap Summer Gathering of Writers. This is her first book.

ABOUT THE PHOTOGRAPHER

Stephen E. Strom spent his professional career as an astronomer. In 1964 he received his AM and PhD degrees from Harvard University. He has held appointments at Harvard University, State University of New York at Stony Brook, University of Massachusetts Amherst, Kitt Peak National Observatory, and the National Optical Astronomy Observatory. He retired from NOAO in May 2007. Strom began photographing in 1978. He studied both the history of photography and silver and nonsilver photography in studio courses with Keith McElroy, Todd Walker, and Harold Jones at the University of Arizona. His work, largely interpretations of landscapes, has been exhibited widely throughout the United States and is held in several permanent collections. His photography complements poems and essays in three books published by the University of Arizona Press—*Secrets from the Center of the World* (1989), a collaboration with Muscogee poet Joy Harjo; *Sonoita Plain: Views of a Southwestern Grassland* (2005), a collaboration with ecologists Jane and Carl Bock; and *Tseyi (Deep in the Rock): Reflections on Canyon de Chelly* (2005), coauthored with Navajo poet Laura Tohe—and in one book published by the University of New Mexico Press—*Otero Mesa: America's Wildest Grassland*, with Gregory McNamee and Stephen Capra (2008). A monograph comprising forty-three images, *Earth Forms*, was published in 2009 by Dewi Lewis Publishing. His most recent publications include *Earth and Mars: A Reflection* with Bradford Smith (University of Arizona Press, 2015), *Death Valley: Painted Light* with Alison Deming (George F. Thompson Publishing, 2015, distributed by the University of Arizona Press), and *Tidal Rhythms: Change and Resilience at the Edge of the Sea* with Barbara Hurd (George F. Thompson Publishing, 2017).